D0467835

EDSELS®, LUCKIES®, & FRIGIDAIRES®

EDSELS, LUCKIES, & FRIGIDAIRES

Advertising the American Way

ROBERT ATWAN
DONALD MCQUADE
JOHN W. WRIGHT

A Delta Special

For
HELENE,
SUZANNE,
VIRGINIA

A DELTA SPECIAL

Published by
Dell Publishing Co., Inc.
1 Dag Hammarskjold Plaza
New York, New York 10017

Edsel ® is a registered trademark of the Ford Motor Company.
Luckies ® is a registered trademark of the American Tobacco Company.
Frigidaire ® is a registered trademark of the General Motors Company.

Delta ® TM 755118, Dell Publishing Co., Inc.
Printed in the United States of America
First printing—March 1979

Designed by Giorgetta Bell McRee

Library of Congress Cataloging in Publication Data

Atwan, Robert.
Edsels, luckies, and frigidaires.
Bibliography: p.
1. Advertising—United States—History. 2. United
States—Civilization. I. McQuade, Donald, joint author.
II. Wright, John, 1941–   joint author. III. Title.
HF5813.U6A87   659.1'0973   78–21503
ISBN 0–440–53487–9

FOREWORD

I grew up surrounded by the advertisements found in EDSELS, LUCKIES, AND FRIGIDAIRES almost as closely as I lived my formative years with my immigrant Greek parents.

Without being aware of it during those media-limited years, seeing and hearing advertising was as vital to my two sisters and me—and probably to most of our peers in the heartland and the boondocks—as how Dick Tracy and Smilin' Jack were doing. I think it's fair to say that I was nourished by radio (particularly by its advertising) and by the comics (particularly by their marvelously simple graphics). Then, through those gifts that I happened to possess as a graphic designer, I became an adman.

Wandering through this lustrous study of advertising shows us that inventive, romantic, outrageous, seductive, delightful thinking and writing has preceded us—and that many sharp minds before us knew down deep what they were doing, and what America was about. They moved us, thrilled us, conned us, sold us. That's why I love every page of this volume. During the sixties and seventies a handful of creative art directors have brought about a revolution in advertising with their bold, clear imagery. As these pages show, this audacious use of graphics works magically with great headline concepts to create truly memorable ads.

Of course, there has always been awful advertising, and of course, the worst advertising is the message of fools that insults our intelligence and treats us like children. There has always been vulgar advertising, replete with diagrams of sinus passages and offensive vignettes of women discussing the relative merits of their laundry detergents. But the worst sin in advertising is to be boring, and the sad fact is that ninety percent of all advertising is literally invisible for this reason: You turn to it, look at it, flip the page, and immediately forget what you have just seen. Likewise, far from capturing our attention, most television commercials have become a signal to get up and get a beer. But the great ads, when they do occur, truly enrich our daily lives, our language, our visual perception of things—and confer a new dimension on our very culture.

My job is to sell products. If I don't, I'm out of business. But to sell a product with talent, with theater, with drama, with outlandishness, and yes, with wit, is what it's all about. A great adperson does advertising that makes a product (and the ad itself) famous. The people who do advertising merely to *explain* the good qualities of a product simply don't understand advertising. Great advertising makes the advertising a benefit of the product!

I create images to catch people's eyes, penetrate their brains, warm their minds, touch their hearts, and cause them to act. To use a more outrageous image: I liken great advertising to poison gas. Shoot it out there, attack the eyes, nose, throat, heart, nervous system—and watch them drop like flies. Not everyone agrees with me. Indeed, much of the advertising in this splendid volume is not *my* style of selling the human race. But the work in EDSELS, LUCKIES, AND FRIGIDAIRES beautifully summarizes a large, rich portion of that continuing American mystique, the art of advertising.

George Lois

PREFACE

This collection has been put together on the basis of several related premises. Advertisements frequently contain two kinds of information: a verbal or pictorial description of the product or service being sold, and the effects—real or imagined, stated or implied—such products or services will have on the purchaser's private or public life. As such, advertisements tell us in miniature a great deal about an entire civilization, its actual material life and interlocking collective fantasies. Our criterion throughout has been to select ads that amply represent this comprehensive approach to people and products.

Another basic premise is that advertisements, to be effective, must embody the accepted values and attitudes of large numbers of people. We feature primarily—though not exclusively—advertising designed from a decidedly middle-class point of view. Advertising is, after all, as its cultural critics like to point out, an unabashedly middle-class mode of expression. But with ninety-five percent of Americans regarding themselves in those terms, that point of view is likely to embrace far more cultural variety than disparaging views may want to acknowledge.

From a vast amount of material, we examined literally hundreds of thousands of advertisements in public and university libraries, at collectors' fairs and exhibitions, and in numerous special collections. With the exception of a few newspaper ads, posters, and trade cards, our selections were made from magazines that had or have large circulations. This was done for both historical and practical reasons: for decades magazines consistently handled compelling advertising, and no other type of advertisement prints as well in book form. We then culled for this collection a representative sample organized around topics generally considered to be among the major elements of social history. Of the general interest magazines, we consulted *Time, Life, Newsweek, Look, American, Colliers, Saturday Evening Post,* and *TV Guide.* Of the women's magazines: *Ladies' Home Journal, Good Housekeeping, Woman's Home Companion, Mademoiselle, Vogue, Harper's Bazaar, Seventeen, Cosmopolitan, Family Circle,* and *McCall's.* We also drew a number of the older ads from such once-popular sources as *Harper's Weekly, Century, Everybody's, Literary Digest, McClure's, Munsey's, Pearson's, Scribner's, Smart Set, Vanity Fair,* and the old *Life* and *Cosmopolitan.* A few of the ads appeared first in *Ebony, Essence, Esquire, Fortune, The New Yorker, Popular Science Monthly, Penthouse,* and *Playboy*—more specialized publications but still with enormous readerships.

The advertisements in this book were selected for their documentary value. Accordingly, they represent important developments in American social history. They are meant to reflect many of the principal cultural and material trends that have marked the various stages of social change. They are in no way intended either to endorse or deprecate any of the manufacturers, agencies, or individuals involved in their creation.

Given the overwhelming amount and diversity of advertising source material, we naturally had to rely on a great deal of expert and discerning assistance. The cooperation and contributions of a number of people made the preparation of this book a far more manageable enterprise than we had at first expected. We are especially indebted to Trudy Baltz and Ellen Chodosh for both their indefatigable searching and their perceptive suggestions. We also received valuable help from William Berry, Tony Bonanza, David Follmer, Leonide Goldstein, John McDermott, Richard Mikita, James Monaco, Frank Moorman, Patricia Peters, Brian Reilly, Esther Schor, Jean Shapiro, Lolly Sullivan, and William Vesterman. We would like to thank the following for securing for us difficult-to-obtain advertisements: Connie De Luca, Bob Gallagher, Lee Lanzarotta, Mary Lyons, James Nichols, Debbie Rogers, and D. P. Sheridan. Michael De Simone and Donald and Joanne Siegel generously provided us with scarce back issues of hundreds of magazines. We are particularly grateful to William U. Harris and John Leypoldt for the fine quality of their photographic work. For making available to us his extensive collection of American advertisements, we'd like to give special thanks to Jerald Mastroli (258 East 33rd Street, New York, New York 10016). We recommend his work to anyone interested in this kind of research.

Advertising agencies often provided indispensable assistance. For their professional advice and for making materials available to us, we'd like to thank Ruth Klaber, Akwell Advertising; Robert Bach, formerly vice president of N. W. Ayer; Sharon Brown, DKG Advertising; Doris Willens, Doyle Dane Bernbach; Jan Dwyer, Epstein, Raboy Advertising; Jean

Boutyette and Robert Koretz, Foote, Cone and Belding, Ron Holland, Holland and Callaway; Harold Gully, Leo Burnett; Marian Lindholtz, Marsteller, Inc.; Tina Decker Long, Regis McKenna, Inc.; Jose Ferrioli, Rosemary Nelson, and Mark Stroock, Young & Rubicam.

We would also like to express our appreciation to the staffs of the following libraries for their expert guidance: the Queens College, Columbia, Princeton, and Yale Libraries; the New York Public Library (most especially the patient and resourceful members of the Picture Collection); the Boston Public Library; the Library of Congress; the Smithsonian; The New-York Historical Society; the American Antiquarian Society; the Museum of Connecticut History; and the New York Academy of Medicine.

The following corporations and copyright holders kindly granted us permission to reprint their work: AT&T, Avon, *Esquire*, Future Homemakers of America, General Foods, General Motors, Hearst Corporation, International Cigar Company, International Harvester Company, Maidenform, Inc., Schlitz Brewing Company, Seven-Up Company, Singer Company, Sony Corporation, Sperry-Univac, Volkswagen of America, Inc., Weider Health and Fitness, Whitman's Chocolates.

Finally, it is a pleasure to express our gratitude to the dedicated people at Delta Books—especially Ann Watson and Martha Kinney—who have labored long and hard but with kindness and patience. To the designer, Giorgetta McRee, a special note of thanks; her excellent work may well have first drawn you to this book.

Robert Atwan
Donald McQuade
John Wright

New York
October 1978

CONTENTS

INTRODUCTION

The historians and archeologists will one day discover that the ads of our times are the richest and most faithful daily reflections that any society ever made of its entire range of activities.

> Marshall McLuhan,
> *Understanding Media*
> (1964)

In contemporary America no one questions the proposition that everyday life in the Space Age changes so rapidly that modes of behavior now regarded as customary will soon pass into oblivion. This realization has so altered, some would say distorted, our sense of history that the recent past has taken on the look and feel, the texture, of a dying civilization. Over the last century, moreover, the records of daily existence have been extended and enriched, first by advancements in printing and photography, then by the development of the electronic mass media. As a result, radio and television programs, popular magazines and novels, movies, and even the comic strips of only a few decades ago have been imbued with a historical significance traditionally reserved for those paintings, plays, literary works, and mythological tales commonly called classic.

The strong public interest in American popular culture has recently produced a spate of books, serious and otherwise, all purporting to show us how we *really* were. Nostalgia buffs, eager to share the thrills of discovering the whacky and wonderful, daffy and delirious "good ol' days," have recently been joined by anthropologists, sociologists, historians, and cultural critics who hope to uncover the underlying codes governing the behavior of people in mass society. Just as old beer cans and bottle caps have become "collector's items," so soap operas, Superman, and Sam Spade are now topics for impenetrable dissertations and monographs. But these remarks are not meant to disparage the enterprise itself. For by steering a course somewhere between the approaches of the lighthearted and the heavy-handed, one can find valuable insights into a part of American life too long ignored by traditional investigators of our past.

Advertising, an industry now consuming some forty billion American dollars a year and the professional energies of tens of thousands of talented people, has been subjected to all kinds of studies. Most of them are part of a long-term debate about advertising that deals with significant questions of economic priorities, environmental consequences, and political ideologies: Does advertising truly stimulate the economy? Does advertising encourage unnecessary and potentially harmful consumption? Is advertising necessary in a capitalist democracy? Other books, in prose and picture, have examined advertising from a variety of social, cultural, and professional perspectives. These include linguistic and iconographic analyses, nostalgic compilations of old ads, evaluations of media strategies and effects, and the reminiscences of prominent advertising personalities.

With these as the precedents it is necessary to state clearly the intentions of the present volume. This is, first of all, a book about *things*—the essential as well as the superfluous goods of industrialized society. It is also about the everyday aspirations, fears, and desires of the American public. On another level, the cultural assumptions and behavioral values reflected in the language, settings, plots, and characters of most advertising make this also a book about the changing nature of American society.

The book is divided into three general parts, each containing several more specific groupings. In Part One, "Advertising and Social Roles," we have chosen examples of the types of men and women—both black and white—most frequently found throughout the history of American advertising. Like all forms of popular culture, advertising relies on archetypes and stereotypes to get its message across quickly and easily to large numbers of people. The character types appearing in Part One are depicted performing everyday tasks and assuming traditional roles that reflect the public attitudes society, with the vigorous help of advertising, has encouraged over the years: the woman as helpmate in home and office, the man as corporate leader or "rat race" victim, the black servant with the ready smile. These characters, furthermore, are not mere oddities or caricatures of an imaginary past, but rather part of a network of images from films, novels, the press, and the broadcast media that continually interact to reinforce acceptable modes of behavior.

Also included in Part One are several examples of a generally neglected form of advertising—ads addressed to other advertisers. Depictions of men and women created by the media themselves (in this case magazines) to attract new advertisers date back to the turn of the century. Because these ads are targeted to such a highly informed audience as the advertising community itself—which must be attuned to every nuance of social change —they are particularly valuable in tracing the shifting image of the American consumer.

After focusing on the characteristic roles in a consumer society, we move in Part Two to the objects of consumption themselves. One of advertising's principal functions over the last century has been to keep Americans posted on the latest marketable adaptations of the technological discoveries that have profoundly altered nearly every aspect of their lives. In "Advertising and Material Civilization," we have included images of inventions that have transformed our working and leisure habits: everything from automobiles and airplanes to washing machines, refrigerators, dishwashers, and computers. Advertising functions well when it disseminates news of material progress, but it thrives when it creates new and memorable relationships between the public and the inventions manufacturers turn into purchasable products.

But obviously advertising is also engaged in more mundane announcements, and in Part Two are included sections featuring what people wore, how and what they ate, and what kinds of gadgets and contraptions fascinated them from one generation to the next. Fads and fashions in clothing, food, and automobiles are pictured here in all their tarnished glory—what was once some copywriter's confident proclamation of sophisticated, up-to-date know-how is now too casually dismissed simply as an occasion for nostalgic disbelief.

Since this is a book about advertising as well as a book about American life, we have included several sections demonstrating how the two are intertwined. Part Three, "Advertising and the Strategies of Persuasion," shows how effective advertising frequently depends on several very basic human concerns: fear, fame, and sex. All three help the advertiser grab the audience's attention, but they also demand that the advertiser be acutely aware of contemporary standards of taste and decorum as well as the fickle nature of popularity in a media-dominated society. Even the harshest critics of Madison Avenue have agreed that the creators of advertising are keen observers of the social scene. In fact, the most famous people in the profession—from Claude Hopkins and Leo Burnett to Shirley Polykoff and Jerry Della Femina—have always insisted that their success depended on a first-hand familiarity with the way most people actually lived and talked and a genuine concern for what those people thought about the world around them.

Few things in that world have changed more dramatically than America's attitudes toward sex. Sexual innuendo (e.g., "A Skin You Love to Touch") began to spice up advertisements in the years before World War I, but it was not until the 1920s that sex became a fairly steady feature of American advertising. Over the last decade, sex, sexiness, and, as some would have it, sexism have become increasingly explicit. The endorsement technique, on the other hand, has a longer and more commercially complicated history. The use of public figures, star performers, and popular athletes in advertisements dates well back into the nineteenth century. Celebrities and advertising have both profited from a remarkably symbiotic relationship: advertising-sponsored media help create famous personalities who, to complete the commercial cycle, in turn reinvest their fame in the advertising of consumer goods.

Throughout this volume surface many examples of Dr. Samuel Johnson's famous dictum: "Promise—large promise—is the soul of advertisement." Here are the perennial promises of health, success, romance, and happiness. But in the section called "Afflictions and Anxieties," we present the darker side, the human fears advertising incessantly plays upon—illness, failure, rejection, loneliness, incurable virginity. The blatant use of such emotional appeals characterizes American advertising from its earliest days and, according to some observers, differentiates it from the advertising of any other society. The history of this type of advertisement from the most outlandish claims of the patent medicines a century ago to the more cautious, government-supervised ones of today can tell us something about the interaction of advertising and human nature. It also discloses a great deal about the depth of American medical ignorance and gullibility as well as the reasons behind the increased activity of regulatory agencies.

If we seek an institution that was brought into being by abundance, without previous existence in any form, and, moreover, an institution which is peculiarly identified with American abundance rather than with abundance throughout Western civilization, we will find it, I believe, in modern American advertising.

David M. Potter
People of Plenty
(1954)

The roots of American advertising can be traced to colonial times, and several key elements, including the basic structure of the agency business, were established as early as 1860. But only in the decades following the

Civil War, when the effects of industrialization had penetrated every part of the country and every stratum of society, did advertising acquire its first distinctly modern role of stimulating the consumption of the goods and services created for a new kind of civilization—one dedicated to the now dubious proposition that unlimited consumption is a fundamental privilege of the American way.

The history of the United States since 1870 is the chronicle of sweeping economic and social change. Urbanization, immigration, technological breakthroughs, and the growth of big business from corporations to conglomerates all helped at one time or another to reshape the face of the nation and transform the everyday lives of its people. In 1870, nearly half of the forty million Americans lived on farms; roughly speaking, 75 percent of the entire population were considered residents of rural areas. Most people produced at least some of their own food and much of their own clothing. A hundred years later, the population had quintupled to 200 million, but only 5 percent remained on farms, and 25 percent in rural areas. By 1970, most Americans lived in cities or suburbs, worked in offices or factories, and depended entirely on their salaries to purchase the essentials of life which now came pre-packaged, pre-shrunk, pre-fabricated, and even pre-digested.

That most of us now regard such unprecedented social and technological transformations as historical clichés indicates how thoroughly the style and quality of everyday life have been affected. But national identities depend on just such commonplaces. In this the first post-agricultural age, Americans have learned, for example, how technology builds on past discoveries to create still newer inventions that rearrange daily routines and often rapidly reshape social patterns. As a result, the way we lived only thirty or forty years ago can today seem quaint and sometimes strange; and what were believed to be immutable laws of social behavior may well now strike us as irrelevant, unjust, or cruel. Although studies of the various popular media have contributed to our awareness of these rapid changes, seldom have advertisements been used systematically as verbal and pictorial documents to reveal—subtly or dramatically—the social and material transformations of the last hundred years.

Advertising, at least in its modern sense, arose as a necessary part of an industrial economy, a means of selling mass-produced goods to masses of people inexpensively. According to figures recently compiled for *Advertising Age*, expenditures for advertising stood at approximately $22 million in 1860. By 1880, that figure had climbed to $175 million, and within one decade to $300 million. The number of advertisements increased in direct proportion to the quantity of products manufactured, which in turn increased because of the expanding markets advertising helped create. By 1890, multiple brands of baking powder, boxed cereals, bicycles, packaged soaps, as well as scores of patent medicines, had become familiar retail items in the advertising pages of newspapers and popular magazines.

Revenue from advertising has been the principal support of newspapers since colonial days and the rise of the "penny press" in the 1830s. Alexander Hamilton noted in 1803 that "it is the advertiser who provides the paper for the subscriber." Toward the end of the nineteenth century, enormous numbers of ads sustained the publishing empires of Hearst and Pulitzer. Then, as now, newspaper ads had a predictably "newsy" quality, announcing goods and services to be purchased immediately and locally—usually from large department stores. Their immediate impact and wide circulations account for the fact that the largest percentage of advertising dollars have always gone to newspapers.

Magazines developed quite differently. In 1860, there were 575 magazines in the United States, most of them regional or local publications with meager circulations and very little advertising. As reading matter for a small and predominantly genteel literary set, magazines could not be considered an ideal medium for advertising. Between 1880 and 1900, several factors coalesced to change all that. The expansion of railroads made possible nationally distributed products; the invention of the rotary press allowed larger and cheaper print runs, increasing readership and thus making magazines more attractive to the advertisers of nationally distributed goods. Even the government cooperated by drastically reducing postal rates for reading material. In 1890, the introduction of inexpensive halftones permitted newer magazines to compete with such established and expensive publications as *Century* and *Harper's*. Halftones not only reduced the cost of advertising graphics, but also added an attractive, contemporary look that helped to push the total number of American magazines over the 5,000 mark by 1895.

By the 1890s, advertising had clearly become the key factor in transforming magazines into a mass media industry. Most of the older, traditional magazines cost between twenty-five and thirty-five cents, a price that, at the time, limited their market to the fairly affluent. In the depression year 1893, one of the new popular magazines, *Munsey's*, with a solid circulation of 40,000, slashed its cover price to ten cents in the hope of attracting more readers and thereby significantly increasing its profits solely from advertising. Rates were based on the easy-to-remember formula of one dollar per one thousand circulation. By 1895, *Munsey's* circulation had jumped astoundingly to 500,000 and other publications soon followed suit. *McClure's*, for example, soared from 8,000 to 250,000 in two years. By the turn of the century, 50 magazines were nationally distributed, and several, such as *Ladies' Home Journal*, could boast of circulations hovering around one million copies a year. Advertising supported all of them.

By 1900, advertising was a $500-million-a-year business. Preparing copy had evolved into a specialized craft that could be learned in schools and through correspondence courses. Advertising in a highly competitive atmosphere required sophisticated strategies of persuasion that went beyond mere announcement, price quotation, and attractive graphics. As a result, several accomplished practitioners began to write "how-to" books as well as articles in such trade journals as *Printer's Ink, Judicious Advertising*, and *Brains*. In these publications can be found the beginnings of a vast body of virtually unexplored advertising literature that analyzes and explains the consumer's relationship to the everyday things of American life. Moreover, in 1900 the first of many treatises called "The Psychology of Advertising" was published, thereby inadvertently acknowledging that a great deal of advertising expertise in the twentieth century would depend on an understanding of human desires, emotions, and motivations.

The foundations of the modern advertising business had been established by the early twentieth century. Inexpensive color reproductions, coupons, and test markets had all been introduced by 1910 and helped turn advertising into a billion-dollar business. New media, new methods, and an ever-increasing number of products would keep advertising's dollar volume growing throughout the century while at the same time generating millions and millions of ads.

> *Advertising, of course, has been part of the mainstream of American civilization, although you might not know it if you read the most respectable surveys of American history. It has been one of the enticements to the settlement of this New World, it has been a producer of the peopling of the United States, and in its modern form, in its worldwide reach, it has been one of our most characteristic products.*
>
> Daniel Boorstin,
> "The Rhetoric of Democracy"
> (in *Democracy and Its Discontents*, 1974)

Many talented writers and social observers have continually noted the capacity of advertising to reflect, for good or ill, the American way of life. From Mark Twain's satirical barbs in *A Connecticut Yankee in King Arthur's Court* (1889) through Marshall McLuhan's pithy attacks in *The Mechanical Bride* (1951) and Betty Friedan's perceptive analysis of the "sexual sell" in *The Feminine Mystique* (1963), advertising has always figured strongly in treatises committed to exposing the folly of "the system." Fifty years have passed since Robert and Helen Lynd made use of advertisements in their pioneering sociological study of *Middletown* (1929). Since then, such noted social scientists as Margaret Mead, Clyde Kluckhohn, and David Riesman have also turned to advertising as a valuable tool in formulating more "objective" interpretations of American civilization. Since 1950, several social historians—especially David Potter and Daniel Boorstin—intent on finding the roots and the significance of our mass consumption society, have insisted on the need to include advertising in any serious study of modern American life. In *People of Plenty* (1954), Potter identifies advertising as the "institution of abundance," a peculiarly American force that "now compares with such long-standing institutions as the school and the church in the magnitude of its social influence." And Daniel Boorstin goes so far as to call advertising "the rhetoric of democracy," "the characteristic folk culture of our society."

Advertisements clearly form one of the most significant sets of cultural artifacts available to those who wish to understand the changing nature of American society. Because advertising reflects the attitudes of huge segments of society—not exclusively those of intellectuals, artists, and statesmen—it is in many ways a dependable barometer of the accepted values and customs of particular historical periods. By tracing in a selective and systematic manner these visual and verbal artifacts, a surprisingly accurate view of American mores and ideals comes sharply into focus. Taken as a whole, the illustrations and text will, we trust, demonstrate advertising's importance as a mirror of social values and as a running commentary on the changes and continuities in American civilization.

Part
ONE

Advertising and Social Roles

90 % of the family income is expended by the women of a household. Every wife and mother at the head of a home holds the clasp of the family pocketbook. Want to reach this woman behind the pocketbook? Three million of her kind read the advertising pages of McCall's Magazine. Six hundred thousand are paid subscribers.

D. L. DAVIS, Advertising Manager
113 West 31st St., New York

1904

As this turn-of-the-century example demonstrates, it has long been a practice of magazines to woo advertisers by offering them pictorial and verbal descriptions of their readership. In ads for women's magazines the most popular theme has always been woman's almost absolute power over the family purse. An interesting contemporary example created for Ladies' Home Journal in 1977 appears on page 43.

WOMEN

The largest expenditures for advertising have invariably been made by America's leading manufacturers of food and beverages, soap and soap powders, over-the-counter drugs, and items for personal hygiene, such as toothpaste, mouthwash, and deodorants. Today the annual advertising budgets of such well-known corporations as General Foods and Bristol-Myers are in the neighborhood of $200 million, while those of General Mills, Colgate-Palmolive, and Warner-Lambert hover around $100 million. But no one has come close to the staggering sum of $460 million spent in 1977 by Procter & Gamble, makers of Ivory, Cheer, Tide, Bold, Spic and Span, Comet, Crest, Pampers, Crisco, and Duncan Hines cake mixes— among other things. Almost all of this money, together with the collective energy of writers, artists, film crews, media planners, and media buyers, is spent in the hope of reaching the female consumer. Because women decide which new products will survive and which established brands will get the greatest market share, advertising and marketing people habitually refer to the consumer as "she." Most industry estimates say that as much as 80 percent of all advertising is beamed directly at her.

The advertising community's obsession with the needs and desires of the American woman has been a constantly observable phenomenon of business history for most of this century. Dozens of articles, several complete books, and large portions of many others have been written to demonstrate proven methods for cajoling or persuading the female consumer, and for piquing, arousing, or stimulating her curiosity. Advertisers and their agencies have invested millions of dollars to have hundreds of psychologists and sociologists spend thousands of hours asking all sorts of women innumerable questions about their home life, their sex life, their mothers, their fathers, their income, and the income of their friends. In the 1950s a few grown men spent hundreds of hours secretly studying the eye movements of women as they marched around a supermarket, in the vain hope of unlocking the key to feminine buying impulses. In a different era, advertisers nurtured and supported an important form of early radio entertainment—commonly called the soap opera—because its popularity with housewives was instantaneous. Nearly five decades later the popularity of soap operas continues, despite the fact that they have moved to television where the viewer can actually see what's happening.

Like most deep and long-lasting relationships, the love affair between advertisers and American women has not been without incident. As the nation's primary purchasers women have been at the forefront during every phase of the consumer movement dating from the struggle for pure food and drug laws at the turn of the century, to the fight against fraudulent advertising of drugs and cosmetics during the Great Depression, and the current protest against advertising directed to children. Only recently, however, have women seriously questioned the images of "the American woman" that advertisers have created. Over the last decade or so, as the debate about woman's place in American society has intensified, advertisers, more than any other contributors to the mass media, have been subjected to the harshest criticisms of feminist groups, radical and otherwise. This is, perhaps, only just, since advertising has played such an important, some would say pivotal, role in creating and sustaining our ideal vision of the middle-class family and woman's function in it.

This view of the American family can be seen as early as the years immediately following the Civil War when the concomitant developments of industrialization and urbanization caused rapid and dramatic social change. As the percentage of American families living on farms steadily declined, new patterns of social behavior became necessary. In the most general terms, if a predominantly agricultural society required the family to form a tightly knit economic unit, the industrial setting invariably fragmented it. On the small, self-sustaining farm, husbands, wives, and offspring lived and worked together, but in the cities the man earned a wage away from the home in an office or factory while the woman remained at home, cleaning, cooking, and raising the children. Of course she had done those same things on the farm, but she had also performed important economic functions such as preserving foodstuffs, spinning, sewing, making clothes, even processing ashes into soap. When the family moved to the city where these everyday items were bought for cash, the task of choosing what and how much to buy devolved to the wife. She was no longer a producer or processor; she was a consumer. But because she was required to use money given to her by her wage-earning husband, the fact of increased economic dependency was added to the long catalog of traditions and laws that made women unequal in almost all spheres of life. In 1898, Charlotte Perkins Gilman, a leading intellectual and an outspoken critic of the new social order, summed up the position of the urban middle-class woman in *Women and Economics*: ". . . all that she may wish to have, all that she may wish to do, must come through a single channel and a single choice. Wealth, power, social distinction, fame—not only these, but home and happiness, reputation, ease and pleasure, her bread and butter—all must come to her through a small gold ring."

Although few of Gilman's contemporaries shared her pessimistic attitude about these developments, the makers and shapers of American popular culture throughout the twentieth century have vividly affirmed the accuracy of her views in poems, songs, and stories, on film, in print, and over the air waves. Until very recently the centrality of marriage and the married state in the life of every woman remained an unchallenged assumption in our most popular movies, novels, and magazine fictions, as well as on radio and television dramas and situation comedies. The creators of advertising, because their work is derived from the content of media, and because of their penchant for playing on our emotions, have always invoked the hopes, fears, joys, and failures commonly associated with marriage to sell a wide variety of products.

From the makers of mouthwash and toothpaste who urge women to realize that bad breath causes spinsterhood to the purveyors of life insurance who reveal the terrors of the widow left alone in a hostile world, almost all major advertisers have employed themes from the mythology of marriage in their persuasive efforts. If ads for beauty soaps, creams, and cosmetics hold out the promise of love and romance as a prelude to marriage, those for household cleansers and detergents promise to ease the daily chores that may destroy a woman's illusion of wedded bliss.

Helping the housewife to avoid drudgery has remained a key theme in advertising for everything from expensive household appliances to everyday packaged foods. Whether the ad is for vacuum cleaners or canned soups, washing machines or instant coffee, frost-free freezers or frozen french fries, the ease, comfort, and convenience of the American housewife is traditionally employed as a major selling point. Inherent in this constant concern for the housewife's well-being is the advertiser's unspoken recognition of just how difficult and boring housework can be.

Although ads depicting the housewife as a drudge exist throughout the history of advertising, realism has rarely been considered an effective mode of persuasion. Most people, advertisers discovered, prefer fantasy and glorification of their workaday lives, especially when someone's trying to sell them something. Ironically, as the woman's home-centered tasks grew easier with the invention of "labor-saving devices," her traditional roles of

No Man Has a Right to Ask Any Woman to Get Down on Her Knees to Scrub the Floor

The one thing now demanded of housework is that it be efficient. For a woman to get on her knees and scrub a floor is wholly inefficient, because every few minutes she must stop and lift a hundred pounds (her own weight), because to shuffle along on her knees is even more than inefficient—it is barbarous.

At Wanamaker's or the Modern Kitchen, New York, ask to see the *Oliver Sanitary Floor Cleaner*, or ask JAMES O. LeFEVRE, New Paltz, New York, for a descriptive folder. Our Money-Back Guarantee insures every advertisement

1904

caring for the house and raising the children were imbued with a falsely exalted significance. As a result, such magazines as *Good Housekeeping* and *Ladies' Home Journal* were laden with images of the American woman as a self-sacrificing mother who surrenders all aspiration for the children's sake, or as a dedicated homemaker whose love of a sparkling clean home transcends every concern—save that of fetching her husband a cold beer, or preparing a hearty, nutritious meal.

Not surprisingly, other female archetypes and stereotypes familiar to consumers of the popular mass media were also easily assimilated into the everyday worlds imagined by the practitioners of advertising. The shy but lovely single girl, the triumphant bride, the cheerful wife, the gossipy next-door neighbor are all character types still being used to sell a wide variety of products. The so-called independent woman who, though married, doesn't keep house, but has a job, drives her own car, and participates in major purchasing decisions, usually appears in ads for expensive or exotic items in such magazines as *The New Yorker* or *Harper's Bazaar*, read in high-income households.

So far we've been talking about advertising created from the woman's point of view, or, as some would have it, the woman's point of view as seen by the men who have always dominated every aspect of the advertising business. In any event, the results have been both an idealization of women's domestic roles in an industrialized society and a reflection of what that society regards as the most useful and satisfactory life for its women. The image of women in advertising directed to men, however, provides a different, but not less interesting, perspective.

This is especially and most obviously true in ads that use women as "sex objects." Even in the days before the Sexual Revolution women were frequently displayed in scanty costumes and alluring poses, usually in ads for such exclusively masculine items as cigars, automobile equipment, and shaving paraphernalia. During the 1950s and 1960s the list of products that used this method increased, as did the sexual explicitness of the ads when magazines of self-proclaimed male sophistication (*Esquire, Playboy, Penthouse*) allowed the advertising to imitate the editorial and pictorial content of the book (see the section on sex).

Another kind of advertising that has traditionally made use of women to sell goods to men is that for office equipment: adding machines, typewriters, dictaphones, and so on. Because men usually purchase the machines that are run by women, this form of advertisement can be found in such business publications as *Fortune*, trade magazines, and in general-interest magazines with large numbers of male readers—*Saturday Evening Post, Time, Life*, for example. Although these ads occasionally provide interesting historical pictures of women at the office, they are more valuable in revealing attitudes about women's work. Predictably, all of the women are pictured as clerks, telephone operators, or secretaries and, generally speaking, represented as recognizable caricatures: If they're young they're attractive and bubble-brained; over thirty, they're efficient and virginal, though not by choice. These characteristics serve to remind the reader that a woman's job is a means to meeting a man, not a stepping-stone in a lifelong career.

In a society so totally and overtly devoted to the ideal of female domesticity, a woman worked outside the home only when she had to, that is, when she was single or when her husband's salary was insufficient for the family's needs. And if a woman's work was viewed as temporary, at least in relation to a man's, it was quite easy for her functions to be considered appendages to the important tasks performed by men: Nurses assisting doctors, and stewardesses taking care of tired businessmen are the most frequent examples found in print advertising. Until the advent of television, advertisments were so preoccupied with the social and cultural assumptions of the middle class that they only occasionally offered us glimpses of the working-class woman as an unskilled laborer on an assembly line, or as a domestic in the homes of the rich (see especially the section on blacks).

In recent years the very notion of work—of what we do and how it affects our individual and collective psyches—has emerged as a subject of increasing importance to historians and sociologists alike. To those concerned with the social position of women, whether with the intention of fostering change or merely observing it, the study of women working outside the home has become the key focal point and the most significant yardstick for measuring "progress" in feminist terms. Between 1910 and

1940 the percentage of all American women working outside the home remained fairly constant at 25 percent; furthermore, in 1940 only 15 percent of all married women were employed. Within only two subsequent decades those figures changed dramatically: By 1960, 40 percent of all women held outside jobs, and 30 percent of all married women, double the earlier number. Many reasons can and have been cited to explain this unprecedented shift in social arrangements, but all commentators have agreed that the economic and psychological impact of World War II was crucial.

As in World War I, this conflict required the direct involvement of millions of men while demanding a vastly expanded industrial and agricultural output. To meet the seemingly endless needs of the first truly mechanized war in history, more than six million women entered the labor force between 1942 and 1945. By the end of the war a total of twenty million women were employed, many of them in jobs always held by men during peacetime. What follows is a leading historian's description of what they did:

> *Women responded to the manpower crisis with an unprecedented display of skill and ingenuity. The beautician who overnight became a switchman for 600 Long Island Railroad trains represented but one example of women's readiness to assume new responsibilities. . . . A former cosmetics salesgirl from Philadelphia operated a 1700 ton keel binder. In Gary, Indiana, women maneuvered giant overhead traveling cranes and cleared out blast furnaces. Elsewhere, women ran lathes, cut dies, read blueprints, and serviced airplanes. They maintained roadbeds, greased locomotives, and took the place of lumberjacks in toppling giant redwoods. As stevedores, blacksmiths, foundry helpers, and drill press operators, they demonstrated that they could fill any job, no matter how difficult or arduous.*
>
> William Chafe,
> *The American Woman*
> (1972)

It may be impossible to measure the effects of such experiences with anything resembling scientific accuracy, but it is reasonable to assume that hundreds of thousands of women had their first taste of meaningful work outside the home while simultaneously observing that home life itself did not collapse as a result. It may even be safe to speculate that for the first time society recognized that the power of a machine was indifferent to the sex of its operator. In any event, at least one fact remains verifiable: The percentage of women working never declined again. However, only the advantage of historical hindsight allows us to see the importance of this.

The postwar generation quite understandably attempted to create a better society by preserving the shape and structure of social institutions as they existed before the conflict. The baby boom, the record number of housing starts—especially in the suburbs—and the rise in church attendance all indicate a desire to reaffirm the values of middle-class family life. In such a society women's traditional roles of wife, mother, and consumer could only be heightened in importance. But when the values of an imaginary, idealized past mingled with the realities and new possibilities of a rapidly changing technological age, confusions and contradictions were the predictable result. Conflict would soon follow, and advertising would be a central issue.

During the 1950s, as the so-called mass-consumption society shifted into high gear, the economic and social roles of advertising took on a new importance. In order to sell the enormous number of prosperity's products, the essential as well as the superficial (both of which existed in a multitude of brand names), the amount of dollars devoted to advertising more than doubled in one decade. Thanks in part, as well, to the establishment of a national commercialized television system, annual advertising expenditures rose from $5.7 billion in 1950 to almost $12 billion in 1960.

As the ads proliferated in proportion to the increased sums, so too did the number of old familiar scenes depicting women pampering their husbands, chauffeuring their children, making sandwiches, scrubbing floors, washing dishes, ironing clothes, baking cakes, shopping in the supermarket, and teaching their daughters to do the same. A boom in the sale of household appliances was accompanied by a spate of advertising in which women smiled ecstatically as their husbands and children presented them with new refrigerators, freezers, stoves, washing machines, driers, dishwashers, toasters, blenders, waffle irons, and the whole gamut of gadgets essential to the functioning of the American home. Ironically, the leisure time these inventions provided soon enabled millions of women to leave the home and return to work. The traditional advertising image of the housewife was on the way to losing its validity.

The first sounds of discontent were voiced in the early 1960s by educated middle-class women who said they wanted more from life than the housewife's role could offer. Armed with college diplomas and sophisticated birth control methods, they demanded the right to have a career as well as a family; they insisted on their ability to compete with men for jobs that required education, training, and judgment, not brawn and muscle. In these women's opinion, advertisers and other communicators continued to create outmoded scenes and old-fashioned characters because they were easy and comfortable, and because they had always worked. At first the complaints were isolated incidents, quiet rumblings muffled in part by the media's coverage of the civil rights movement and the escalating war in Vietnam. Before the end of the decade, however, the woman's issue had exploded onto the front page of every newspaper and into the major stories of all the news broadcasts.

The media hoopla that enveloped the women's movement during the late 1960s and early 1970s actually helped to obscure the fact that true social change had begun. While newspapers and television chose to show pictures of women marching and chanting, burning their bras, and publicly proclaiming their love for a member of the same gender, in reality the birthrate dropped while the divorce rate soared, inflation skyrocketed, and wives and mothers returned to work in unprecedented numbers. The advertising community, like most social observers, failed to recognize the nature of the transformation taking place. Although much was made of the new sexual innuendo and even bravado present in advertising to women, most of this was localized in magazines designed for young career types, *Cosmopolitan* being the most obvious example. But in ads found in general periodicals and the established women's magazines, as well as in television commercials, the image of the woman's world had changed very little. As late as 1971, according to an article in the *Journal of Marketing Research*, an analysis of the roles portrayed by women in thousands of magazine advertisements could only lead to the following conclusions: A woman's place is in the home, women do not make important decisions or do important things, women are dependent and need men's protection, and men regard women primarily as sex objects who are not interesting as people.

Advertisers, their agencies, and the major industry associations all protested. But their assertion that advertising reflected the way American women really lived proved more damnable than redeeming. Over the last few years constant complaints by various women's organizations have resulted in slight but recognizable changes. Relatively minor achievements, such as de-emphasizing the home setting or having a woman demonstrate knowledge in such a recognizably male area as car repair have not, however, hidden the increasingly blatant use of sex, even on television, to sell cigars, shaving cream, and sports cars. In addition, the most important objective of the women's groups—the portrayal of women in roles outside the home and in jobs other than clerical ones—has met with only limited success.

Operating on the theory that the cumulative effect of traditional images can be to prevent social change by *not* presenting alternative career and lifestyle possibilities, leaders of the women's movement asked the advertisers to show women acting as doctors, physicists, business executives, and in once all-male occupations, such as telephone installers, letter carriers, or taxi drivers. Although every important advertising journal and trade association has agreed this should be done, change has taken place very slowly. One reason is that some large advertisers fear a negative response from the millions of housewives who are offended by advertising that indirectly implies that their way of life is passé. Sustained cooperation has come, perhaps predictably, from those who would most benefit by it: whiskey manufacturers who have found a new group to sell to; and institutional advertisers such as the utilities or the aerospace industry, who have nothing to sell the general reader of advertisements but who seek the goodwill of the educated public and the government.

Perhaps, as some have said, the whole image issue has been greatly exaggerated because the forces impelling social change are so strongly established and so deeply rooted. The advertisers would be only too glad to drop the whole subject and get on with the business of trying to sell the female consumer by finding out how she lives. And what is most striking today is the continuation of the trend toward women working outside the home no matter what their age, class, or marital status might be. About 50 percent of all American women work, and an incredible 54 percent of married women with school age children now hold jobs (double the percentage of right after the war). What kind of work they do, and why, are questions advertisers are only beginning to ask.

In 1975 a new agency called Advertising to Women, Inc. was started with the avowed intention of reaching the contemporary woman, the confident, career-oriented woman who was now unabashed by her sexuality. The publicly announced results of the agency's market research demonstrated that the love affair between women and business still had the same premises as before, only now women's consuming power was even more important. According to the new agency today's women not only directly decide what to purchase for the running of the home, they also make "60% of all vacation-destination decisions, nearly 50% of color-TV brand selections, over 46% of wine-brand decisions, and 30% of new car selections."

12

1896

"So long as the woman's place is consistently that of a drudge, she is, in the average of cases, fairly contented with her lot. She not only has something tangible and purposeful to do, but she has also no time or thought to spare for a rebellious assertion of such human propensity to self-direction as she has inherited."

Thorstein Veblen, *The Theory of the Leisure Class* (1899)

Woman is the great civilizer. If it were not for her man would revert to whiskers and carry a club.

Woman does much for the Gillette because it is her presence, her influence, that puts the emphasis on good clothes, clean linen, and a clean shave.

She admires the clean, healthy skin of a man who uses a Gillette. She does not approve the ladylike massage-finish of the tonsorial artist. The massaged appearance ceased to be "class" largely because she said so.

There is something fine and wholesome about the Gillette shave. It does not reek of violet water and pomades.

The use of the Gillette has a decidedly good effect on the skin. It gives a healthy look that suggests the outdoor rather than the indoor man.

Then think of the comfort—the convenience—the morning shave in less time than the morning dip.

A million men will buy Gillettes this year. Now is the time to get yours.

Standard Set with twelve double-edge blades, $5.00. Regular box of 12 blades, $1.00; carton of 6 blades, 50c.

King C Gillette

GILLETTE SALES COMPANY, 34 W. Second Street, Boston
New York, Times Building   Chicago, Stock Exchange Building   Gillette Safety Razor, Ltd., London   Eastern Office, Shanghai, China   Canadian Office, 63 St. Alexander Street, Montreal
Factories: Boston, Montreal, Leicester, Berlin, Paris

1910

EQUAL RIGHTS! — SURE!

THAT is one of the big reasons why an International Time Recorder should be installed in every Business Institution.

❧ The employer has a right to every minute of the working-day of the people on his payroll.

❧ The employee has a right to be paid for all his time.

❧ And that is just what the International Time Recorder does. It precludes the possibilities of mistakes in computing time and wages.

❧ When Mary fusses unduly with her curling-irons and is late, it makes note of the fact in flaming red—indisputable evidence of her tardiness—and she is "docked."

❧ Next day she's right on time! for she can't afford this depletion of her exchequer—and neither can her employer. Equal rights—sure! ❧ The International Time Recorder cuts out waste, prevents error, shows "who's who," and is an invaluable aid to efficiency, economy and success. ❧ The International Time Recording Co. make error-proof, fool-proof, cost-saving machines of every description. ❧ Drop them a postal, stating your business and position, and they'll show you how to dam the waste and stop the leaks.

INTERNATIONAL TIME RECORDING COMPANY

LONDON OFFICE:
International Time Recording Co., Ltd., 30-32 Farringdon Road, London, E. C. England

of New York
Lock Box 26
Endicott, N. Y.

BERLIN OFFICE:
International Time Recording Co., m. b. H., 135-136 Alexandrinenstr., Berlin, S.W., Germany

1912

These two ads represent the extreme views of women as depicted in advertising directed to men. On the one hand she is seen as a civilizing agent, the force that prevents men from descending into barbarism (a theme frequently found in popular Western stories); on the other, she's the butt of many jokes because she is more concerned with her hairdo than her job, more interested in her curling irons than in true equal rights. It is interesting to note that the class of women in each ad is so easily identifiable.

Stop Waiting for the Wash-Woman

"Late again. Half the morning gone and the wash isn't even started!"

How many times it happens, doesn't it? How many times the hours grow into days while you wait for Mary, Ann or Maggie to "show up!"

How many times you have to hunt around, through your friends or through the employment agency at the eleventh hour for a substitute!

It is easy to stop this wash-day uncertainty.

Put a Gainaday in your basement and you won't even have to wait for Monday. Any day, any hour, this efficient electric washer and wringer is ready to take care of your heaviest wash or your daintiest laces.

It gives you better than hand-method results with none of the wear and tear. Its revolving cylinder handles all the clothes as carefully as you handle laces in a wash-pan. It thoroughly cleanses everything from rugs and overalls to the daintiest of fabrics.

You'll like the sturdy, swinging wringer because you can wring the clothes from washer to rinse water, from rinse water to blue water and from blue water to basket without moving the machine. During the last two operations another wash can be going through the machine.

The Gainaday is safe—every working part is entirely covered up, all electric connections are heavily insulated and even the wringer has a safety catch. The Gainaday slides around on the floor as easily as a baby tender.

It's guaranteed for five years.

Write today for a copy of our Picture Story Circular; then we'll tell you how easily you can obtain one of these efficient machines.

Pittsburgh Gage & Supply Co.
3010 Liberty Ave.   Pittsburgh, Pa.

Gainaday
★
Washer   Wringer

1916

The style, tone, and point of view of the copywriter all make this an extremely interesting piece of social history; but note, too, his puzzling use of Irish names. (For later examples of blacks portrayed in domestic roles see the section on Blacks.)

Are You Keeping Up With Your Husband?

ARE you still the attractive, alert, up-to-date woman he married? Are you keeping up with the interesting things in life as he is, or are you devoting all your time, strength and thought to housework?

The busiest man in office, shop or profession manages to have time to meet people and progresses mentally as he succeeds financially. But many a wife, intending to help her husband, gets along without many household aids, and thus is forced to confine her activity to the narrow sphere of housework. This is false economy from the financial standpoint, and wrong from the standpoint of companionship.

SIMPLEX IRONER
"THE BEST IRONER"

Hand ironing is tiring and aging work, which can and should be eliminated. The SIMPLEX Ironer will do your entire ironing in an hour or two instead of your spending a whole day at it. The hours gained can be put to more profitable and enjoyable use.

Once you have used the SIMPLEX, you will find it indispensable. Any SIMPLEX dealer will install a machine in your home where it can best be demonstrated. Where there is no dealer we shall be glad to send a SIMPLEX on approval.

Send for our book "Clean Linen in Abundance" and our illustrated story "Aunt Eliza from Boston" which tells of the joy the SIMPLEX brought into one home.

Our Service Department will plan and arrange your home laundry—no obligation.

AMERICAN IRONING MACHINE CO., 503, 168 N. Michigan Ave., CHICAGO

We also make Ironing Machines for the Small or Hand Laundry, Hotel, Institution, etc. Write for catalog.

And... "I promise
to keep that schoolgirl complexion"

Thousands are doing it through this simple rule
in natural skin care, followed in this way:

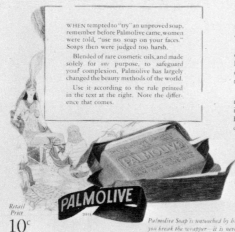

WHEN tempted to "try" an unproved soap, remember before Palmolive came, women were told, "use no soap on your faces." Soaps then were judged too harsh.

Blended of rare cosmetic oils, and made solely for *one* purpose, to safeguard your complexion, Palmolive has largely changed the beauty methods of the world.

Use it according to the rule printed in the text at the right. Note the difference that comes.

WOMEN used to lose the priceless charm of youth, then struggle everlastingly to regain it. Today, by following natural and proved ways in skin care, they keep it.

Start by avoiding the use of unproved ways on your skin. A good complexion is too priceless for experiment. You can retain natural charm and freshness through the years simply by taking ordinary precautions with your skin.

Foremost skin specialists of the world recommend soap and water cleansing as the first rule in skin care. Leading beauty experts employ it. Results are proved on every side. Try it—it will do much for you.

The rule to follow if guarding a good complexion is your goal

Wash your face gently with soothing Palmolive Soap, massaging the lather softly into the skin. Rinse thoroughly, first with warm water, then with cold. If your skin is inclined to be dry, apply a touch of good cold cream—that is all. Do this regularly, and particularly in the evening. Use powder and rouge if you wish. But never leave them on over night. They clog the pores, often enlarge them. Blackheads and disfigurements often follow. They must be washed away.

Avoid this mistake

Do not use ordinary soaps in the treatment given above. Do not think any green soap, or one represented as of olive and palm oils, is the same as Palmolive.

And it costs but 10c the cake! So little that millions let it do for their bodies what it does for their faces. Obtain a cake today. Then note the amazing difference one week makes.

Soap from trees!

The only oils in Palmolive Soap are the soothing beauty oils from the olive tree, the African palm, and the coconut palm—and no other fats whatsoever. That is why Palmolive Soap is the natural color that it is—for palm and olive oils, nothing else, give Palmolive its natural green color.

The only secret to Palmolive is its exclusive blend—and that is one of the world's priceless beauty secrets.

THE PALMOLIVE COMPANY, (DEL. CORP.), CHICAGO, ILLINOIS

Palmolive Soap is untouched by human hands until you break the wrapper—it is never sold unwrapped

Retail Price
10c

PALMOLIVE

1927

In a society that regards marriage as the most important part of a woman's life, few advertising images can match that of the young, beautiful bride for sheer attention-getting power. She has been used to sell everything from soap, makeup, and lingerie to hope chests, silverware, and pots and pans. Brides themselves have always been a very special audience for a broad range of advertisers because in the months preceding the wedding they make so many major purchases. Bride's magazine was founded in 1934 to meet this specialized advertising audience, and it was so successful that a competitor called Modern Bride was issued in 1949. Both are still popular among brides-to-be: in 1978 they had a combined monthly circulation of over 500,000.

COPYRIGHT 1917 BY THE PROCTER & GAMBLE CO., CINCINNATI

TO the one who washes the dishes Ivory Soap means freedom from red, rough hands. It is so mild and pure that no matter how often used it leaves the tenderest skin soft, smooth and white.

To the one who does the drying Ivory Soap means faultlessly washed dishes. It cleans them so thoroughly that it is easy to make the glassware sparkle, the silver shine and the china look its best.

The cost of using Ivory Soap for washing dishes is but a few cents a month more than for ordinary soap. Do you wash your dishes with Ivory Soap?

IVORY SOAP.... ★ .... 99 44/100 % PURE

IT FLOATS

The Woman Who Never Went Out

*What happened when she realized there was
more in the world than the view from her kitchen window*

I HURT—that sudden flash of seeing herself as others must see her. A drudge—that's what she was. One of the army of women past whom the world whirls gaily, while they grow older and more faded and colorless—till finally one morning they wake up and realize that their chance to play has slipped away forever.

She had never meant to let it happen—it had come upon her so gradually she couldn't remember how it began.

When first she was married she went out quite often—to little tea parties, to luncheons, and to "showers" given for her friends when they were married, too. And in the evening she would go to the movies with her husband and they'd stop in at the Greek's for a sundae on the way home, quite as they had done when they were engaged.

But before she knew it her friends stopped inviting her—she was always "too tired," or didn't have time. And now, as she stood among her pots and pans, it seemed to her that that was all she ever did. Was it really months since she had been to a party—or did it only seem so? Oh, how she hated that kitchen—even the view from the window was always the same!

*   *   *

What should she do? It was inconceivable that she should simply walk out and let the door close behind her, as Nora did in The Doll's House. No such dramatic solution was needed, anyway. It was a matter for sane thought, for constructive effort—

So she sat down to think it over calmly.

Corned Beef Metropolitan
Cream Libby's Corned Beef and place on platter. Dot with sliced ripe olives and garnish with toast points and hard boiled egg slices. Quickly prepared and delightful to eat!

In the end, as she wrote us in one of the most interesting letters we have ever received, it simmered down to the conclusion that she had

The best deviled eggs you ever ate—stuffed with veal
Remove yolks from hard boiled eggs which have been cut in quarters. Mash yolks with Libby's Veal Loaf and arrange mixture on egg quarters. Garnish with parsley

let her job run away with her. She saw that she had allowed her housekeeping to absorb not only all her time but her interest and vivacity. And she resolved to turn over a new leaf—to start at once to get the upper hand of her job—to run her house, instead of letting her house run her!

As soon as she really tried, her letter said, she discovered countless ways to relieve the burden of her housekeeping "chores." It would take too long to describe all of them, but one which she stumbled on may prove helpful to you, too. She began to use Libby's Packaged Meats.

This woman is only one of many who have told us how these almost-ready-to-serve meats have helped them solve the problem of setting a good table and still having time left for other interests. For women everywhere

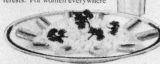

Just right when they're hungry—Vienna Sausage and eggs
Heat and split Libby's Vienna Sausages and arrange on plate with mound of scrambled eggs. Such tender, savory little sausages you never tasted!

are learning that there are no finer meats obtainable than Libby's Packaged Meats—Corned Beef, Dried Beef, Vienna Sausage, Veal Loaf and a long list of other delicacies.

They are packaged in Chicago—meat center of the world—where the choicest meats are available to the Libby kitchens. Only cuts from fresh Government inspected meats are used.

They come to you in air-tight containers which, when opened, reveal the meats as fresh as on the day they were packed. You will find that Libby's meats have a flavor and tenderness that home cooking of ordinary meats cannot approach. Shown on this page are a few suggestions for new

Dried Beef with rice and tomato sauce—try it!
Boil one cup rice until tender in salted boiling water, drain dry and moisten with tomato sauce. Serve with Libby's Dried Beef, creamed and garnished with parsley

and delightful ways of serving these meats. Begin tomorrow to let Libby's meats save time for you.

"Book of Five Minute Meats"—Free
WRITE for the Libby "Book of Five Minute Meats," a book of simple recipes devised by Libby's expert chefs to lighten the burden of cooking and save time for the homemaker. Every dish is attractively illustrated in full colors and is accompanied by complete cooking instructions. Write for your copy today. It is Free.

Your grocer has Libby's Packaged Meats or will gladly get them for you.

LIBBY'S MUSTARD—Try Libby's Mustard with Libby's meats. An unusually good mustard—not too "tangy," not too mild, delightful in flavor, it adds a touch of savoriness that puts an edge on the dullest appetite.

Libby, McNeill & Libby
105 Welfare Bldg., Chicago
Libby, McNeill & Libby of Can., Ltd., 45 E. Front St., Toronto, Ont., Can.

1920

"It is not that women are really smaller-minded, weaker-minded, more timid and vacillating; but that whosoever, man or woman, lives always in a small, dark, place is always guarded, protected, directed and restrained, will become inevitably narrowed and weakened by it. The woman is narrowed by the home and the man is narrowed by the woman."
Charlotte Perkins Gilman, *The Home, Its Work and Influence* (1910)

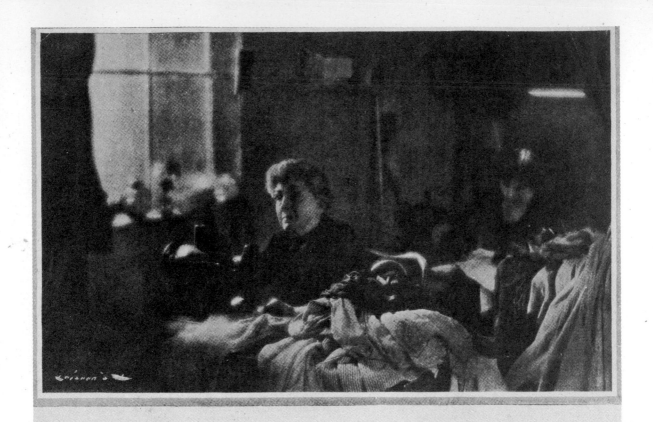

The little grey lady

Toil—toil—a merciless cycle of toil is all she knows. Daily the lines on that pitifully beautiful old face grow deeper. Daily those slender, needle-scarred fingers tremble more and more.

Someone is responsible for this—glaringly responsible. A husband, a brother, a son has failed in his imperative duty.

Because life insurance provides a way to give to old age the comforts and consideration it so richly deserves, this forlorn spectacle is less general today than in bygone days. May the time soon come when it will be completely obliterated!

THE PRUDENTIAL INSURANCE COMPANY of AMERICA
EDWARD D. DUFFIELD, *President*   HOME OFFICE, *Newark, N.J.*

1925

By necessity, life-insurance advertising has always been preoccupied with themes of death and destitution. Until very recently these ads were directed exclusively to men and, in order to make their point, used pictures and descriptions of the women who would be, so to speak, left behind. Implicit in this kind of advertising is a sense that women's dependency on men reaches beyond the grave. See a later example on p. 36.

The woman who does a man's work

She must prove her worth every day. She must keep young, alert, responsive. There can be no let-up

"A woman can't live on her past achievements. I find I must prove my worth every single day," says a successful business woman.

THE modern woman finds herself frequently called upon to do a "man's work."

There can be no shirking in her busy life. She must withstand the same strain on her nerves—the same steady grind, hour after hour and day after day—that a man's work requires.

She cannot give way to the vagaries and nerves and weakness so long considered characteristic of the "weaker sex." For her competition is not alone with men—but with her own healthy, eager sisters.

The secret of youthfulness

WHETHER in business, the arts, the home or in society—the modern woman must *keep* young. The real secret of keeping young lies in preventing the usual feminine illnesses. Every such illness weakens the system; and the woman of today cannot afford simply to *appear* young. Her whole system must be responsive, awake, keen.

Most typically feminine illnesses can be prevented. A well-known New York physician, chief gynecologist of one of the large hospitals, says, "Most of these illnesses are the result of bacterial infections." For this reason, physicians are recommending regular feminine hygiene as a necessary preventive

measure. And "Lysol" Disinfectant is the accepted antiseptic for this purpose. It is *safe* and it is *effective*. It insures the complete antiseptic cleanliness which is so vital.

"Lysol" Disinfectant is completely soluble in water. Tests made by pouring "Lysol" into water, stirring well and then examining this solution under the microscope show that every single drop is clear and transparent—there are no undissolved globules. This means that "Lysol" is 100 per cent effective in destroying harmful germ life.

At the same time, "Lysol" is *neutral*. It contains no free alkali nor free acid. Diluted in correct proportions, it is non-caustic. It does not irritate. No antiseptic could be safer for the delicate internal tissues.

And "Lysol" is economical; one-half teaspoonful to one quart of water is all that is required to make the proper antiseptic solution for feminine hygiene.

Send for Booklet

CORRECT, vital facts about feminine hygiene are included in a new booklet, which gives complete information and directions for the many personal and household uses of "Lysol" Disinfectant. Every woman should know and follow the rules of personal hygiene contained in this booklet. Mail coupon for free copy.

Manufactured only by LYSOL, INC., 635 GREENWICH ST., NEW YORK CITY
Sole Distributors: LEHN & FINK, INC., NEW YORK
Canadian Agents: Harold F. Ritchie & Co., Limited, 10 McCaul St., Toronto

COMPLETE directions for use are in every package. The genuine "Lysol" Disinfectant is put up only in brown glass bottles containing 3, 7 and 16 ounces; each bottle is packed in a yellow carton. The 3 ounce bottle also comes in a special non-breakable package for travelers (50 cents). Insist on obtaining genuine "Lysol" Disinfectant. Sold by all drug stores.

Lysol Disinfectant
Reg. U.S. Pat. Off.
The ideal personal antiseptic

Use "Lysol" as an antiseptic solution
One-half teaspoonful to one quart water
For feminine hygiene
When baby comes
For wounds
For the sickroom
For the bathroom

Use "Lysol" as a disinfecting solution
Two teaspoonfuls to one quart water
For the kitchen
In the toilet
For sweeping
For floors, cellars, dark corners

SIGN AND MAIL THIS COUPON TODAY

LEHN & FINK, INC.,
Dept. B-2, 635 Greenwich St., New York City.

Mail me, without charge, your booklet which gives complete information about the use of "Lysol" for feminine hygiene.

Name

Address

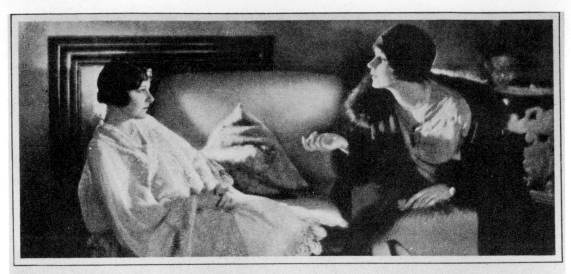

"Why *in the* world do you continue *to* empty *the* filthy contents *of* a cleaner bag

. . . *When Modern Sanitary Methods Are Available in the Air-Way Sanitary System?"*

Grace—"Oh, I'm so sorry you're ill, Anne. I was over to Mother's and she told me about you, so I rushed right over."

Anne—"I'm certainly glad you came. I've been upstairs in bed since last Thursday, but the Doctor said I could come down on the davenport today. It's not so lonesome and I'm feeling better already. I'll be all right in a day or two."

Grace—"I hope so. Where did you get that awful cold?"

Anne—"I don't know unless it was the other day when I was cleaning. I ran the vacuum cleaner around and then went right outdoors to empty the bag. I was warm and didn't think about a wrap. The bag was pretty full and I had to shake it and then turn it inside out and brush it. I stayed out in the cold longer than I had intended. That night I began to cough and here I am."

Grace—"That's probably just where you caught cold. Why in the world do you continue to empty the filthy contents of a cleaner bag anyway? Running out into the cold to shake out the bag! You ought to be scolded. You're so up-to-date with everything, I am amazed that you have not bought an Air-Way Sanitary System."

With Air-Way you never have to empty a bag."

Anne—"Never have to empty a bag? Where does the dirt go?"

Grace—"It's collected and sealed in a Sanitary Dust Container. When the container is filled, just detach it and either burn it or throw it away. Then put in a fresh dust container. I'll use about a dollar's worth of dust containers in a year. It's a dollar invested in my health. No dust blows back on my person or clothing. Really this is the only sanitary way to dispose of the collected dirt that I have ever seen."

Anne—"It sounds wonderful. Just think of not having to shake out that dirt."

Grace—"It is wonderful. You know I had a heavy old cleaner, but I gave it to my laundress when I saw how much easier and better the Air-Way would do my work. It's so light that it's really a pleasure to use. It polishes my hardwood floors, cleans my radiators, mouldings, lampshades, overstuffed furniture—in fact, everything that doesn't have to be washed. And you ought to see how much brighter my rugs look."

Anne—"Did you say it polished floors?"

Grace—"It certainly does. My floors never looked as well. Then there's something else, the Insector. You know how I always dreaded moths. Well, now I use the Air-Way Insector regularly and spray everything with Air-Way Moth Control. It's a dry chemical, not one of those liquid insecticides."

Anne—"I need some of that Moth Control."

Grace—"This Moth Control comes out of the System in a spray of tiny crystals which dissolves into a powerful penetrating gas that seeps into cracks and crevices. It isn't just a surface treatment. It goes very much deeper. I never saw anything like it. I use it regularly, just as directed."

Anne—"Well, I certainly must buy an Air-Way. No more bag shaking for me. Where can I get one?"

Grace—"Look in your phone book under the "A's" for Air-Way Branch. It's always listed that way. They'll send a man out to show you one right here in your home. And you'll certainly be amazed at what it will do. You'll thank me for advising you to get one."

Air-Way is represented in hundreds of cities and listed in the telephone books under "Air-Way Branch of (your city)." Sold direct—not in any store. A telephone call will bring a trained, gentlemanly, bonded representative to demonstrate Air-Way in your home.

Air-Way
SANITARY SYSTEM
It has raised the standard of sanitation in the home

If you do not find an Air-Way Branch listed in your phone book we will gladly supply you with complete information about The Air-Way Sanitary System. Just write your name and address on the margin of this page and send it direct to the factory.

AIR-WAY ELECTRIC APPLIANCE CORPORATION, TOLEDO, OHIO, U. S. A. - AIR-WAY LTD., TORONTO, CANADA

1929

This is a very interesting ad for reasons that go beyond the quaint, outdated language ("davenport," "wrap," "scolded") and the pomposity inherent in calling a vacuum cleaner a "sanitary system." Although it was written about fifty years ago the ad contains the essential elements of many television commercials directed to the female consumer. Set in the home, it is a dialogue between two women, one strong and knowledgeable who explains the value of the product to the other, her weaker and ignorant friend.

In 1880 only 4 percent of all employed women worked in offices, the rest were engaged in agriculture; in 1890 the percentage of working women in offices had soared to 21 percent. By 1920 women represented almost 50 percent of all bookkeepers and accountants, and over 90 percent of all typists and stenographers. As David Potter, a distinguished social historian, commented: "As a symbol, the typewriter evokes fewer emotions than the plow, but like the plow, it played a vital part in the fulfillment of the American promise of opportunity and independence. The wilderness may have been the frontier for American men, and the cabin in the clearing the symbol of their independence, but the city was the frontier for American women and the business office was what gave them economic independence and the opportunity to follow a course of their own."

"American Women and American Character" (1962)

24

Let Me SEE Your Wares

"I am the purchasing agent of America. I buy four-fifths of all things that are bought in stores.

"I buy little which I do not see. Seeing arouses my desire. Seeing satisfies my caution. I must see or I won't buy.

"I must see clearly. I must see things well displayed in good light. Good lighting in your display windows draws me into your store. Good light inside shows that your store is neat, clean, sanitary, modern—a safe place to buy. Let me SEE your wares!"

THERE are trained National Lamp Works lighting specialists in all parts of the country, maintained for the sole purpose of rendering experienced counsel on store window and interior lighting. Their services cost merchants nothing. Get in touch with them now. Find out whether your lighting measures up to modern requirements—whether, indeed, you have the necessary minimum of ten foot-candles of illumination in all parts of your store.

Write us and we will arrange for a free survey, which will show you whether you have enough light to *see* by and to *sell* by. National Lamp Works *of General Electric Co.*, Nela Park, Cleveland, Ohio.

NATIONAL GE MAZDA LAMPS

MAZDA- the mark of a Research Service ...

1929

These ads appeared in the year that the mass-consumption economy reached its first apex. After the onset of the Depression the role of woman as principal consumer would not be romanticized and glorified again until the 1950s.

Through the turnstile
to a land of ADVENTURE!

A unique plan of shopping that
2,500,000 women are using today

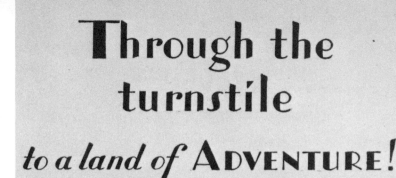

Just walk through the turnstile and help yourself! Take what you please from the shelves, examine it, arrive at your own decision—at Piggly Wiggly

WOMEN like to tell their friends about this unique method of shopping. They enjoy discussing its advantages. Old customers send us thousands of new ones every week.

In a few swift years women have made this plan of household buying a nation-wide vogue.

With their new, wide knowledge of real values, the women of today want to *choose for themselves*. When they shop for foods, they want no clerks trying to urge and persuade them. To them, this special plan is an easy way to give their families more delicious meals at less expense.

Make your own decisions

Within easy reach, on open shelves and stands, the choice foods of the world are

Choose for yourself, help yourself —at Piggly Wiggly

waiting to be looked over at Piggly Wiggly. Beyond the turnstile, a land of adventure!

Famous packages, familiar jars and cans, fresh inviting fruits and vegetables —each item with its big square price tag, at Piggly Wiggly. And no clerks—just help yourself.

Finer foods—lower cost

You linger or hurry as you please. Take what you like in your hands, examine it at leisure. You compare prices—make your *own decision*, uninfluenced by salesmen.

PIGGLY WIGGLY
STORES
The finest kinds of each food selected for you to choose from

A SERVICE NOW OFFERED IN OVER 800 CITIES AND TOWNS

An easy way to serve more tempting meals—and spend less: Piggly Wiggly

And ideas for your menus come flocking, while you shop at Piggly Wiggly!

Most important of all, you save money week in and week out at Piggly Wiggly. Consistently lower prices are assured by our unusual and economical plan of operation.

To serve finer food, to cut grocery costs —this is why 2,500,000 women are using this method of buying every day. To surprise your husband both at the table and with your monthly expenses try this plan. Visit the Piggly Wiggly store in your neighborhood and choose for yourself!

A few years ago only one Piggly Wiggly store —today over 3,000, used daily by 2,500,000 women!

1929

'And....
did you notice the bathroom?'

At that moment the hostess re-entered the room. She just barely overheard. But it was more than enough. She began talking about Junior, about bridge, anything — but like chain lightning her mind reviewed the bathroom. She saw it suddenly as a guest must see it, saw the one detail that positively clamored for criticism. She vowed to change it immediately — to make a simple change that thousands have discovered does more than any other one thing to improve and modernize a bathroom—replacing the old-fashioned wood toilet seat with a handsome, new, all-white Brunswick.

This big improvement can easily be made in any bathroom. The new Brunswick White Seat is especially designed so you may install it yourself.

The Brunswick patented 9-ply reinforcement feature enables us to guarantee it for a lifetime, yet it costs no more. The white pyralin sheet covering will not crack, split, wear off or discolor.

For charming bathrooms decorated in colors the new Brunswick Seat is made in pearl-finish pyralin in nine lovely colors.

Phone your plumber for a new Brunswick Seat. Send for free copy of our booklet, "Bathroom Magic", which gives details of white and colored seats. The Brunswick-Balke-Collender Co., Dept. U-4, 623 South Wabash Ave., Chicago.

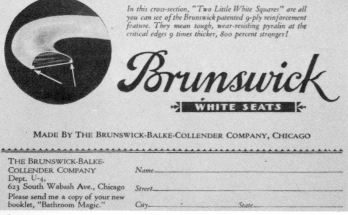

In this cross-section, "Two Little White Squares" are all you can see of the Brunswick patented 9-ply reinforcement feature. They mean tough, wear-resisting pyralin at the critical edges 9 times thicker, 800 percent stronger!

Brunswick
→ WHITE SEATS ←

MADE BY THE BRUNSWICK-BALKE-COLLENDER COMPANY, CHICAGO

THE BRUNSWICK-BALKE-
COLLENDER COMPANY
Dept. U-4,
623 South Wabash Ave., Chicago
Please send me a copy of your new booklet, "Bathroom Magic."

Name_____

Street_____

City_____ State_____

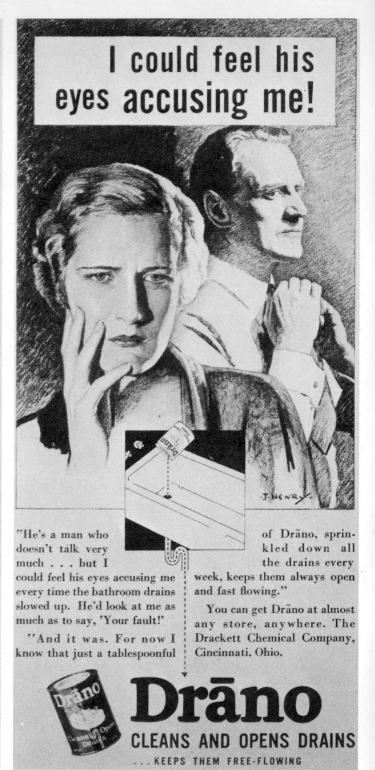

I could feel his eyes accusing me!

"He's a man who doesn't talk very much . . . but I could feel his eyes accusing me every time the bathroom drains slowed up. He'd look at me as much as to say, 'Your fault!'

"And it was. For now I know that just a tablespoonful of Drāno, sprinkled down all the drains every week, keeps them always open and fast flowing."

You can get Drāno at almost any store, anywhere. The Drackett Chemical Company, Cincinnati, Ohio.

Drāno
CLEANS AND OPENS DRAINS
... KEEPS THEM FREE-FLOWING

1930   1932

During the Depression advertising took on a decidedly gloomy air. This was due, in part, to drastic cutbacks in advertising budgets that resulted in less expensive black and white photographs replacing the vibrant four-color illustrations that had characterized the ads of the 1920s. Generally speaking, the mood and tone of the ads were decidedly different as fear of failure became a national pre-occupation, at least in the world of advertising. For women these fears naturally centered on the home, and although the ads usually dealt with relatively minor problems of clogged drains or choice of hats, they often implied that the possibility of male displeasure caused the greatest apprehension.

She said, "I'M AFRAID I DON'T LIKE IT"
She thought, "I'M AFRAID HE WON'T LIKE IT"

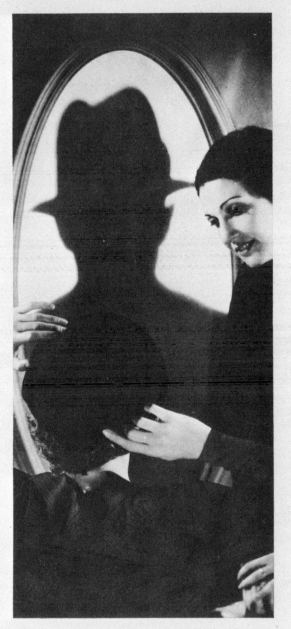

WHEN a woman buys a hat that causes her to be looked at with just the right kind and degree of interest, it's a good hat. Even if it was made out of four diaper pins and the New York Times for August 11, 1902, it would still be a good hat.

A woman's hats are not bought to keep the rain off, nor (being more or less invisible to the wearer) to please the woman. They are bought for people to look at. And "people" usually means "men."

The above is one of the small number of facts remaining to us nowadays which are both delightful and true. Few would deny it. And yet few seem to realize how far this happy proclivity of women for striving to please men goes.

When a woman buys shirts for her husband, she buys the kind she knows he likes. When she buys perfumes for herself, she is thinking of her husband's tastes. When she buys food for her family, she averages her likes with his and the children's before she names a brand. And when it comes to radios, automobiles, electric refrigerators and such important things, a family conference decides.

Back of her, when she buys, stands the shadow of a man, ready to help or hinder the sale according as he thinks well or ill of your goods.

This isn't a silly or a slavish habit of women. It is a dignified and sensible acknowledgment that since men and women have to live together, when a woman spends man-earned money it pays to spend it on something that pleases them both.

Those manufacturers are well advised who arrange to have men, as well as women, see their advertising. The so-called Family Group magazines are a means to this end, for they are read by men *and* women. And in one of them—Redbook—the cost of reaching both sexes is 30% *less* than the cost of reaching one sex through other media. Even if it didn't help your sales to have men see your advertising, it would cost less to reach *women alone* in Redbook!

Sell the family and you sell all. Redbook Magazine, 230 Park Avenue, New York City.

THE SHADOW OF A MAN STANDS BEHIND EVERY WOMAN WHO BUYS

*W*hat she *really* wanted was Children

It is curious how some minor fault may alter a person's life. Take the case of Miss Nickerson.

If you live in New York you may have seen Miss Nickerson walking up Park Avenue. A lithe woman in her late forties, with a streak of grey or two in her black hair, and a suggestion of a double chin. You would realize that once she must have been very beautiful. With her are two Pekingese dogs—always. Their pictures, with Miss Nickerson, frequently appear in the rotogravure sections.

People say that Miss Nickerson makes a fool of herself about them; that she acts downright silly. Having them sit at the table with her while she dines, for example. Putting each one in his little French bed. Sending them out for an airing in her car, jacketed as well and certainly more beautifully than children. Talking baby talk of the most banal kind to them.

The whole attitude sounds silly enough, but in Miss Nickerson's case it is not silly. It is tragic. Because these two pets of hers represent a bitter compromise with life.

If ever a woman was born who yearned for love, marriage, motherhood and children, Miss Nickerson was the woman. All of them were denied her.

What kind of sly trick had life played upon her? Why had fate singled out for punishment this great-hearted, charming woman? Many, many times she must have wondered about it herself.

After her debut in June, 1904, it seemed almost certain that she would marry a titled young English army officer whom she had met on the Riviera, when the Nickerson yacht had been in foreign waters. Nothing came of it.

Then in rapid succession other men paid serious court. At least so it seemed. But one by one they, too, drifted away. She didn't seem to be able to hold them. The years passed quickly and still Miss Nickerson was unmarried. Occasionally men still felt the force of her beauty and charm—but not for long.

When she was past forty, she seemed to give up any idea of romance. Most of her time and her money were devoted to her many charitable enterprises. The Nickerson Home for Crippled Children. The Nickerson Education Foundation. She busied herself in a round of activities for the good of others.

To those who did not know her, she seemed to be like a thousand other New York women. Sophisticated. Cold. Indifferent. But if you could see her at the end of the day, mothering the two Pekingese, you would realize that she was none of these things; that she was simply a lonely and disappointed woman.

Halitosis (unpleasant breath) is the unforgivable social fault. The insidious thing about it is that you yourself never realize when you have it. And even your best friend won't tell you. The one sure way to make sure your breath is beyond suspicion is to use Listerine systematically as a mouth wash.

For obvious reasons names and places referred to are fictitious

For him... and him... and him...

"I pledge myself to guard every bit of Beauty that he cherishes in me"

To help you in keeping this pledge, trust the one leading beauty soap that's made with Olive and Palm Oils!

Today, those moments with him are fleeting, rare, and...infinitely precious. For his sake, and yours, be at your lovely best, whenever you're together.

Turn now, as so many charming women are doing, to Palmolive for your beauty care. For, since the dawn of history, Olive and Palm Oils have been treasured as Nature's finest aids to feminine loveliness. And Palmolive *alone*, among all leading soaps, is made with Olive and Palm Oils!

No wonder Palmolive is the largest selling beauty soap in all the world! You can truly feel the difference in its silk-and-cream lather. You can truly trust its gentle help in keeping your skin soft and fresh and radiant as the dawn.

Palmolive costs *so* little! Why not let it do the nice things for your body that it does for your face? Keep your pledge of beauty with Palmolive. Guard your loveliness . . . 'til he comes marching home!

REMEMBER PALMOLIVE'S BEAUTY OILS...

olive and palm oils — no others — go into the making of Palmolive. Look for the olive color.

PALMOLIVE

1943

WAFS

Women's Auxiliary Ferrying Squadron
Theirs is the man-sized job of ferrying war planes from factories to air-bases for Uncle Sam. Expert flyers, each and every one . . . *THEY ARE THE BEST.*

With us It's CHESTERFIELD

GOOD TOBACCO, YES . . . THE RIGHT COMBINATION OF THE WORLD'S BEST CIGARETTE TOBACCOS

It is not enough to buy the best cigarette tobacco, it's Chesterfield's right combination, or blend, of these tobaccos that makes them so much milder, cooler and definitely better-tasting.

Good Tobacco, yes . . . but the Blend — the Right Combination — that's the thing.

SMOKE CHESTERFIELDS AND FIND OUT
HOW REALLY GOOD A CIGARETTE CAN BE

Molly Pitcher, 1944

Molly Pitcher, Revolutionary heroine, symbolizes the spirit of America's women who take over the work of men at war.

Women are doing a big job on the Pennsylvania Railroad

More than 48,000 experienced Pennsylvania Railroad men have entered our armed forces. Yet, wartime's unusual needs for railroad service are being met . . . thanks in great part to more than 23,000 women who have rallied to the emergency. From colleges, high schools and homes, these women—after intensive training—are winning the wholehearted applause of the traveling public.

You see them working as trainmen, in ticket and station masters' offices and information bureaus, as platform ushers and train passenger representatives, in dining car service. Yes, even in baggage rooms, train dispatchers' offices, in shops and yards and as section hands. The Pennsylvania Railroad proudly salutes these "Molly Pitchers" who so gallantly fill the breach left by their fighting brothers-in-arms.

★ 48,128 in the Armed Forces

248 have given their lives for their Country

Pennsylvania Railroad
Serving the Nation

BUY UNITED STATES WAR BONDS AND STAMPS

1944

During World War II American women, like their counterparts in other industrialized nations, played a vital role in the creation of materials essential to gaining final victory. Between 1942 and 1945 more than six million women entered the work force, two million of them in heavy industry, performing functions usually reserved for men. As welders, riveters, lathe operators, and so on, in shipyards and ammunition factories, as unskilled workers on assembly lines in defense plants, women did their part to unleash America's vast, and overwhelming, production capabilities. In a fashion similar to the work of the government's official propaganda agencies, many advertisers included pictures and descriptions of this "new" American woman, praising her work and associating their products and services with her accomplishments.

1945

Historians and sociologists have noted that the fear and loneliness experienced by so many American women during World War II helped to intensify their already highly romantic notions of home and family. In the post-war years descriptions of married life and motherhood were often suffused with a saccharine tone, especially in advertising. Despite the idealization of the homemaker's role, an astonishing 25 percent of the women interviewed by pollster Elmo Roper in 1946 said they would rather have been born men.

1945

Creators of advertising have always been faced with the problem of how to present a product in a recognizable setting that still manages to catch the consumer's attention. During the 1940s and 1950s the primacy of children in the lives of American women was sometimes depicted with startling—and effective—exaggeration.

34

1951

Sis uses 750 dishes a month

Dad uses 570 dishes

Junior uses 720 dishes

Mom uses 770 dishes a month
(and one guess who does them all!)

Get out of the kitchen sooner!

It's so nice outdoors—but *you're* stuck inside—with 3500 dishes to do! (When you include pots and pans, that's how many an average family uses each month.) But Lux Liquid can help you get done *fast!*

Unlike powders that have to dissolve, Lux Liquid goes to work *instantly.* It cuts under grease, lifts it up, floats it away. With even a quick rinse, Lux Liquid gets china, silver, glassware—*sparkling* clean!

And Lux Liquid is Lux-mild on hands. Thrifty, too—one can outlasts several boxes of the leading powder. A teaspoonful does a dishpanful. Get Lux Liquid!

HOW LUX LIQUID CUTS UNDER GREASE AND FLOATS IT AWAY!

Thick gravy was poured on this dish and let stand for 10 minutes until it hardened

Just as soon as the dish is placed in the water Lux Liquid starts to do its work

Lux Liquid's special action cuts under the grease, lifts it up and floats it right off

A quick rinse and the dish, as you can see, is beautifully and hygienically clean

LUX LIQUID IS THE NEXT BEST THING TO A DISHWASHING MACHINE

and it's Lux-mild on your hands

1956

"The problem lay buried, unspoken, for many years in the minds of American women. It was a strange stirring, a sense of dissatisfaction, a yearning that women suffered in the middle of the twentieth century in the United States. Each suburban wife struggled with it alone. As she made the beds, shopped for groceries, matched slipcover material, ate peanut butter sandwiches with her children, chauffered Cub Scouts and Brownies, lay beside her husband at night—she was afraid to ask even of herself the silent question—'Is this all?' "

Betty Friedan, *The Feminine Mystique* (1963)

Could your wife hold down a second full-time job?

Keeping house and caring for the kids fills a woman's day—and more. But what if she had to earn a living, too?

Your wife will never have to face this double duty if you protect yourself with Life Insurance under the Travelers umbrella. And the same policy that protects your family when you are working can guarantee a retirement income for you and your wife when you stop working.

You can also get your Car, Health and Homeowners Insurance from your Travelers agent—save time, and perhaps money, by letting one man handle everything. You'll find him listed in the Yellow Pages under "Insurance." Call him today.

Remember, you can get all types of insurance under the Travelers umbrella.

The TRAVELERS INSURANCE Companies
HARTFORD 15, CONNECTICUT

The phone company wants more installers like Alana MacFarlane.

Alana MacFarlane is a 20-year-old from San Rafael, California. She's one of our first women telephone installers. She won't be the last.

We also have several hundred male telephone operators. And a policy that there are no all-male or all-female jobs at the phone company.

We want the men and women of the telephone company to do what they want to do, and do best.

For example, Alana likes working outdoors. "I don't go for office routine," she said. "But as an installer, I get plenty of variety and a chance to move around."

Some people like to work with their hands, or, like Alana, get a kick out of working 20 feet up in the air.

Others like to drive trucks. Some we're helping to develop into good managers.

Today, when openings exist, local Bell Companies are offering applicants and present employees some jobs they may never have thought about before. We want to help all advance to the best of their abilities.

AT&T and your local Bell Company are equal opportunity employers.

38

Women of the future will make the Moon a cleaner place to live.

Presenting: Tomorrow's Lestoil!
Nothing, nothing, nothing cleans like it.
It leaps through dirt, soaks up grease, and makes everything fresh and new.
Its solvents, cutting agents and steady, tireless <u>action</u> make your day lighter.
Everything in your beautiful house can be cleaned, immaculately.
(Tomorrow's Lestoil® makes Standard International grow some more.)

1968

In 1968, as the possibility of America actually landing a man on the moon became more certain, some advertisers tried to foresee ways in which the housewife might use everyday products in outer space. The earthly vision of women as service personnel assisting men in a wide variety of ways continued, although the nuances were less subtle.

39

Think of her as your mother.

She only wants what's best for you.
A cool drink. A good dinner. A soft pillow and a warm blanket.
This is not just maternal instinct. It's the result of the longest
Stewardess training in the industry.
Training in service, not just a beauty course.
Service, after all, is what makes professional travellers prefer American.
And makes new travellers want to keep on flying with us.
So we see that every passenger gets the same professional treatment.
That's the American Way.

Fly the American Way
American Airlines

1968

Who is the Olivetti girl?

And why are people saying such terribly nice things about her.

The Olivetti girl is a secretary/typist who's been attracting lots of attention lately for her amazing performance on the typewriter. Because no matter how fast she types she rarely makes a mistake! Now, she may be prettier than other typists, but she's not necessarily any brainier. Then what makes an Olivetti girl such a phenomenal typist? Her brainy Olivetti Electric Typewriter, of course! This typewriter can actually think for itself. Because it has a brain inside that makes the four most common typing mistakes absolutely impossible. No flying caps!
No improper spacing!
No shading or ghosting!
No crowding or piling!
That's why an Olivetti girl can really belt it out. And is sharper, looser, never uptight. That's why an Olivetti girl has more fun. And that is why people are saying such terribly nice things about her.

P.S. to Office Managers:
You never have to overspend for an Olivetti Electric Typewriter! Because we have six different models, priced from $265 to $705, each matched to a specific secretarial work load. (Did you know that mismatched typewriters are costing American business millions of dollars a year?) To get more information, see the Yellow Pages for the nearest Olivetti office.

olivetti
The American Dream Machines

office typewriters
portable typewriters
calculators
accounting machines
adding machines
electronic billing systems
microcomputers
computer terminals
office copiers

1972

Despite the fact that the look and texture of social change were present every-where during the 1970s, the nature of woman's work as well as the manner in which advertisers displayed it remained relatively constant. In 1970, according to the Census Bureau, 95 percent of all receptionists, typists, and stenographers, and 98 percent of all secretaries were women. In addition, women made up only 4 percent of those managers and administrators earning more than $15,000 a year, and only 2 percent of those making over $30,000.

A WOMAN'S WORK IS NEVER DONE.

She had breakfast with the national sales manager, met with the client from 9 to 11, talked at an industry luncheon, raced across town to the plans board meeting and then caught the 8:05 back home. Women are playing a greater role in business. And commercial airlines are helping that come about with Boeing jetliner flights to nearly every major city in the U.S. For women in business, as well as men.

BOEING
Getting people together

1977

42

You're always hearing about the inequality between men and women in offices...that girls and men do the same work but girls get paid less. Frankly, I never worried about that...I decided long ago just to do the most fabulous, energetic job I could and not try to worry about "equality." Well, what happened is that I've just had a wonderful promotion...and I now have a secretary of my own. I always knew men were wonderful, especially in offices! All the time I was getting on with my job one particular magazine inspired me and gave me helpful advice. They really are for career girls. I like that magazine. I guess you could say...I'm That COSMOPOLITAN Girl.

Photographed by Francesco Scavullo

If you want to reach me you'll find me reading
COSMOPOLITAN

1969

The intention of both these ads is to attract appropriate advertisers for each magazine. In style, tone, and content they represent a significant departure from the earlier one for McCalls in 1904 found on page 2. This ad also offers an interesting comparison with the ads for Playboy and Hustler (see pages 79 and 80).

I tell him where to GIT off.

Marriage is a 50/50 proposition. Vacation decisions are more like 60/40. 60 hers. Ever since honey chose the honeymoon, she's been choosing the Group Inclusive Tours, fly 'n' drives, 'n' sun 'n' funs. She's off and flying. Into all the areas of purchase that used to be male dominated. A whole new fleet of consumers. For planes and pleasure islands. Cars and credit cards. And wise, indeed, is the forward-thinking advertiser who sees the feminine writing on the wall—and on the checks. And speaks to her directly. Your next move is deciding how best to reach her. Simple. Look to the judgment of a century of traditional advertisers to women. And place your ads in Good Housekeeping. It's simply the best package for your advertising dollars. Not just because it gives you the absolutely lowest CPM in the women's field. But because an ad in the editorial environment of Good Housekeeping stimulates more consumer confidence than it does in any other woman's magazine. Proven. In survey after survey. If you want to reach women in any new frontier area—fly with us. You'll go places.

She's a tougher customer than ever. You never needed Good Housekeeping more.

SP 1

COPYRIGHT © 1977 THE HEARST CORPORATION

1977

MEN

The status of the mythical American male has slipped noticeably in recent years, his sovereignty diminished on any number of fronts—from the battle-field and corporate board room to the bar and the boudoir. An accelerating technology, the feminist movement, and the demoralizing impact of the Vietnam War have converged to force many American men to question the security of their personal identities. The old image of the ruggedly simple, self-confident, success-oriented American male has been beset by confusions in roles and responsibilities. As an appreciable number of contemporary men reevaluate their definition of the successful American male, advertising reminds them of the traditions that supported their collective self-image and supplies them with graphic new versions of whom and what they ought to be.

The relationship of men to the American economy evolved through a cumulative series of roles: producer, wage earner, consumer. One predicament of the modern male is that he is expected to blend all three into a stable personal identity. The American man must now be a rugged achiever in the mythic frontier fashion, a resolute "breadwinner," and yet a sensitive "free spirit" in domestic and social relations, as well as a credit card-carrying member of a consumer economy.

Over the years, advertising has cultivated the American male's three major economic roles and capitalized on the variety of self-images that derive from them. In the early days of the republic, few consumer goods distracted the predominantly self-reliant American frontiersman and farmer. But since that time nearly every segment of the future they helped design has given a commercial boost to this antiquated self-sufficient lifestyle. Contemporary advertising is filled with variations of this heroic male standard. Consider all the mug shots of those attractive, hard-nosed, independent smokers willing to pay any price for taste and satisfaction. With its emphasis on brand loyalty and consumer sovereignty, most of today's advertising reminds us of just how culturally ingrained these values of decisiveness and self-determination are; they also remind us how these values can become trivialized.

As the frontier receded, the identity of the broad-shouldered, sinewy American male harnessing the power of the natural world was forced to adapt to less salutary urban conditions. Since the late nineteenth century, a strain of advertisements has consistently promised a "new life" to those men who feel "only half alive." The advertising of Eugen Sandow, Earle Liederman, and later Charles Atlas offered the prospect of not only "biceps like steel" and "arms and legs rippling with muscular strength" but also the "vitality to do things you never thought possible." Most recently, there is Joe Weider's "miracle of Charlie Kemp," who made the transcendental leap "from a pathetic, undesired, unloved loser whose only companions were dogs—to a prize winning 'Mr. America Physical Achievement Award' body surrounded by the world's most beautiful girls." Such blurring of the literal and figurative, of fact and fiction, dramatically reveals advertising's particular responsiveness to the ways men are traditionally depicted in American culture.

The discrepancies between exemplary behavior and reality, between masculine images and the actualities of a functional masculine life, are most readily apparent in advertising's representations of men as wage earners. In the late nineteenth century—not long after technology, mass production, and advertising had lured many men to cities in the service of big business—male consciousness had to take on the pressures of a new economic identity. Once the sole determiners of their own goals and tasks, American men were now told when to report to work, what to do while there, and when to leave. And as soon as they arrived home, they were expected to consume the goods they had so monotonously helped assemble. In the overpowering presence of mass production, as highly organized corporate enterprise replaced self-initiated work, the traditional role of the aggressive, independent male became more an image than a reality. Specialization and mechanization further narrowed the scope of men's labor and responsibilities. The vast majority of factory workers and businessmen exercised little, if any, control over the results of their own efforts and, more often than not, judged their work to be an insignificant element in a much larger pattern of production. Confined to the routinized movements insisted on by influential "time-study" experts, and isolated from the meaning of their labor, modern workers found few opportunities to measure their own on-the-job resourcefulness.

Unnerved by Chaplinesque assembly lines or by the shuffle of counting-room invoices, male identity came to depend more on take-home wages than on either the nature of the work or the goods produced. Earning a "decent wage" became the most widely advertised sign of manhood. Many men responded by relentlessly driving themselves over the limit and equating their own personal well-being with that of the corporation. A recent *Fortune* article quoted an executive speaking about his boss: "He's a very hard person to work for. You have to make a decision about whether you want to devote twenty-four or twenty-five hours a day to the business. If you don't, you gotta leave, because there's no place for you." Many of these "organization men" could wind up, as one advertisement describes, as little more than "burnt-out furnaces of energy." If, as psychologist Erik Erikson contends, work ideally serves as the backbone of identity formation and a release for creative energy, then the everyday actualities of working conditions prevented most men from fulfilling basic psychological needs. Men began to talk of their jobs as a "rat race," a "grind," a "treadmill."

Given this anxiety-laden environment, men eventually grew more vulnerable than their legendary predecessors—those pre-industrial, "inner-directed" men. For each corporate executive with access to the corridors of power, ten men paid the price for even aspiring to such privileged fellowship. The incidence of business-related ailments rose sharply in the early twentieth century. Insurance agency and pharmaceutical advertising focused on heart disease, ulcers, alcoholism, and a host of minor illnesses. During the Depression, a popular cereal advertisement (Kellogg's All-Bran, p. 57) made the cruel point dispassionately clear: "a sick man has no place in business." As usual, advertising tried to have it both ways. It portrayed both the successes and the failures. It encouraged the male drive to succeed, then portrayed the awful consequences of too relentless a drive. It endorsed the role, and, if that failed, it also endorsed the remedy.

To compensate men for their increasingly confused identities, advertising, for the most part, shows them as the "masters" of their personal and domestic lives. This image depends on the tradition of a breed of rugged industrial folk heroes: Sam Patch, Mike Fink, Casey Jones, John Henry, assorted steelworkers, and the like. These cultural figures may be considered another form of indemnification—just as today truck drivers give themselves cultural and job status through a commercialized image that turns their work into something more than being simply long-distance delivery men. Advertisements in male-oriented magazines addressed the breadwinner and father with the kind of serious, deferential tone that for many was so strikingly absent from their working lives. Ads for insurance and automobiles, for example, created the impression that each potential consumer was a successful wage earner who would make only an informed decision about a product or service. Women's magazines, on the other hand, featured advertisements that continued to show men almost exclusively in their occupational roles. And when it came to such matters as which brand of cereal or coffee to buy, the men were invariably depicted as unable to get by without the "little woman's" help. Despite this portrayal of the wife as helpmate, advertising has most often emphasized images of male authority, especially when it comes to major consumer purchases.

The frontier experience had democratized the American home and rendered the old-fashioned roles of father and husband less awesome by the end of the nineteenth century. One foreign visitor, here to observe the "aristocracy in America," noted in 1883 that "the family, which is a monarchy in the old world, has become, like everything else, a republic in the new. The father is not king; he is simply a president." But by the early twentieth century the state had become an obsolete model for the family. In its place, the corporation began to supply men with new images and criteria for running their homes. Advertising began to show the average man managing his home with the same kind of efficiency and authority the "captain of industry" used to head a corporation. In a late 1930s Dodge advertisement, a husband and wife in bed discuss the merits of a major consumer purchase with all the intensity of a top-level management meeting. In each instance, the "executive officer" inevitably made the final decision, but usually not without some spirited opposition.

The role of a strong, decisive provider bears, as advertisements suggest, its own special anxieties. The father must be even more successful at home than he is at work. Advertising has turned this role, and the pressure associated with it, into the myth of the vanishing American father. The customary props for this identity include the three-button suit, an attaché case, and the three-martini lunch. As a 1940 Budweiser advertisement demonstrates, the "image" is that of a white picket fence, a frisky dog, a cold bottle of beer, two exemplary children, and a devoted wife waiting for "their hero" to arrive on the next bus. Yet most fathers, in order to provide such comfortable circumstances for their families and to serve as models of strength, virtue, and industry, must be away from home for a long stretch of each day. As the advertisement for "Grouchy Husbands" (p. 56) ironically notes, a loss of stature eventually follows. Family members rarely get to see and appreciate the father's work. And in most modern American "bedroom communities," the father normally has neither the time nor the strength to display leadership in community affairs.

In a four-page public interest advertisement circulated in 1961, the American Dairy Association warned of the nation's "growing need for strength in its people as well as in its machines" and lamented the decline of American masculinity. The ad noted that nearly 60 percent of this country's youth (as compared to less than 9 percent for European children) could not pass simple tests of muscular strength and flexibility. In addition, the ad reported that one of every two American men called to military duty was being rejected as "unfit." And when an "ordinary day" in the life of a "middle-class suburban dweller," "Mr. Joe Citizen," was studied, the findings were even more alarming. With nearly every conceivable electrical appliance within reach, Joe Citizen's most strenuous activities each day ranged from kissing his wife good-bye each morning to "unwinding" in front of the television set each night. On weekends, the ad observed, Joe "drives to the country club, mounts an electric golf cart, plays 18 holes, [and] joins the boys back in the clubhouse for a few drinks." Satisfied that he's put in a good day's exercise, Joe returns home to reward himself with a big meal.

The ad describes Joe's wife, Jill, in slightly more invigorating terms. As an "average suburban" homemaker, she gets far more exercise each day walking, washing, cooking, and dusting than does her husband, who "no longer hikes the dusty trail to bring home the buffalo meat and hides to feed and clothe his family." Embedded in the descriptions of this advertisement are several indications of shifting male and female roles in contemporary American society. Today, in the thick of the feminist movement, Joe's wife most probably is no longer simply the obsequious mate who prepares meals, cleans house, and raises children. So too, Joe has quite likely come to question advertising's images of him as a buffalo hunter and workaholic. By now, he may well even estimate the personal "costs" of overtime, promotions, transfers, and commuting. As a personnel officer at a large west coast plant put it, "The values of the work force have changed. A man may be just as dedicated to the company, but he wants more balance —his recreation, his family, his community activities."

Contemporary advertising reveals that men, having been culturally conditioned to regard themselves as physically superior and psychologically more sturdy than women, are discovering just how vulnerable they can be. "Crusher Lizowski" in the 1978 ad for "Homemaking, the misunderstood profession," shares—equally with his wife—child care and housekeeping chores as well as the responsibility for "establishing values in our home." In the aftermath of the women's movement, Crusher refuses to be locked into the predetermined roles of history and advertising. No longer the "lord and master" of the house or the monarch of the bedroom, he is, as he says, "into" macramé and Japanese cooking.

What is so interesting about the Crusher Lizowski advertisement is that it epitomizes the history and range of male images in American advertising. His wrestler's face and brawny hands mark him as ruggedly masculine. Yet he is also anxious, if not insecure: "Nobody kids me when I put on an apron. Not in front of me at least." But what finally sets Crusher apart from the majority of men is his willing assumption of a role reversal: "I do most of the cooking around the house." Many men would militantly oppose the redefined male roles promoted in this advertisement, but the ad, designed primarily to show women that some men actually do think the way Crusher does, winds up proving that many women endorse the same stereotypes as men. A large, physically imposing male is presented in what would seem to be an unaccustomed role. How dependent is this ad on a traditional male image? How impressive would the advertisement be if, say, the fragile-looking orchidologist featured in Lord Calvert's "Men of Distinction" campaign (1945) put on Crusher's apron? The "Homemaking" ad with Crusher Lizowski reminds us that while a balance of images and a full spectrum of roles are expected of men in advertisements, in the end the most conventional male identity still shapes public responses.

Contemporary advertising requires that men be both physically imposing and emotionally sensitive, a wrestler and a helpmate. Advertisers must now stake a claim to a number of subsidiary male identities in order to establish consumer confidence in the products they sell. In a 1972 advertisement, "Roger reads *Esquire*," Mrs. Roger Davis admiringly announces that her husband is "the only man I know who can get high on 18th-century literature in the evening and spend the morning watching a boxer he sponsors work out in the gym." A good-looking actor who had also been a college professor, Roger Davis is loved for "his originality and style": he goes to the race track with "a copy of Robert Frost under his arm." Contemporary advertising shows more and more men with Roger Davis's seemingly endless skills, men who are dissatisfied with being "just" a professor, athlete, or truck driver. Advertising expects every man to incorporate a number of strikingly different roles if he is to amount to anything. That most of these roles are paradoxical or extremely difficult to achieve simultaneously only adds to male anxiety and confusion.

Of all these proliferating male identities, the male as consumer is the most recently acquired and self-consciously tended to. It is also the identity now most deliberately cultivated by advertisers. Until the mid-1960s, when men began to question the work ethic, ads characteristically featured them in occupational roles or traditional domestic settings, where they functioned primarily as agents of authority or voices of approval. Men didn't depend on consumer goods for their identities; they simply controlled or endorsed their wives' choices. More often than not, advertisements showed men in relation to products after purchases had been made or could safely be assumed. As the ads for Marlboro, Corina, 7-Up, and Mustang make clear, men were depicted as busily enjoying or envisioning the benefits of a product or designing ingenious adaptations of its use. Now, however, ads are much more clearly targeted at men as consumers themselves, and they are depicted in ways that suggest they are relying on products to help determine their own identities.

One group of practitioners of advertising "psychographics" has recently established five basic categories of male consumers: "Ben, the self-made businessman," "Scott, the successful professional," "Dale, the devoted family man," "Herman, the homebody," and "Fred, the frustrated factory worker." Fred, for example, represents 19 percent of the male population. He "married young," is "now unhappy and cynical," and spends much of his spare time scanning "girlie" magazines and fantasizing about a life as a swinger. Scott, who accounts for 21 percent of the men, is a smooth-talking, confident, shameless professional who carries three major credit cards as badges of success. These psychological portraits, however tentative the boundaries separating them, are unified by the consistent urge to consume. For each figure, functioning as a consumer serves as the latest, and perhaps most enticing, outlet for much of the aggression repressed by the pressures and constraints of his work. Unable in most circumstances to convert decisions into vigorous, independent action, these men have shifted the focus of their decisions to leisure activities and the consumer goods that now dominate ways to relax or have fun.

"Leisure" has become the most dynamic component of the consumer economy. By the mid-1960s Americans were spending over $30 billion each year on recreational equipment. Shopping for a new boat, golf clubs, skis, or the latest hunting or fishing gear can now compete for men's time with, say, going to ball games or prizefights. In fact much of the intensity, compulsiveness, and frenetic behavior associated with work has been applied to recreational and consumer activities. Advertisements routinely pressure men into feeling obliged to have "fun." For many men, leisure and shopping are now even more demanding activities than their jobs.

Traditional masculine values of superiority, accomplishment, status, and security have irrevocably become associated with work and leisure. And they have come to depend—more so than ever before—on the purchase of consumer goods. A 1972 ad for The Bank of New York, for example, features a distinguished businessman in front of an elegant hotel. The headline asks: "How much are you worth this morning?" In responding, male readers are expected to point to more than the salaries they earn or the fluctuating values of the stock portfolios and bank accounts they have accumulated. Their "worth" is also measured by the everyday purchases they make: the clothes they wear, the liquor they drink, the cigars they smoke, as well as, of course, the cars they drive and the homes they sleep in. The latest version of the American "Renaissance Man" is the consumer, the man who shops with a discerning eye for the "best deal" on toothpaste, after shave, hair spray, record albums, airline tickets, and designer labels. As anthropologist Margaret Mead has observed, "Maleness in America is not absolutely defined, it has to be kept and re-earned every day."

Advertising encourages men to adopt certain modes of behavior and profits from the anxieties nurtured by those images. New male images do not replace old ones; they compound and complicate male identities. Contemporary advertisements expect men to adopt the qualities of human perfectability previously attributed only to heroic figures in epic literature. Ads implicitly criticize men for not living up to the expectations associated with such roles but do not question the role itself. Given such circumstances, the current challenge for American men is to develop the psychological resiliency necessary to adapt to the pressures and anxieties generated by the confusion of overpowering self-images proliferated in advertising.

Every Woman Admires a Tall Man

If you are short, you will appreciate the unpleasant and humiliating position of the little man in the above illustration. But you are probably unaware that it is no longer necessary to be short and uncomfortable.

The Cartilage Company, of Rochester, N. Y., is the owner of a method whereby any one can add from two to three inches to his stature. It is called the "Cartilage System" because it is based upon a scientific and physiological method of expanding the cartilage, all of which is clearly and fully explained in a booklet entitled "**How to Grow Tall**," which is yours for the asking.

The Cartilage system builds up the entire body harmoniously. It not only increases the height, but its use means better health, more nerve force, increased bodily development and longer life. Its use necessitates no drugs, no internal treating, no operation, no hard work, no big expense. Your height can be increased, no matter what your age or sex may be, and this can be done at home without the knowledge of others. This new and original method of increasing one's height has received the enthusiastic endorsement of physicians and instructors in physical culture. If you would like to add to your height, so as to be able to see in a crowd, walk without embarrassment with those who are tall, and enjoy the other advantages of proper height, you should write at once for a copy of our free booklet "**How to Grow Tall.**" It tells you how to accomplish these results quickly, surely, and permanently. Nothing is left unexplained. After you read it, your only wonder will be "Why did not some one think of it before?" Write to-day.

THE CARTILAGE COMPANY, 74 P, Unity Building, ROCHESTER, N. Y.

1904

Let the Men wash

if they won't get you Pearline. Let them try it for themselves, and see if they don't say that washing with soap is too hard for any woman. This hard work that Pearline saves isn't the whole matter; it saves money, too—money that's thrown away in clothes needlessly worn out and rubbed to pieces when you wash by main strength in the old way.

That appeals—where is the man who wouldn't want to have the washing made easier—when he can save money by it?

The country's future is written in the faces of the young men. They are clean-shaven faces. In the store, the counting-room, the classroom, the office —in work and sport out of doors—the men who do things shave for the day just as they dress for the day.

The use of the Gillette Safety Razor is almost a universal habit with men of affairs. It is not solely a question of economy—though it means a great saving. It's a matter of comfort, of cleanliness, of time.

The Gillette is a builder of self-respect. The man who doesn't care how he looks does not care much about anything else.

The Gillette is a builder of regular habits.

Own a Gillette—be master of your time—shave in three minutes. No stropping, no honing.

You don't have to take a correspondence course to learn how to use it. Just buy it and shave.

Thirty thousand dealers sell the Gillette. If there is no one in your neighborhood send us $5 and we'll send the razor and twelve double-edged blades by return mail.

Write and we will send you a pamphlet—Dept. A.

King C Gillette

GILLETTE SALES COMPANY, 38 W. Second Street, Boston
New York, Times Building   Chicago, Stock Exchange Building   Gillette Safety Razor, Ltd., London
Eastern Office, Shanghai, China   Canadian Office, 63 St. Alexander Street, Montreal

GILLETTE SALES COMPANY, 38 W. Second Street, Boston
Factories: Boston, Montreal, Leicester, Berlin, Paris

1910

King Gillette's patented safety razor not only spared men frequent trips to the barber shop but also provided them with an opportunity each day to be the "master" of their own time and helped to establish male conformity in dress and personal hygiene.

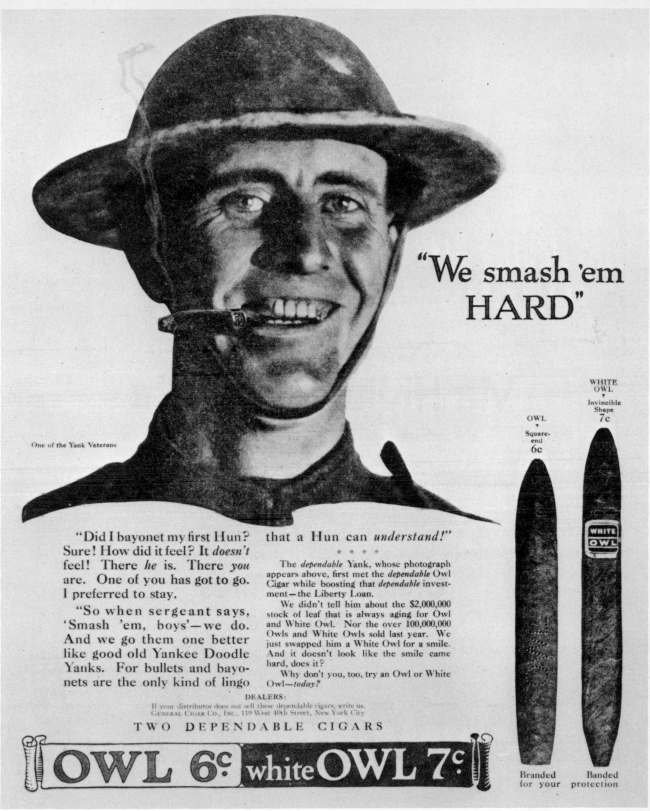

"We smash 'em HARD"

One of the Yank Veterans

WHITE OWL ▾ Invincible Shape 7c

OWL ▾ Square-end 6c

"Did I bayonet my first Hun? Sure! How did it feel? It *doesn't* feel! There *he* is. There *you* are. One of you has got to go. I preferred to stay.

"So when sergeant says, 'Smash 'em, boys'—we do. And we go them one better like good old Yankee Doodle Yanks. For bullets and bayonets are the only kind of lingo that a Hun can *understand!*

* * * *

The *dependable* Yank, whose photograph appears above, first met the *dependable* Owl Cigar while boosting that *dependable* investment—the Liberty Loan.

We didn't tell him about the $2,000,000 stock of leaf that is always aging for Owl and White Owl. Nor the over 100,000,000 Owls and White Owls sold last year. We just swapped him a White Owl for a smile. And it doesn't look like the smile came hard, does it?

Why don't you, too, try an Owl or White Owl—*today?*

DEALERS: If your distributor does not sell these dependable cigars, write us. GENERAL CIGAR CO., INC., 119 West 40th Street, New York City

TWO DEPENDABLE CIGARS

OWL 6c white OWL 7c

Branded for your

Banded protection

1918

Cigar manufacturers fought the dramatic increases in cigarette sales prior to World War I with intense advertising efforts appealing directly to patriotism, and by endorsing General Pershing's declaration: "You ask me what we need to win this war. I answer tobacco as much as bullets." But in light of the prices of White Owls, the cigar might have enjoyed greater sales if it had heeded the advice of Vice President John R. Marshall (1913–21) that "What this country needs is a really good five cent cigar."

Grouchy Husbands

EVERYTHING a moment before had been peaceful—and even comparatively quiet. Perhaps the youngster did make a slight disturbance at play, but it was unintentional—not anything over which a normal father should hit the ceiling. Perhaps some remark was made, innocently enough—but from the eruption which followed it might have been criminal!

What is the cause of outbursts like that? Unreasoning fits of temper on the part of men who ordinarily are kindly husbands and fathers!

It isn't often that overwork is the cause. Men are made for work. Work leaves the healthy brain and healthy body pleasantly relaxed—not taut and straining. Responsibility shouldn't fray the nerves. Men are miserable without it. They really love their homes and families.

But when this love is manifested by periodic explosions over nothing—when any little disturbance is a signal to fly off the handle—something is decidedly wrong!

The chances are that the man isn't well. Nerves! He would be the first to deny it, of course.

Why men fly off the handle

"Never felt better in my life!" he sputters. But he doesn't. His very vehemence is indication of the trouble which is secretly worrying millions of men in America. They are fagged. They are wearing out prematurely. Instead of the glowing health which should be theirs, "the prime of life" finds many of them a burden on their feet, tired at the beginning of the day as well as at the end of it, irritable, exacting, pessimistic. They are not "sick," no; but certainly they are not well.

And nine times out of ten the reasons are these: they neglect exercise; they don't get enough sleep; they shun fresh air; they eat too much, and eat the wrong things. And worst of all, they unthinkingly load their systems with artificial stimulants—with drug stimulants—which contribute *nothing of real value* to their well-being, but which slowly and surely rob the body of its reserve strength.

Perhaps the most widespread offender among these artificial stimulants is caffein. It has no food value. It *seems* to give new energy, but this is a delusion. Actually it whips and goads the tired nerves to action when what they really need is rest.

Various forms of abuse have resulted in an alarming health record in America. The United States Life Tables for 1920 show that Americans pass the period of full health and vigor at the age of 31. These are cold, hard figures. But they become warm, human, illuminating, every time a grouchy husband goes on the warpath over nothing!

In 2,000,000 homes, people are eliminating one form of abuse by making Postum their regular mealtime drink. It is all wheat, skillfully blended and roasted. Instead of caffein, an artificial stimulant, it gives only the healthful elements of whole wheat and bran. It is delicious!—rich, full bodied, with the appetizing flavor of roasted wheat.

Here is a drink which every member of the family can enjoy together, with no fear of sleeplessness, ragged nerves, headache, indigestion—with no sign of a grouch! Made with hot milk instead of the usual boiling water, it is the ideal drink for children, too.

You—the wife, the mother—are in a wonderful position to improve the health of your family. Your most important contribution, perhaps, will be the selection of food which builds up, instead of tearing down. Postum is not a cure-all—but it is one easy step in the right direction!

Get Postum at your grocer's—or accept the offer of Carrie Blanchard, famous food demonstrator.

Carrie Blanchard's Offer

"I want you to make a thirty-day test of Postum. I want to start you out on your test by giving you your first week's supply, and my own directions for making it. You will be glad to know, too, that Postum costs much less per cup.

"Will you send me your name and address? Tell me which kind you prefer—Instant Postum or Postum Cereal (the kind you boil). I'll see that you get the first week's supply and my personal directions right away."

FREE—MAIL THIS COUPON NOW!

© 1925, P. C. Co.

Postum is one of the Post Health Products, which include also Grape-Nuts, Post Toasties (Double-thick Corn Flakes), and Post's Bran Flakes. Your grocer sells Postum in two forms. Instant Postum, made in the cup by adding boiling water, is one of the easiest drinks in the world to prepare. Postum Cereal is also easy to make, but should be boiled 20 minutes.

A sick man has no place in business

THE tempo of modern business is a pace that only healthy men in full stride can hold. The man who is sick—or half-sick —is soon outstripped by competition.

The leaders of business have conserved their youth with the same care with which they saved their first thousand dollars. They know that the most severe bankruptcy is that of the body.

Early in their lives these men discovered what famous physicians know to be true . . . that one of the greatest physical liabilities is constipation. Its poisons often spread through the body. Sometimes this poisoning goes on for years, dragging down vitality, smothering enthusiasm, stealing efficiency. Undoubtedly, many men whose chances were brilliant have failed to reach their high objective because of improper elimination.

What a pity—when constipation can be overcome so easily. Just eat a delicious cereal: Kellogg's ALL-BRAN. This supplies the roughage needed to sweep the intestines clean of all poisonous wastes.

Two tablespoonfuls daily are guaranteed to prevent and relieve both temporary and recurring constipation. In stubborn cases, use ALL-BRAN with each meal. Isn't this far better than taking pills and drugs—which so often form dangerous habits. Kellogg's ALL-BRAN also provides iron to build up your blood.

Perhaps on many occasions you have seen men ordering ALL-BRAN in a dining car, or at a hotel. Try ALL-BRAN with milk or cream, fruits or honey added. Have your cook make it up into bran muffins, breads, omelets, etc.

Kellogg's ALL-BRAN is served wherever you go. Made by Kellogg in Battle Creek.

• • •

You'll enjoy Kellogg's Slumber Music, broadcast over WJZ and associated stations of the N. B. C. every Sunday evening at 10.30 E.S.T. Also KFI Los Angeles, KOMO Seattle at 10.00, and KOA Denver at 10.30.

If directors met
IN THE WASHROOM

Would you be on the carpet?

Would you be "on the carpet?" Washroom conditions—toilet seats to be frank—tell a story louder than words. Right, they build good will—secure tenants, hold old customers and effectively bid for new ones.

What if tomorrow brings a close inspection of that building you're trying to lease, an unexpected big customer or a delegation on whom you must create the right impression? Will you have to dodge the washrooms?

The larger your business and the more intimate its public contacts, the greater is your responsibility. Many in high places little dream of the conditions that prevail in washrooms for which they are ultimately responsible—toilets that advertise policies and management.

It is important that you look *personally* into this matter of toilet seats and sanitation. You may be amazed at what you discover.

It's easy to get right. Church Sani-Black Seats are a sound, long-term investment. The first cost is the last. They endure as long as the building. Your letterhead or the coupon will bring you an actual cross-section sample, together with a free copy of "Commercial and Industrial Sanitation." C. F. Church Mfg. Company, Holyoke, Mass.

Church Sani-Black Seats are indestructible, the result of moulding a thick rubber coat under 216,000 pounds hydraulic heat pressure.

Modern Buildings Church Sani-Seat equipped include:

Empire State Building
Chrysler Building
Bank of Manhattan
Columbia-Presbyterian
  Medical Center
Fisher Building
N. Y. Central Building
Irving Trust Building
Rockefeller Center
  (Radio City)

and hundreds of others from coast to coast.

FOR SALE BY ALL PLUMBING STORES

CHURCH *sani-black* SEATS

Division of American Radiator & Standard Sanitary Corporation

C. F. CHURCH MFG. CO., Dept. F1, Holyoke, Mass.

Without cost or obligation, send me Sani-Black Seat cross-section and copy of "Commercial and Industrial Sanitation".

Name
Company
Address

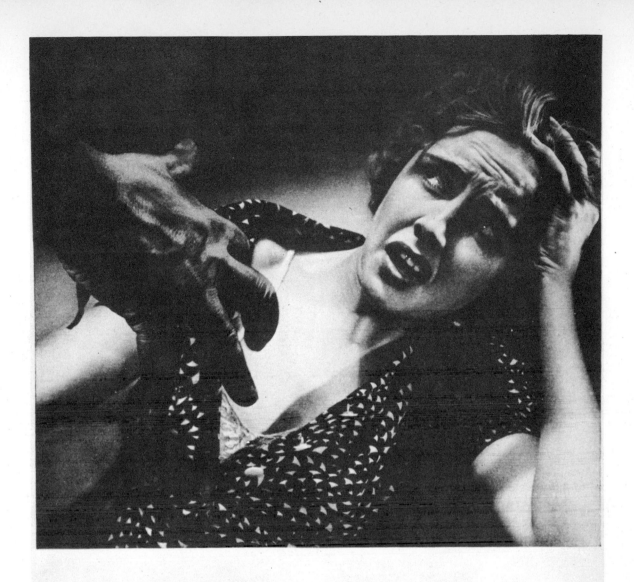

That this shall not be
<u>Your</u> Sister!

Will a yellow hand of lust fall roughly on the white shoulder of *your* sister?

"Not while I've an ounce of manhood in my soul or a drop of blood in my body!" Naturally, that's your answer. BUT . . .

. . . if yellow feet ever reach American soil, yellow hands will clutch American women! Will that happen? That's largely up to you and the other red-blooded young men of America.

Words won't stop them. Prayers won't stop them. The "other fellow" won't stop them. But YOU can stop them! You, with a hard-hitting Yankee rifle in your hands!

Every hour you delay you give those yellow hands the chance to draw closer to *your* sister . . . *your* wife . . . *your* sweetheart. Come on! JOIN UP NOW! Show them that you're *white* . . . that "*You're not yellow!*"

★

Join now!
you're <u>needed</u> now!

★

1938

The above advertisement was never intended to be run. It was devised by a team of copywriters three years before America's entry in World War II to show what wartime enlistment propaganda might look like.

THOUGHTS AT THIRTY-NINE

I'm 39 today.

Not old, as somebody once said, for a cathedral. But well past the starry-eyed stage for a man.

And I've gotten rid of some of my starry-eyed ideas.

Does that mean I'm worn down and disillusioned? No—I don't think it does. Not when I remember the kick I got out of landing that 3½ pound brook trout on the Tenabeck last spring.

But I'm beginning to see some things as they really are.

That dream every kid has of being rich some day. I don't think it's coming true, as far as I'm concerned.

The securities I bought in '29—well, why go into

that again? This house . . . it will be mine some day, but there is that boom price to write off. The job . . . good even at cut pay . . . but after all, how many people get rich on jobs?

No, I'll probably never be rich. But I'm losing no sleep over it . . . for I've fixed things so I'm even surer that I'll never be poor.

I've seen to it that I'll have money when I need it. I've done it the only way I know of for the man who hasn't an estate behind him . . . by taking full advantage of insurance.

If anything happens to me, my life insurance policies cover the rest of my mortgage, take care of Mary, and send the boys to college. If I live, there will be

an income that will let us have a mighty comfortable time.

My accident insurance takes up where my life insurance leaves off. My house is covered by fire insurance. Automobile insurance protects me when I drive.

I've looked ahead, calculated the hazards of life and guarded against them.

And at 39 I've greater peace of mind than I've ever had before.

Moral: Insure in the Travelers.

The Travelers Insurance Company, The Travelers Indemnity Company, The Travelers Fire Insurance Company, Hartford, Connecticut.

M-229 B-9-8I PRINTED IN U.S.A.

1935

Sid Ward, a one-time traveling salesman for Jell-O in Ohio and later copy chief of the Young and Rubicam agency, reported the unusual response to this ad: "It drew fan mail. A lot of people wrote to say it was just the way they felt about their insurance. Others said it had given them fresh understanding of what insurance could do. Travelers' agents reported prospects with stars in their eyes and tear sheets in their hands."

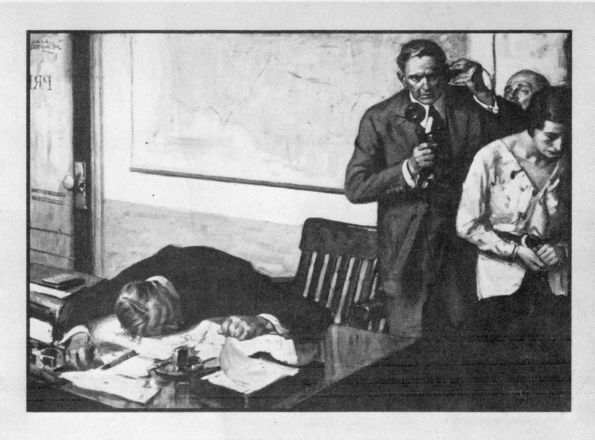

... 41 YEARS OLD

"HUMPHREY HOBBS collapsed in his office at 11:30 this morning," says a recent newspaper report. "After examination, Dr. Griffin stated that he had died of heart disease. Mr. Hobbs was 41 years old."

We hear of such tragedies among young and middle-aged people far too often. Scarcely a day passes that we do not read of some person in the prime of life being taken by "heart trouble." And, unfortunately, the number of deaths from this cause is increasing.

The group of diseases generally covered by the phrase "heart trouble" claims more victims than any other disease—more than tuberculosis, cancer, or pneumonia. It takes one out of every six people over 40 years old.

There are various types of heart dis-ease. Some of them result from infectious germs, which, it is believed, frequently enter the body through bad teeth or diseased tonsils. Excesses, such as over-eating, may be important factors because of the unusual strain they put upon the heart. Even exercise, usually so beneficial, may be overdone and carried to harmful extremes. Far too often the cause is simply overwork.

Heart disease may be so insidious in its onset that the person afflicted is, for some time, often entirely unaware of it. But it *does* give warnings, although these warnings may not be recognizable by the patients themselves.

In most instances a physician can detect the earliest symptoms. It is then of course that he has the best chance to control the disease. But at any time it is usually possible for scientific medical care to bring about a decided improvement in the patient's condition.

*See your doctor before
he HAS to see you*

The fact that in every civilized country, except ours, the death rate among the middle-aged *decreased* between 1921 and 1927, while with us it *increased*, is a warning that should not go unheeded.

Nearly everybody is quick to call a physician when he is ill. But remember that it will pay you also to take timely inventories of your health, through occasional examinations by your own physician *while you are still feeling well.*

The proverbial "ounce of prevention" may add years to your life.

**BUILDING
THE FORTRESSES
OF HEALTH**

One of a series of messages telling how the worker in medical science, the physician, and the maker of medicines are surrounding you with stronger health defenses year by year. Parke, Davis & Company, Detroit, Michigan; Walkerville, Ontario.

PARKE, DAVIS & CO.

THE WORLD'S LARGEST MAKERS OF PHARMACEUTICAL AND BIOLOGICAL PRODUCTS 1931

"We know that men stand a 500 percent greater risk of a coronary than women, and, in the past two decades, deaths from heart attacks have jumped 14 percent among men aged 25 to 44, while declining among women in the same age group. . . . Characterized by intense striving for achievement, competitiveness, aggressivity, impatience, a preemptive speech pattern and a constant awareness of the pressure of time and responsibility, the candidate for a coronary is a living embodiment of the ideals of the [male] Mystique."
Harvey E. Kaye, from *Male Survival* (1974)

62

"Don't let daddy lick me again!"

An old, old problem solved in an up-to-date way

1. **MOTHER:** Oh, John, why don't you let him alone? He's only a child.
FATHER: Well, *somebody* has to make him listen to reason.

2. **MOTHER:** That's the first time I ever heard of a hairbrush being called "reason"!
FATHER: Let's settle this right now! He needs that *stuff* and he'll take it whether he likes the taste or not!

3. **MOTHER:** That's right, Mr. Know-it-all—get him all upset and leave it for me to straighten him out.
FATHER: Aw, don't get yourself in a stew!

4. **MOTHER:** I'm *not!* All I know is that Millie Bliss used to jam a bad-tasting laxative down her boy until her doctor put a stop to it. He said it could do more harm than good!
FATHER: For Pete's sake, what laxative *can* we give him?

5. **MOTHER:** The one Millie uses—not an "adult" laxative, but one made especially for children...Fletcher's Castoria. It's mild, yet works effectively. Millie says it's SAFE...and her boy *loves* its pleasant taste!
FATHER: O.K. I'll get a bottle. But boy, he better like it!

6. **MOTHER:** Would you believe it, John? I never saw a spoonful of medicine disappear so fast!
FATHER: I wouldn't have believed it if I didn't have my glasses on. I guess this Fletcher's Castoria is OKAY!

What about the child of 5...8...or 11?

THE SYSTEM of a child even up to 9 and 11 is still NOT an adult system...is still too delicate for a strong, "adult" laxative.

So Fletcher's Castoria is recommended not only for infants, but for all children up to 11 and 12 years of age.

Play safe...and get a bottle of Fletcher's Castoria today. The Family-Size bottle saves you money. Look for the signature, Chas. H. Fletcher.

Chas. H. Fletcher **CASTORIA**

The modern—SAFE—laxative made especially for children.

1940

Their Hero Arrives on the Next Bus

Thinks of himself as Daddy — just a fellow like millions of others making the most of every day…working with a purpose and then relaxing to live with his family and friends. His age? He feels so young that the years don't matter. He's the best playmate his wife and youngsters ever had. And why not? No setting sun sees him bringing home the cares of the day. No rising sun fails to find him refreshed and eager to greet the new day. * * *

Advice to Wives: One of Home's greatest charms for Daddy is the icebox — especially when well stocked with Budweiser and other good things. It gives the busy man-about-town the urge to be a gracious man-about-home.

Live Life…Every Golden Minute of it…Enjoy Budweiser…Every Golden Drop of it

ANHEUSER-
BUSCH
*Makers of the
World-Famous Beer*

Budweiser

TRADE MARK REG. U. S. PAT. OFF.

A Beverage of Moderation

TRADE MARK OF
ANHEUSER-BUSCH, INC.
ST. LOUIS, MO., U. S. A.

MAKE THIS TEST

DRINK BUDWEISER FOR FIVE DAYS. ON THE SIXTH DAY TRY TO DRINK A SWEET BEER. YOU WILL WANT BUDWEISER'S FLAVOR THEREAFTER.

COPR. 1940 ANHEUSER-BUSCH, INC., ST. LOUIS, MO.

"SURE, THERE'LL BE A PARADE..."

I know what I'm up against.

I know what the odds are.

I know what they mean by "lost at sea."

But *I'm* going to make it . . . nothing can stop me!

Sure, when this war's over there'll be crowds and cheers and ticker tape and confetti. Sure, there'll be handshakes and pats on the back and good wishes. Sure, but what's bringing me back is bigger than that . . .

I want what I've been fighting for . . . a fighting chance!

Maybe some folks would say I was crazy, if they could hear me talking out loud this way . . .

Maybe they'd laugh and say, "Listen, buddy, get wise. . . . the trouble with guys like you is—you keep trying to do it the hard way . . ."

Well . . .

It wasn't easy learning how to swim, but I did . . . and now I won't drown. It wasn't easy to stick it out when the going got tough, but I did . . . and now *nobody* can make me quit. It wasn't easy finding out how to steer a course by the stars and the sun, but I did . . . and now, even from out here, I'm going to find my way home!

The girl I'm going to marry wasn't easy to win . . . because she's the finest girl in the world.

The job I'm coming back to wasn't easy to get . . . because it was the swellest job any guy ever had.

The future *I'm* after is so big nobody's ever going to hand it to me on a silver platter!

That's why I want a fighting chance . . . a chance to move *up* . . . an opportunity to go ahead. That's why I want to plan a future of my own in a land and a world where *every* man is free to make the most

of his ability . . . where there'll be plenty of work days and plenty of pay days . . . with no limits on how high you can rise . . . how far you can go.

That's the America I left behind me.

That's the America I'm fighting for.

That's the America I want when I get back.

* * *

Here at Nash-Kelvinator we're building Pratt & Whitney engines for the Navy's Vought Corsairs and Grumman Hellcats . . . Hamilton Standard propellers for United Nations bombers . . . governors, binoculars, parts for ships, jeeps, tanks and trucks . . . readying production lines for Sikorsky helicopters. All of us devoted 100% to winning this war . . . to speeding the peace when our men will come back to their jobs and homes and even better futures than they had before . . . to the day when together we'll build an even finer Kelvinator, an even greater Nash!

NASH-KELVINATOR CORPORATION
Kenosha • Milwaukee • DETROIT • Grand Rapids • Lansing

NASH
AUTOMOBILES
KELVINATOR
REFRIGERATORS • ELECTRIC RANGES

1944

"It's a ring for your nose,"
said my wife sweetly

"VERY FUNNY, very funny," I said. "What comes next?"

"I merely decided," she went on, patiently, "that if you're going to keep on being so bull-headed about things, you might as well wear a ring in your nose and look the part."

"But I AM NOT . . ." I started to shout.

"Shhhh!" she broke in. "Just let me remind you—among other things—that you *positively* refuse to wear anything but blue suits. I tell you you'd look very nice in a brown suit, but you won't even try one on. Not you!"

"I know what I like," I said.

"Of course you do, dear. You know what you like before you even *try* a thing. Remember that perfectly silly argument we had about Postum last night?"

"I did NOT argue," I blurted out, "I merely TOLD you . . ."

"That's right," she said, "when I suggested that we have Postum for dinner, you *told* me you'd heard Postum was just a substitute for coffee. You *told* me you heard it didn't even taste like coffee. You *told* me you would have no part of it. Period."

"That's not being bull-headed," I complained.

"Oh no?" said my wife. "Then why didn't you listen when I told you that Postum is *not* just a substitute for coffee? It isn't *supposed* to taste like coffee, any more than tea is supposed to taste like coffee.

"Furthermore, why didn't you listen when I told you Postum is a swell, delicious, full-bodied drink in its own right . . . that it's got a rich, hearty flavor all its own . . . that millions of people would rather smack their lips over a cup of Postum than any other mealtime drink in the world?

"Did you give the slightest heed to those perfectly true statements? You did not!

"You didn't even listen," she said, "when I told you that many people find themselves feeling better after they change to Postum."

So, finally, to keep her quiet, I tried Postum.

So, I liked it.

So, I'm mad!

NOTE: Postum, besides being a grand, full-flavored drink, is truly economical. Costs less than ½¢ a cup. Comes in two forms: Postum, the kind you boil, drip, or percolate; and Instant Postum, made instantly in the cup by adding boiling water. Postum is a product of General Foods.

Postum —ONE OF AMERICA'S GREAT MEALTIME DRINKS

TUNE IN: The Aldrich Family, Thursday nights, NBC Network. One of America's great radio programs, written by Clifford Goldsmith, sponsored by Postum.

MR. JOHN LAGER—DISTINGUISHED ORCHIDOLOGIST

For Men of Distinction... LORD CALVERT

EACH bottle of Lord Calvert is numbered and registered at the distillery . . . for so *rare*, so *smooth*, so *mellow* is this "Custom" Blended whiskey that it has never been produced except in limited quantities. For years the most expensive whiskey blended in America, Lord Calvert is intended especially for those who can afford the finest.

LORD CALVERT IS A "CUSTOM" BLENDED WHISKEY, 86.8 PROOF, 65% GRAIN NEUTRAL SPIRITS. CALVERT DISTILLERS CORPORATION, NEW YORK CITY.

1945

"Snob appeal might seem to be the most obvious feature of this type of ad, with its submerged syllogism that since all sorts of eminent men drink this whiskey they are eminent because they drink it. Or only this kind of whiskey is suited to the palate of distinguished men, therefore a taste for it confers, or at least displays an affinity for, distinction in those who have not yet achieved greatness. If greatness has not been thrust upon you, it is no fault of this ad, which generously thrusts the inexpensive means to greatness upon you. . . . What really emerges from this item is the notion of distinction and culture as being a matter of consumption rather than the possession of discriminating perception and judgment."

Marshall McLuhan, *The Mechanical Bride* (1951)

1952

Now's the time for JELL-O
GELATIN DESSERT
SIX DELICIOUS FLAVORS

Take a peek at Mr. America of 1962! Like most American men (ahem!) we'll bet he enjoys a big dish of shimmering Jell-O. And you can give him all he wants, too! A Jell-O gelatin dessert is not only good for him, but it costs just pennies to serve.

1952

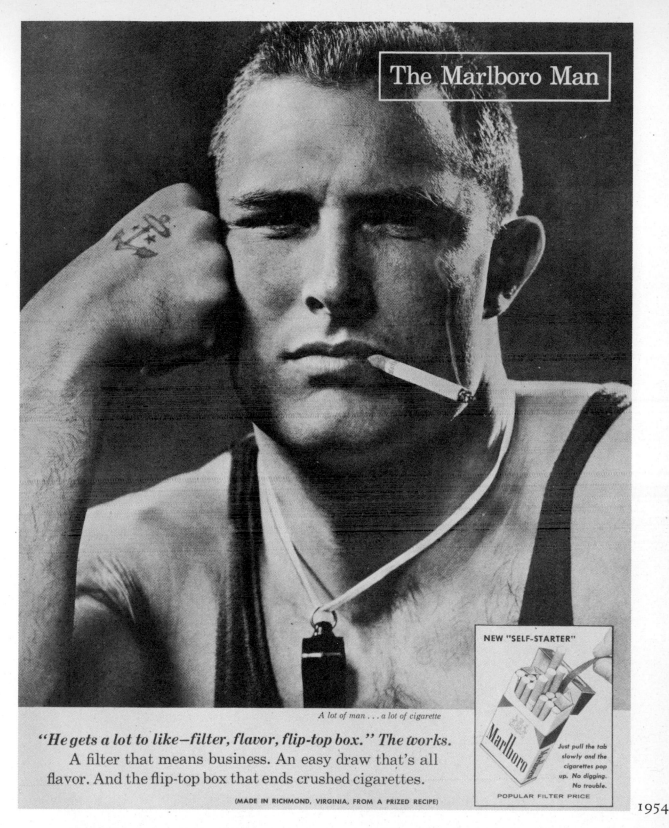

The Marlboro Man

A lot of man . . . a lot of cigarette

"He gets a lot to like—filter, flavor, flip-top box." The works.
A filter that means business. An easy draw that's all
flavor. And the flip-top box that ends crushed cigarettes.

(MADE IN RICHMOND, VIRGINIA, FROM A PRIZED RECIPE)

NEW "SELF-STARTER"

Marlboro

*Just pull the tab
slowly and the
cigarettes pop
up. No digging.
No trouble.*

POPULAR FILTER PRICE

1954

*Marlboro cigarettes were identified as a "feminine high-style cigarette" when the
company decided to go masculine. Marketing researcher Pierre Martineau offers
this analysis of the campaign's strategies: "1. No women were shown in the advertising. 2. All models were very virile men . . . 3. The models were also chosen
as successful, forceful personalities to inspire emulation, identification with an
admirable figure . . . 4. To reinforce the notion of virility and also to hint of a
romantic past, each man had a plainly visible tattoo on his hand. . . . This symbol
gave a richness to the product image, bringing it all into focus."*
                                        Motivation in Advertising (1957)

Madam! Suppose you traded jobs with your husband?

You can just bet the first thing he'd ask for would be a telephone in the kitchen.

You wouldn't catch him dashing to another room every time the telephone rang, or he had to make a call.

He doesn't have to do it in his office in town. It would be mighty helpful if you didn't have to do it in your "office" at home.

That's in the kitchen where you do so much of your work. And it's right there that an additional telephone comes in so handy for so many things.

Along with a lot of convenience is that nice feeling of pride in having the best of everything—especially if it is one of those attractive new telephones in color.

 P.S. Additional telephones in kitchen, bedroom and other convenient places around the house cost little. The service charge is just pennies a day.

Bell Telephone System

Confessions of a neophyte cigar smoker

I walk into a restaurant a little unsure of just how to hold my Corina Cigar as I move to my table.

Several women sneak glances at me.

The waiter seems more respectful today.

I think of Albright at the office calling me "Sir" this morning.

I'm seated and I take a puff. This Corina is so flavorful I'm not even tempted to inhale.

I order . . . seems to me my voice is a little deeper and stronger.

I look forward to dinner. Food tastes better lately.

Afterward I relax and light up another Corina Lark. The flavor is

mild . . . so even a beginner like myself enjoys it. I see why Corina Larks are the largest selling 15¢ cigar most everywhere.

I gaze at the pretty girl at the next table. Switching to cigars was a good idea. Switching up to Corina was a better one.

The girl smiles . . .

Thirst getting into the act?

Bring on the *real thirst-quencher!*

Are the funny lines sticking in your throat? Is your mouth as hot as a spotlight? Enter: 7-Up! What a welcome relief—that first chilled sip. What a delicious feeling as you finish the bottle and discover thirst is really gone! Not hidden. But gone. (Because 7-Up stimulates your mouth's natural moisture!) Audition a bottle now. It's *always* 7-Up time!

FOR FRESH TASTE, THIRST QUENCHING, QUICK LIFT . . . "FRESH UP" WITH SEVEN-UP!

Should a man in his 50's be allowed out in a Mustang?

Let's consider what might happen. To begin with, he'll go around with
a mysterious little smile on his face, new spring in his walk. Mustang acts
on a man that way, what with standard equipment like bucket seats, husky
200 cubic-inch Six, all-vinyl interiors, floor-shift, wall-to-wall carpeting,
the works. Driving a Mustang can be like finding the Fountain of Youth!
Then there's this: Mustang might give a man an incurable taste for luxury.
Options include Stereo Tape System, air-conditioning, front disc brakes,
power steering, big smooth 289 cubic-inch V-8. Finally, remember
Mustang's low price. It will give a man a sense of spending
power he's never had before. Do you know a man in his 50's
who'd like all this to happen to him? *You do!* Well, welcome
him to 1966—and tell him to get into a Mustang fast!

America's Favorite Fun Car
MUSTANG
MUSTANG
MUSTANG

1966 Mustang Hardtop

A PRODUCT OF
Ford

I am the greatest wigmaker in history.

I am Armando Ghedini. I spit on ugliness. I especially spit on wig ugliness. For years I fight wig ugliness.

My only weapon is my mind. My mind says, "Bring out a woman's mood, Armando."

So I make the Nomad™. It is wash and wear. It has curls to comb. It comes in 26 colors. And makes you a gypsy lady.

Is there anything more beautiful than a gypsy woman who lives in the city? I ask you.

Many think I am wrong. Many think wigs should be neat. Functional. I say no! Wigs should be mad, jealous, happy, sad, messy—wonderful!

Like women. Like Nomad. Like me.

Be grateful for Ghedini.

NOMAD. From the Ghedini Collection at fine department stores and beauty salons everywhere.   North American Hair Goods Co., New York, San Francisco, Hong Kong.

1970

"Roger reads Esquire"

Photographed by Francesco Scavullo

Mrs. Roger Davis

"He calls it the only 'men's lib' magazine. Meaning, he says, Esquire recognizes the fact that man has a mind as well as a body. I think that's kind of well put, but then Roger was an English major at Columbia ('61) and taught at UCLA before he became an actor. He has a way of saying things that I find very apt. I think that's one of the main reasons I became Mrs. Roger Davis. Most of the women Roger meets are slightly bowled over by his good looks and the fact that he's a TV star. (Alias Smith & Jones' Hannibal Hayes). But I loved him for his originality and style. He's the only man I know who can get high on 18th century literature in the evening and spend the morning watching a boxer he sponsors work out in the gym. Or, go see how his racehorse, Royal Bupers does at the track with a copy of Robert Frost under his arm. He's that way about places, too. So we live in Beverly Hills and New York — and we'd like to have a home in Rome — Roger's favorite city in Europe. But wherever we are — life is interesting — because my husband is an interesting man."

The Esquire Man: He's got a sense of style.

1972

When Clay Felker took over as editor of Esquire in February 1978, he dedicated the magazine to "The American Man and the New Success": "There is an increasing recognition that life must be better balanced between achievement in their professional and personal lives. In short, the American man is demanding more out of life and yet doesn't quite know how to get it."

A NEW JOE WEIDER SCIENTIFIC <u>WEIGHT-GAINING</u> BREAKTHROUGH

The end of the SKINNY BODY!

<u>He's "Drinking-On" A-POUND-A-DAY Our New Delicious Fun-Way!</u>

Thousands are doing it—Monthly...WHY NOT YOU? Here's a totally new breed of
nutritional "wildcat" that's guaranteed to put an end to your muscle-starved, hungry-looking
skinny body—through a new, scientifically blended, delicious milkshake-flavored drink.
It fills out your body and face—for a fresher, more exciting, fun-going you!

From near death by tuberculosis, emphysema, chronic bronchial asthma, collapsed lungs, alcoholism and drug addiction, this sickly 5'10" skinny 110-lb. weakling gained 65 pounds of solid muscle—added 12 inches of boulder-sized bulges to his chest, 9½ inches to each arm, 8 inches to each leg, and reduced his waist to 28 inches—to become a body building champion... all through the use of Joe Weider's Trainer of the Champions CRASH-WEIGHT GAIN FORMULA #7 Plan!—That's the **true** story of Charlie Kemp!

A Long History of Physical Weakness Problems

Charlie's trouble started early. All his life he had been frail and sick—by the time he was 10 he had developed asthma, and at 16 his left lung had collapsed. Yet these were only hints of problems that would follow, for during the next three years his left lung collapsed five more times and his right lung collapsed twice—he had cystic emphysema complicated by tuberculosis. This, combined with his sickly appearance, was too much for Charlie's battered ego, and by the time he was 25 he was a bona-fide alcoholic with severe cirrhosis of the liver.

Just when things looked darkest, they got darker. His dismal health brought on narcolepsy, and in order to combat this disease he had to take powerful doses of amphetamines—pep pills. They, in turn, brought on more pernicious complications—loss of appetite and, ironically, insomnia, which required drug depressants. The combination of alcohol and drugs destroyed not only Charlie's physical health but also his mental health, and before long he entered the Seton Psychiatric Institute.

For a full year, psychiatrists bolstered Charlie's psyche, but when he was released, emphysema hit again and his right lung collapsed once more. Was his life really doomed?

Into the hospital again. Surgery curtailed the collapsing of his lungs and removed the diseased portions, and when he was released he found new determination to rebuild his body. But that meant gaining weight—and Charlie, who had to continue taking amphetamines which killed his appetite, began to rely almost entirely on food supplements.

Weider Formula/Method Creates a New Life!

Charlie devoured Joe Weider's CRASH-WEIGHT GAIN FORMULA #7 by the case, altered his eating habits as prescribed for him by Joe Weider, and followed a few simple daily exercises, which helped to turn the weight gains he made into a firmer, more muscular and handsomer body.

His progress was astounding—you see here the gains he made—absolutely phenomenal, especially for a man entering his 40's and a truly great testimonial for the Weider System and Crash Weight Gain Formula #7.

His life changed with him—from a pathetic, undesired, unloved loser whose only companions were dogs—to a prize-winning "Mr. America Physical Achievement Award" body surrounded by the world's most beautiful girls.—This is the miracle of courageous Charlie Kemp!

© COPYRIGHT JOE WEIDER, 1973

110 lbs.

❝Tuberculosis, emphysema, chronic bronchial asthma, collapsed lungs, two lung operations, cirrhosis of the liver, narcolepsy, alcoholic, drug addict, a life in and out of the hospital, psychiatric patient, three packs of cigarettes a day, no SEX desire, unloved—only dogs as companions.❞

175 lbs. **PHOTOS UNRETOUCHED**

❝After years of struggling to stay alive he decided to follow Joe Weider's miraculous Weight-Gaining Plan. The result today is a muscular man of vitality—athletic, handsome, earning $40,000 a year, cured of the sickness that used to plague him, and now—surrounded by beautiful girls!❞

You Can "Build-Up" Too!

Now, that miracle can be yours. If Charlie Kemp, who was a hopelessly sick underweight weakling struggling daily to live, could achieve so much, just think what you—underweight but medically fit—can accomplish by using the same milkshake flavored drink plan that Charlie used.

Start today to put an end to your skinny body by following the exact same successful weight-Gaining Formula that Charlie Kemp and thousands of others are using—Monthly! Just drink 4 zestful glasses of delicious CRASH-WEIGHT GAIN FORMULA #7 daily. It's full of calories, vitamins, minerals, carbohydrates and tastes delicious with your regular meals. It's safe and healthy, made from all-natural nutrients—NO DRUGS—and does all its work in a relaxed manner, piling on pound after pound of handsome weight to flesh out your bones. Combine CRASH-WEIGHT GAIN FORMULA #7 with five simple daily exercises, and watch how you fill our your narrow chest, your skinny arms and spindly legs. Put an end to your skinny body once, for all—in JUST 14 TO 30 DAYS! And, oh yes—it also fills out your face for a healthier, more exciting, fun-loving you, and that's a lot!

BEFORE AND AFTER MEASUREMENTS				
	BEFORE	AFTER	GAINS	
Weight	110	175	65	lbs.
Chest	33	45	12	in.
Arms	7½	17	9½	in.
Thighs	16	24	8	in.
Calves	10	16	6	in.
Waist	29	28	Lost 1	in.

THE DO-IT-YOURSELF GAIN-A-POUND-A-DAY-KIT

It's a one-day supply of CRASH-WEIGHT, chock full of weight-gaining nutrients that can smash the weight-gaining barrier! You want to gain a pound a day? Half a pound a day? Maybe you just want to add a few pounds here and there. You want it easily—enjoyably—without stuffing yourself with heavy-as-lead foods? Now you can do it! It's as simple as drinking a delicious milkshake.

FREE:

"Valuable Weight-Gaining and Muscle-Building Course." This Illustrated Guide sent FREE with each CRASH-WEIGHT FORMULA #7 Kit. Crammed with step-by-step instructions in muscle-building and weight-gaining basics. Filled with all the latest ideas and how to adapt them for your own personal, fun-going weight gains!

I was what you call big on spectator sports. As my enthusiasm grew over the years, so did my waistline.

Last fall, the biggest workout of my week had to be Monday Night Football. I'll bet I was the nation's leading rusher to the refrigerator. And for every touchdown, I must have downed a beer.

Basketball season took me to new heights. Or should I say weights. While the boys were stuffing in the ball, I stuffed in the pretzels.

When baseball came around, so did the hot dogs and chocolate malteds. To me, RBI's meant raisinets batted in. Needless to say, my personal stats were on a steady rise.

Then I hit my big slump. My body was out of condition, overweight and miserable.

It was time to tackle the problem. So I went to the pros — the people at European Health Spas. They're the largest chain of health spas in the country.

Now, thanks to European Health Spas, I'm participating instead of watching. My enthusiasm for sports didn't diminish, but I'm going to. The Spa has the techniques and facilities and I've made up my mind. Together, we're an unbeatable team. Here's one sports fan who is going to stop fanning out.

Confessions of a really big sports fan.

European Health Spas
Physical fitness for men and women

GOOD NEWS FOR AMERICAN BUSINESS:

Those young men you thought wouldn't fit in after they served in Vietnam are fitting in very well.

WILFORD SMITH
COSMETICS EXECUTIVE

Every society that goes through the terrible experience of a war holds its breath in fear it will go through another terrible experience after the war.

And that is the aftermath of war. The returning of the young men. And their return to society.

If ever a postwar period was ripe for problems, it was the period following the end of the Vietnam war.

EVERYBODY'S WAR: NOBODY'S WAR.

A war so unpopular, we had wars against it at home. A war that gave us no victories and no returning heroes.

A war that just…faded away.

Inflation and recession were rearing their heads, simultaneously. Jobs were hard to find.

UP BY THE BOOTSTRAPS.

Yes, there was cause for concern. And a girding for the crime and drug epidemics that were to follow.

They didn't follow. They didn't happen. Those young men were a lot smarter than a lot of us gave them credit for.

Instead, for the most part, the Vietnam veteran picked himself up and started making up for lost time.

He rejoined the millions of other young men of his generation, and the impact of that reunion is being felt today.

A CHANGE FOR THE BETTER.

This generation includes the fastest-advancing, most effective, highest-paid group of young managerial men ever to hit American business.

Their participation in politics has brought forth new openness, new expectancy, new faith.

And results. In 1974, for example, Congress was flooded by the youngest group of electees since World War II.

In education, especially higher education, this new generation is bringing a new reality into focus. The ivory towers are crumbling. In their place a new give and take, a new closer contact between student and school is developing.

The turmoil in ecology, in human rights, in consumer rights, in individual rights was started by this group. And carried on by them. They've seen it through—from the earliest, irrational protestations to today's careful, pragmatic approaches to the solutions.

Yes, this generation is making its mark as few generations have done before it.

In all, we think it's the most vital, alive group of prospects American business has been blessed with since the post–World War II boom.

WANT TO MEET THEM?

At PLAYBOY, we grew up with this generation.

When our magazine was an infant and alert to the slightest sound, we listened to them. Very carefully.

And the more we listened to them, the more they listened to us.

The rapport that developed over the years has given us a larger audience of these maturing young male adults than any other men's magazine, newsweekly or sportsweekly.

We reach 13,621,000 men every month.

Which means, if you're in the market, we can help you. Because, in fact, we are the market.

The Playboy reader. His lust is for life.

1977

According to the account executive for Playboy, this ad is addressed to corporate wives and says, "Playboy readers have grown up. . . . The Playboy man is decent, solid, a guy who has money or is willing to struggle within the system to get it. That's the kind of person they want their sons to be."

WHAT SORT OF MAN <u>REALLY</u> READS HUSTLER?

When Larry Flynt started HUSTLER three years ago, he said it would be a mass-appeal vehicle—a magazine that would mock the myth of pseudosophisticated values glorified by other men's magazines and capture the realism that is the true spirit of Middle America today. Now the figures are in. Our first TGI Survey (Spring '77) proves Larry was right on target! Pick any category and compare HUSTLER with the other two leading men's magazines: You'll see a profile of the typical Middle American male . . . some college men, but *more* high-school men; some managers, but *more* salesmen, craftsmen and foremen. More than 64% of them are married, almost 60% of them make over $15,000 a year, and <u>more</u> of them own homes worth over $25,000! It's a valuable market, with families and money to spend. And HUSTLER delivers it at a lower CPM! We've given you the vehicle—do you have the courage to give us a contract?

HUSTLER Magazine • 40 West Gay Street • Columbus, Ohio 43215 • (614) 464-2070

1977

WE CRUISE ALL SUMMER

Live like a millionaire on your yacht, with an intimate number of adventurous people for a fabulous, full week or weekend voyage to Fire Island, Atlantic City or both. Something Special "Yacht Set Ltd" was conceived for you as special people would want it to be.

For a Fire Island weekend you are picked up by limousine* and taken to the boat basin, welcomed aboard your yacht where we have made all the arrangements for you... beverages, hors d' oeuvres and epicurean dinners. The setting is elegant. We'll transport you, in style over water, through a stimulating vacation.

Drifting by the sparkling lights of New York, you are surrounded by the sounds of the sea and a soft mood where your imagination can run wild.

Arrive at your destination around the bewitching hour. Depending on your program, sleep on the yacht** or at the luxurious Cherry Grove Inn. During the day swim and sun from the beach or even from the deck of the yacht.

At night, dinner at the internationally famous Sea Shack... then dancing and land cruising to the pulsating lights and throbbing disco sounds of the island... have a love affair in the excitement... live out your fantasy.

We sail for home with unlimited beverages again, a gourmet brunch and an equally glorious cruise. Upon docking you are wisked back home by limousine*. The perfect ending to your week/end week of pleasure.

No hassles... your vacation begins minutes after you leave home or work.

Cruise packages from $299 to $599 per person, based on double occupancy and availability. For discriminating people, of course.

includes membership in CMSC, inc.

*Included in all packages except $299 minimum, where it is also available, in Manhattan at $25 additional cost.

**Based on package availability

for information call or write to:

 **Something Special YACHT SET,** LTD.
345 East 93rd. St. New York, N.Y. 10028
(212) 860-9196   suite 29G

EXCLUSIVE REPRESENTATION
Lambda Travel & Communications Network, Ltd.
55 West 42nd Street Suite 1501
New York, New York 10036 (212) 354-0322

The "Jet-Set" is International. Now be part of the New "Yacht-Set"...Launched this year from New York

This advertisement appeared in a recent issue of Christopher Street, *a successful national magazine addressed to the gay community.*

When Crusher Lizowski talks about being a homemaker, you listen.

"I like to cook, and I think I'm pretty good-at it. My specialty is Japanese dishes. Sushi, tempura, teriyaki, shabu-shabu.

"When I'm not on the road, I do most of the cooking around our house. I'm even teaching my oldest son how to cook.

"My wife and I feel that making a home is sharing. Equally. In the drudgery. In the fun. In everything. Especially in the important things like the care and guidance of our children and in establishing values in our home.

"The point is, I don't believe in the old stereotype about being the lord and master around the house while the little woman raises the kids and cooks the meals.

"I don't see anything unusual in that. Nobody kids me when I put on an apron. Not in front of me at least.

"Being a homemaker is, after all, being an adult. Learning how to manage your life.

"Learning how to give. And how to give yourself to the people you love.

"Another thing I'm into is macrame. I'm learning how to make belts and plant hangers.

"Nobody kids me about that either."

This message about homemaking is brought to you as a public service by Future Homemakers of America and this publication. For more information, write: Future Homemakers of America, 2010 Massachusetts Ave. NW, Washington, DC 20036.

HOMEMAKING
The most misunderstood profession.

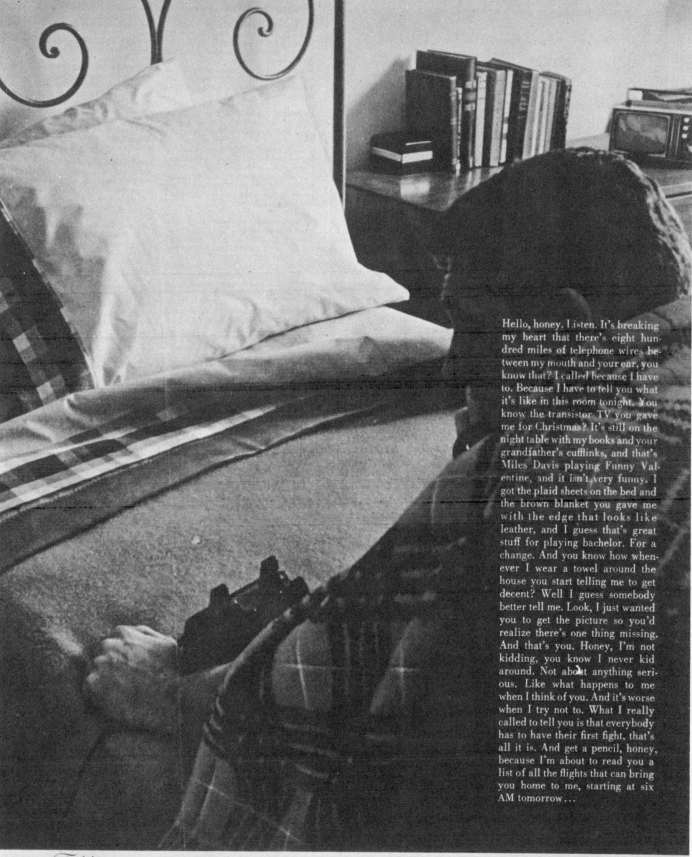

Hello, honey. Listen. It's breaking my heart that there's eight hundred miles of telephone wires between my mouth and your ear, you know that? I called because I have to. Because I have to tell you what it's like in this room tonight. You know the transistor TV you gave me for Christmas? It's still on the night table with my books and your grandfather's cufflinks, and that's Miles Davis playing Funny Valentine, and it isn't very funny. I got the plaid sheets on the bed and the brown blanket you gave me with the edge that looks like leather, and I guess that's great stuff for playing bachelor. For a change. And you know how whenever I wear a towel around the house you start telling me to get decent? Well I guess somebody better tell me. Look, I just wanted you to get the picture so you'd realize there's one thing missing. And that's you. Honey, I'm not kidding, you know I never kid around. Not about anything serious. Like what happens to me when I think of you. And it's worse when I try not to. What I really called to tell you is that everybody has to have their first fight, that's all it is. And get a pencil, honey, because I'm about to read you a list of all the flights that can bring you home to me, starting at six AM tomorrow...

Fieldcrest makes towels, blankets, sheets (Stag collection shown here), bedspreads, automatic blankets, bath rugs, shower curtains. 60 W. 40 St., N.Y.

"MAN—YOU SURE ARE CRAZY!"

SELENA: *Here the boss has been givin' you practically new shirts all these years—and you go and spoil it!*

SAM: All I said was, "Boss, how come you don't buy the kind that won't shrink outa size after they're washed?"

SELENA: *Shootin' off your big mouth!*

SAM: And he says, "What kind of shirts? If you mean that pre-shrunk kind, it's no dice!" he says. "Most of them shrink, too."

SELENA: *And plenty!*

SAM: So I says, "No suh, boss. I ain't talkin' about no pre-shrunk shirts. It's *Sanforized-Shrunk* I mean."

"What's the difference?" he says.

"A lot of difference," I tells him. "Don't you ever read the magazines? Seems this Sanforizing process takes all the shrinkin' out of a fabric, down to a measly

little ole 1%. And boss," I says, "when a shirt's got the Sanforized-Shrunk label on it, I know it *cain't* shrink out of size."

SELENA: *You know too much—that's your trouble!*

SAM: Right off, the boss wants to know where he can get 'em. "Anywheres," I says. "All the stores sell San-forized-Shrunk shirts now—most any style or make you want. Don't cost any extra."

SELENA: *Humph! I s'pose you told him where he could get Sanforized shorts and pajamas, too—so you won't get no more of them, either.*

SAM: We-ell, fact is, I did. But listen, Selena! With that, he peels off a wad of bills and tells me to get him a half dozen of everything, and keep the change.

SELENA: *What change? I ain't seen none of it yet.*

SAM: The change is gwine to be on me! Boy, I got me some of the swellest, fanciest Sanforized-Shrunk shirts you ever seen on anybody!

HERE'S YOUR CHANCE, SELENA—

Tell the missus that Sanforizing will end shrinking troubles in everything made of cotton, linen, or spun rayon.

| Women's Dresses | Slip Covers & Draperies | Nurses' Uniforms | Children's Clothes | Slacks, Work Clothes |

FOR PERMANENT FIT—LOOK FOR THE WORDS—SANFORIZED-SHRUNK

BLACKS

In the struggle to achieve equality in a society ostensibly pledged to that ideal, black leaders from W. E. B. Du Bois to Roy Wilkins and Stokely Carmichael have all said that the greatest barrier to freedom was institutionalized racism. The vast majority of whites would always react with horror when the violent treatment of blacks in the South was publicized, and many would even support the movements for desegregation and equal job opportunity. But after laws were passed, Supreme Court decisions rendered, and tanks rolled onto the lawns of Ole Miss, it was sadly clear that the problem was rooted not in the nation's laws but in its psyche. If true equality was to be gained, the image of blacks in the white mind would have to be radically transformed and, more complexly, the self-image of blacks strengthened and dignified.

That image, a blend of childish simplicity and foot-shuffling dependency, had been born in slavery and given new life in the years following Reconstruction, just at the time advertising was emerging as a national force for selling consumer goods. Not surprisingly, the pictorial representations of blacks for commercial purposes strongly resembled other popular depictions rendered by a predominantly white society. The faithful servant, the kind old darky, the pickaninny with the watermelon, the nostalgic view of plantation life—all of the characters, caricatures, and scenes of racial harmony essential to the mythology of southern rural experience appeared in the advertising pages of America's leading consumer magazines for more than fifty years.

After World War I the scenes shift with increasing frequency to an urban atmosphere, reflecting the massive migrations of blacks to northern cities. The percentage of blacks living outside the South rose from about 10 percent in 1915 to an astounding 25 percent by 1940. Although most settled in the slums and took low-paying jobs in factories and on assembly lines, or as dishwashers and bootblacks, the advertising community joined with the movie and radio industries to present an image of blacks as America's servant class. In the kitchen or the laundry, on trains, or at fancy parties, the black domestic was invariably on hand in the ads happily giving service to the "boss" or "lady," just as radio's Rochester on the Jack Benny show, or Beulah, the black maid, provided a touch of levity to the serious business of running the white middle-class household.

Before 1945 virtually the only popular image of blacks other than the servant's role was the white entertainer in blackface, a minstrel-show tradition standard in the vaudeville and radio routines of such national favorites as Al Jolson and Eddie Cantor. The dumb but lovable characters in *Amos 'n Andy*, the most popular radio program of all time, were created and portrayed by two white men trained in blackface comedy. Incredibly, even the part of Beulah was played on radio by a white man named Marlin Hurt.

During World War II advertisers continued to depict the blacks in a servile role. Indeed, if one examines the vast amount of wartime propaganda issued by this nation's major advertisers, it is difficult to believe that blacks did anything in the war except serve as faithful porters on troop trains. But black men did fight and many died, usually without recognition. As has often been noted, nothing did more to awaken the consciousness of blacks than the experience of fighting to preserve ideals of freedom and equality for a nation that traditionally deprived them of those same rights. To be sure, the image of the black as servant continued for years after the war, even in the advertising for such liberal and sophisticated magazines as *The New Yorker*. Moreover, newly established black magazines (*Ebony* and *Jet*, for example) always contained advertising for skin-lighteners and hair-straighteners, stark symbols of the deep-seated hatred blacks had for their own race. Still, by this time signs of impending dramatic change were unmistakable.

It began with the wide acclaim blacks began to receive in the public worlds of big-time sports and big-name entertainment. The seemingly unconquerable Joe Louis was now openly hailed as the greatest heavyweight of all time, while the brilliant performances of Duke Ellington, Louis Armstrong, and Ella Fitzgerald became an enduring part of America's musical tradition. But the most important event took place in 1947 when, under the glaring scrutiny of the mass media, a young, gifted athlete named Jackie Robinson bravely broke the color line of America's national pastime (see the section on heroes, heroines, and celebrities.) At about the same time, but almost without notice, black groups were filing lawsuits that challenged the entire legal basis for segregation and that would eventually culminate in the violent civil rights struggle.

Advertisements, as well as the popular entertainment presented over advertising-supported media, usually go out of their way to avoid involvement with controversial issues. As a result, the racial upheavals of the late 1950s and early 1960s had the almost immediate and beneficial effect of removing the more offensive black stereotypes from public view. During this period blacks formulated their own ideas about acceptable media images and let it be known that they would vociferously oppose all attempts to impose any they found offensive. This awareness of the profound effects the mass media have on the way we see ourselves meant the end of big-bottomed mammys, smiling Sambos, and stooping Toms. In their place the black middle-class demanded depictions of themselves in normal, everyday situations as families, as husbands and wives, as successful athletes, as up-and-coming young executives, and as sex objects.

By the late 1960s much of the advertising directed to the black consumer employed the popular theme of "Black Is Beautiful" or stressed the African heritage of the audience. Some advertisers, often encouraged by their agencies, began to employ black models in traditional consumer roles, even in ads that would be seen primarily by white audiences. A large part of the always conservative business community remained so suspicious and uneasy, however, that such prestigious periodicals as the *Harvard Business Review* and the *Journal of Advertising Research* felt compelled to carry articles (with dispassionate charts and graphs) demonstrating that the use of blacks in advertising intended for whites had no negative effects on sales. Many black leaders, on the other hand, regarded integrated advertising as another attempt to remake blacks into imitations of the white bourgeoisie, while some black businessmen viewed social change as the beginning of new economic opportunities:

> *The fact that Negroes have billions of dollars to spend and that they can be influenced to buy a wide range of products and services through positive programs that recognize them as consumers, identify with them to buy, is a fact that is gaining increased interest and action from American businessmen. . . . Negroes, as 11 percent of the total population in the United States, consume over 50 percent of the Scotch whisky imported into the nation, consume more than 70 percent of the entire output of the Maine sardine industry, consume more than 49 percent of all the grape soda produced in America, spend 23 percent more for shoes than does the majority white population, and spend up to 12 percent more for food sold in supermarkets to be consumed at home.*
>
> D. Parke Gibson,
> *The Thirty Billion Dollar Negro*
> (1969)

Throughout the 1970s blacks have continued to play an important role in the advertising world. Blacks have entered the business, and recently several agencies owned and staffed entirely by blacks have been started. The advertising itself reflects both the quiet assimilation of the last decade and the growing belief in separatism within the black community. Blacks are frequently found in contemporary ads for luxury cars, expensive clothing, imported wines—all the ingredients of the good life in America once reserved only for whites. Moreover, while only a few years ago every advertiser feared the accusation of black stereotyping, in today's less sensitive atmosphere black preferences in food and clothing, as well as the milder forms of black slang, are frequently employed, especially on television.

Although the public acceptance of blacks as a distinct and powerful consumer group has been long awaited, it has arrived under conditions that unfortunately raise serious questions about its significance. It is possible that advertising continues to present a set of unrealistic stereotypes. The numerous depictions of blacks enjoying America's abundance may be helping to obscure the hard and often unpleasant facts about race and race relations in this country. Because everyone in the imaginary worlds of advertising must now be strictly middle class, advertisements help us to forget that median family income is 50 percent higher for whites ($15,000 a year) than blacks ($10,000 a year), and that unemployment is almost twice as prevalent among blacks.

In examining the images of blacks in American advertising, most of us are startled and even amused by the outmoded attitudes and assumptions of the writers and artists. Most of us are also impressed by the dramatic changes that have occurred over the past twenty-five years. But in these pages we can also see the power of mass-media images to distort reality by reinforcing the majority's preconceived notions about minority groups. In today's media-dominated world we face a more complex situation. So many images have been tailored to meet the demands of pressure groups that the results are often just as unrealistic as those from thirty or forty years ago. We are also exposed to many more media images today than ever before. No one is quite sure what the long-term effects of that increased exposure will be, but for the present we should continually examine the motivations behind the images we see. More than ever we must be willing to take seriously the connection between reality and the media, between the way we wish life to be, and the way it actually is. Advertising, more than any other business or creative enterprise in America, depends so completely on image-making for its survival that we would do well to pay strict attention to its public manifestations.

1875

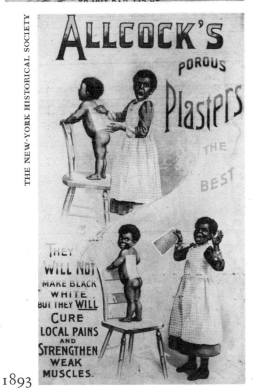

1893

1885

"The history of the American Negro is the history of this strife—this longing to attain self-conscious manhood, to merge his double self into a better and truer self. In this merging he wishes neither of the older selves to be lost. He would not Africanize America, for America has too much to teach the world and Africa. He would not bleach his Negro soul in a flood of white Americanism, for he knows that Negro blood has a message for the world. He simply wishes to make it possible for a man to be both a Negro and an American, without being cursed and spit upon by his fellows, without having the doors of Opportunity closed roughly in his face."

W. E. B. Du Bois, *The Souls of Black Folk* (1903)

90

1902

1907

*Until about 1930 caricatures of blacks were often used as identifying trademarks
in the advertising of many products. The most famous was Aunt Jemima, who's
still around although she's been portrayed in an entirely different way since about
1960; others such as the Gold Dust Twins, Kornelia Kinks, and the Cream of
Wheat chef were well-known in their day. These images served the same advertising purpose as the so-called continuing central characters (e.g., Mr. Whipple,
Madge the Manicurist, and Cora) do in TV commercials today.*

THE HAM
WHAT **AM**

Armour's
QUALITY
PRODUCTS

The Holiday Ham is *Armour's* STAR
—an Oval Label Product!

Ham is the universally popular meat food for all occasions, and Armour's Stockinet Star Ham is the maximum of food utility. More than this it is a standard of quality and value by which over three hundred other Oval Label Products may be judged.

For Stockinet Star Ham is the perfection that comes from fifty years experience in the preparation of foods. All the rich, natural juices and the fine flavor that make it a feast dish have been retained by smoking in the Stockinet

Covering—and it was experience that produced the Stockinet. Buy a *whole* Star Ham. It's economical.

Armour's Stockinet Star Ham, its companion, Star Bacon, and all the other Oval Label Products are not only *banquet* foods because of their delicious flavor, but are *thrift* foods; for, they have high food value as well as good taste.

Ask your dealer for Oval Label Products. Look for the Oval on his store front and on the packages he gives you.

ARMOUR AND COMPANY

1558

The Last Christmas on the Old Plantation

ALL the cousins and aunts and uncles had flocked home for the merriest reunion ever! The rafters of the old mansion fairly rang, from the moment the avalanche of guests and luggage arrived, till the last carriage rattled down the driveway the day after New Year's. Never a shadow of the fast-approaching struggle between North and South that was to make this their last Christmas together. . . .

The kitchen, where Aunt Jemima ruled, a gentle tyrant, had been all in a commotion for days. Such bringing in of plump poultry and little porkers, such baking of pies and plum puddings, such frosting of elaborate cakes as there had been!

Christmas dinner was a repast not soon to be forgotten. But it wasn't that alone which made the Colonel and his guests praise Aunt Jemima till her black face was all aglow with pride. It was her pancake breakfasts!

The children, stuffed like little geese, delight in teasing Aunt Jemima

"Now thrice welcome Christmas Which brings us good cheer"

Oh, those breakfasts! Sometimes she would give them crisp little sizzling sausages, with pancakes. Another day it would be delicate strips of bacon, with pancakes. But always pancakes! Golden-brown ones, and *so* tender, *so* rich-flavored!

Many years later the fame of Aunt Jemima's pancakes reached the North, and she was finally persuaded to sell the recipe. Today every housewife has Aunt Jemima's secret at her command! Aunt Jemima Pancake Flour can be found in every grocery store, and with it the most inexperienced cook can make cakes with the same flavor that delighted those holiday guests on the old plantation!

Try it for muffins and waffles, too

"Lawzee, but dey sho' do keep me humpin' fo' mo' pancakes!"

Look on the top of the package and see how to get the jolly Aunt Jemima Rag Doll Family

The Aunt Jemima people also make a delicious buckwheat flour

AUNT JEMIMA PANCAKE FLOUR

UNT JEMIMA UCKWHEAT OUR MIXTURE

"I'se in town, Honey!"

Copyright 1919, Aunt Jemima Mills Company, St. Joseph, Missouri

1919

Because slaves were never called "Mr." or "Mrs.," white children used the terms "Aunt" and "Uncle" to address elderly blacks in a respectful way. The use of these titles continued in all forms of popular culture well into the twentieth century.

"GIDDAP, UNCLE"

Painted by Edw. V. Brewer for Cream of Wheat Co.   Copyright 1921 by Cream of Wheat Co.

1921

"A COLORED SUPPLEMENT"

Painted by Edward V. Brewer for Cream of Wheat Co.   Copyright 1916 by Cream of Wheat Co.

Why Does a Pickaninny Love Watermelon?

*"I'se comin', you big boy, I heah you calling me.
Ma mouth am watering t' taste yo' sweetness"*
.... *Luscious, red-ripe watermelon — what an over-powering appeal to his craving appetite!*

The tempting taste of Blatz Grape Gum "gets you" in the same way. Simply irresistible. The greatest gum sensation in years. Ask for Blatz, insist on the original grape gum.

Also get acquainted with its peppy companion — Blatz Mint Gum, full of real, old-fashioned peppermint. Sold everywhere. Look for the name, Blatz. There's a world of difference in the taste.

"Everybody Loves It"

Also Blatz Buttons — Grape and Mint Flavors.

Blatz MILWAUKEE **CHEWING GUM**

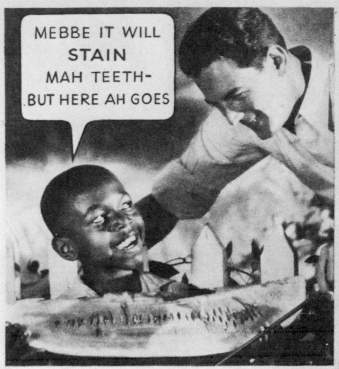

MEBBE IT WILL STAIN MAH TEETH—BUT HERE AH GOES

7 kinds of stains discolor teeth—
Colgate's removes all seven

"Go right ahead, Sambo! Sink those ivories in that luscious watermelon.

"Sure it'll stain your teeth, Sambo. But so does everything else you eat—and drink! All told, your three-meals-a-day leave 7 different kinds of stains on your teeth.

"But you should worry! For Colgate's removes all 7 stains—leaving your teeth beautifully clean—a pleasure to behold."

And that's where Colgate's has a big edge on other toothpastes. Colgate's removes all 7 stains.

Know why? Because Colgate's has two cleansing actions where most toothpastes have only one. And oh! how those teeth of yours need BOTH actions.

For all stains will not yield to one—and if you don't remove them all, they gradually build up, dulling your teeth, clouding their natural brilliance.

So get a tube of Colgate's Ribbon Dental Cream and try it. The emulsive action will dissolve and wash away some of the stains that food and drink leave on your teeth. The safe, gentle polishing action will remove the stains that are left.

At the end of 10 days, look in the mirror —and see the best-looking teeth you've ever owned.

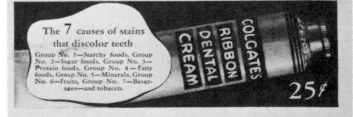

The 7 causes of stains that discolor teeth

Group No. 1—Starchy foods, Group No. 2—Sugar foods, Group No. 3—Protein foods, Group No. 4—Fatty foods, Group No. 5—Minerals, Group No. 6—Fruits, Group No. 7—Beverages—and tobacco.

25¢

Use of the words "pickaninny" and "Sambo" in these two ads presents an interesting example of the political nature of language. To the modern reader, black or white, they are highly charged racial slurs, but the copywriters of fifty years ago did not question their use nor the image they created. These words had been used for centuries, were common expressions even among blacks, and their literal meanings were far from being offensive. "Sambo" is a word and a proper name in a Nigerian language and it means second son; "pickaninny," on the other hand, was brought here by slaves from the West Indies, most likely as a mispronunciation of a Spanish phrase meaning little child. But during the black revolt of the 1950s and 1960s, these words were driven from use not because of their literal meanings but because of their connotations, because of the attitudes they embodied—attitudes clearly visible in the illustrations for the ads.

1934

1935

During the 1930s, images of blacks as servants of whites were used extensively. The portrayal of black maids in these ads is exactly the same as those found in many films of the day, especially those starring Dietrich, Harlow, or Mae West. (For example, in I'm No Angel Mae West utters her famous "Beulah, peel me a grape.")

"How come
dese diffent shirts all say de same thing, Mr. Jack?"

sanforized shrunk · ARROW SHIRTS · a new shirt if one ever shrinks

1935

"Magnolia, you make this sink
sparkle more every day!"

"You mean Bon Ami does,
Missy...I never did see such
a *polishing* cleanser"

BonAmi
"hasn't scratched yet!"

1936

98

1930

"**Yassuh...**
it's *Genu-wine* Hire's"

It's the real *Root Juices*
that make Hires taste better than
imitation root beers

NOW lower prices for bigger bottles of delicious Hires!
Always refreshing and healthful...all the time...every-
where...at home or office, while shopping or driving...for
sale at groceries, restaurants, refreshment stands. Always insist
on genuine Hires. You'll enjoy its natural, wholesome flavor.

It tastes so good – It's good for you

The Charles E. Hires Company, Philadelphia.

5¢
2 GLASS SIZE
10¢
FAMILY SIZE

THE R-J ON
THE LABEL IS FOR
YOUR PROTECTION
—A GUARANTEE OF
REAL
Root Juices
IN HIRES ROOT BEER

1937

*"It seems to me wonderfully symbolic of our age that the only son of Abraham
Lincoln should have become the president of the Pullman Company, that the
son of the man who liberated the slaves politically should have done more than
any other ... to exploit them industrially."*
Van Wyck Brooks, "The Dream of a National Culture" (1917)

SOLDIERS' SHOES!

 Just what distant lands these heavy army brogans are bound for is a military secret.

But one thing is certain. When they step off the train at camp or embarkation point, the men who wear them will be rested and ready for action. On long, cross-country trips, troops are *going Pullman!*

During the first six months of 1942, more than 3,000,000 soldiers, sailors and marines traveled in Pullman sleeping cars—565,200 of them in June alone. That keeps a lot of Pullman cars in constant military service, with lots more standing by for orders day and night.

So far, Pullman has been able to handle its military duties without seriously disrupting civilian passenger service, even with troop travel at an all-time high and civilian traffic running 30 percent ahead of 1941.

But a word of caution is in order. The extent to which Pullman can *continue* to serve civilians depends considerably on *your cooperation.* For example, you can help tremendously if you will follow these four simple *wartime travel rules:*

1. Make your Pullman reservations early.

2. Cancel your space promptly if plans change.

3. Ask your ticket salesman on what days travel is lightest and try to go on those days.

4. Take as little luggage as possible.

We believe you will agree that these are sensible and necessary suggestions . . . easy for most

travellers to observe. When you do so, you help make *capacity use* of all the Pullman sleeping cars that remain available for civilian service after troop train requirements have been supplied. And that means, you help *all* wartime travelers—yourself among them—get the "*sleep* going" they must have in order to "*keep* going" at the pace they must maintain.

Copyright 1942, The Pullman Co.

◀ **"It's sleep that counts!"** says this experienced Pullman passenger. "These days, I don't always get the exact *type* of Pullman space I ask for. But I *do* get privacy and the sleep-inviting comfort of a full-sized Pullman bed, whether I travel in an upper, a lower, a section or a room."

SLEEP GOING—
TO KEEP GOING—

Go PULLMAN

KEEP YOUR PLEDGE TO BUY WAR BONDS AND STAMPS

They spend the most where the most is spent

82% of THE NEW YORKER'S circulation is concentrated in the 41 city-trading
areas where most of the retail dollars are spent. Top stores in those areas
have proved (*by checking charge accounts*) that NEW YORKER subscribers are top
spenders. Ditto when those subscribers travel: They go to the best places in the best style with
bulging wallets . . . which explains why THE NEW YORKER carries more hotel and resort
advertising than any other national magazine. NEW YORKER readers are dream patrons.
They spend the most where the most is spent.

THE NEW YORKER

No. 25 WEST 43RD STREET
NEW YORK, 18, N. Y.

SELLS THE PEOPLE OTHER PEOPLE COPY

1955

1955

The nature of the products being advertised on these pages, as well as the date, the source (Ebony), and the selling techniques (the promise of romance, celebrity endorsement) indicate how deeply complex the problem of race in America truly is.

The Hospitality Decanter makes Walker's DeLuxe an even more elegant gift!

It's Walker's DeLuxe, sir,  in its gift decanter

A gift of Walker's DeLuxe carries with it a great compliment. For this is Hiram Walker's finest straight bourbon — 6 years old, 90.4 proof — a truly elegant whiskey. And now its elegance is accented by the handsome new Hospitality Decanter shown above. May we suggest Walker's DeLuxe in its new Decanter for your own entertaining as well?

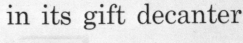

The full distinction of the Hospitality Decanter is revealed by removing the label. There is no extra charge for Walker's De Luxe in Decanters, but we suggest you order early, since the number is limited.

STRAIGHT BOURBON WHISKEY. 6 YEARS OLD. 90.4 PROOF. HIRAM WALKER & SONS INC., PEORIA, ILLINOIS

1940

In their ads, especially those promoting the sale of bourbon, liquor manufacturers frequently used blacks in the role of butler or waiter.

We don't owe nobody nothin'.

Mr. & Mrs. Walter White have lived in Watts, Los Angeles for 21 years.

Mr. White: "I built this house with my own hands. And we own the land."

Ester White: "We grow just about everything we eat... lemons, oranges, grapefruit, chicken, greens, strawberries... we grow it all."

Mr. White: "The man at the garage takes real good care of our Cadillac. He puts the best spark plugs in. What kind's that? That's right, Champion."

CHAMPION
DEPENDABLE
SPARK PLUGS
Toledo, Ohio 43601

20 million people have switched to Champion Spark Plugs.

Kama baba, kama mwana
(Like father, like son)

Through his father, a son's eyes are opened to the world. He learns about pride at his father's side. The pride of being black, of being a man.

He learns, too, about pride in his culture, and that his beautiful natural is the outward expression of that pride.

And nothing grooms and conditions a proud natural better than Afro Sheen. Afro Sheen makes the difference you can see in your hair. Your natural takes on new body . . . lustrous and alive. Afro Sheen, the complete product for father . . . for son . . . and for you . . . naturally.

BUY AFRO SHEEN CONCENTRATED SHAMPOO . . . CONDITIONER AND HAIR DRESS . . . COMB EASY AND HAIR SPRAY.

wantu wazuri use afro sheen

Nobody Else Like You Service.
We stole the idea from your father.

Got a little problem? Just ask dad. It's always been that way. He just can't do enough for you.

At The Equitable, our whole approach to life insurance is built around the same idea.

We call it Nobody Else Like You Service.

When an Equitable Agent plans your insurance program, he or she plans it around your specific needs and goals.

Nobody else's.

And when you buy insurance from The Equitable, you'll always have an Equitable Agent available to answer your questions. And help you plan for your family's needs.

We call that a lifetime of Equitable Service. Nobody Else Like You Service. But don't thank us, thank your dad.

It was his idea.

EQUITABLE

Nobody Else Like You Service
The Equitable Life Assurance Society of the United States, N.Y., N.Y.

108

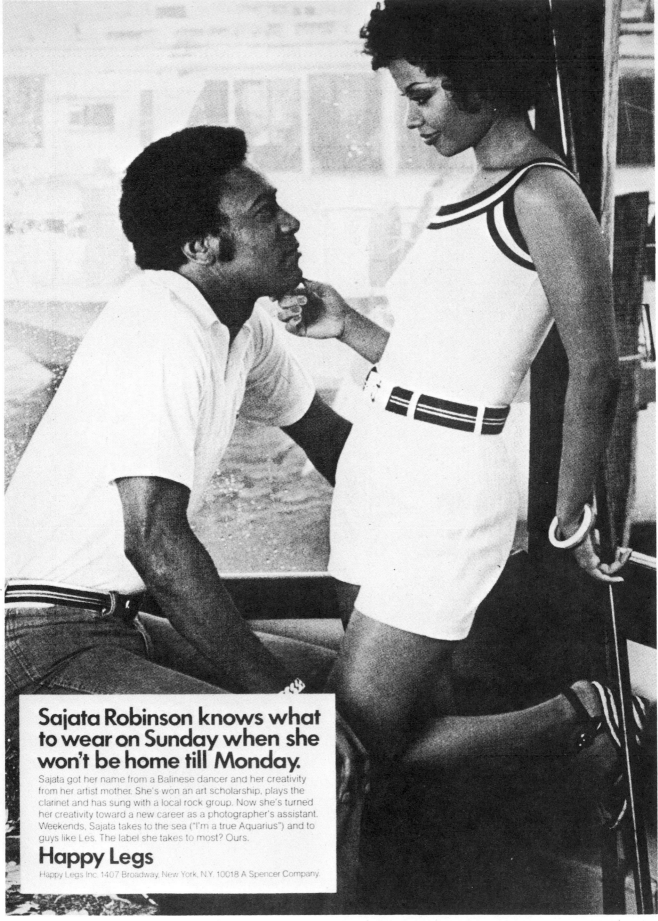

Sajata Robinson knows what to wear on Sunday when she won't be home till Monday.

Sajata got her name from a Balinese dancer and her creativity from her artist mother. She's won an art scholarship, plays the clarinet and has sung with a local rock group. Now she's turned her creativity toward a new career as a photographer's assistant. Weekends, Sajata takes to the sea ("I'm a true Aquarius") and to guys like Les. The label she takes to most? Ours.

Happy Legs

Happy Legs Inc. 1407 Broadway, New York, N.Y. 10018 A Spencer Company.

1976

This is who we are and what we do at General Motors.

"You work around the plant, and you see what care people put into the cars."

Willie Rawles, General Motors Assembly Division, Linden, N.J.

"I'm a utility man. That's like the back-up man. I replace fellas out sick.

"I get to work all over the plant. I have to know the jobs in all the sections—soldering, welding, grinding. I don't get tied down to one job. When you're moving around, it makes the time go fast.

"I've also been training people for the past 12 years. That's part of my job. If a new man comes in, I work with him until he's able to do the job by himself. I get a lot of kick out of that.

"I think the work is a little lighter now than it was 18 years ago when I started. You get more benefits and the job's getting better. The line isn't any slower, but you have more people than years ago.

"I also think it's getting better for blacks now. Eighteen years is a big difference. I have a black boss.

"We have a good group. They work hard to produce a good car. They care. You work around the plant, and you see what care the people put into the cars.

"Building cars is more exciting than working at other places. When you're driving down the street and you see somebody's Cadillac or Olds or whatever, you often think, 'maybe I worked on that car.' It makes you feel good.

"I enjoy working here. I enjoy it very much. It's the best paying job I ever had. I always try to put the best into it. I can't think of any other job that I would rather do."

General Motors
People building transportation to serve people

"My family comes first. That's why I love working as an Avon Representative. I'm my own boss. I work my own hours and my husband and kids never feel neglected."

Hattie Williams
Miami, Florida

"A typical nine-to-five job would just be too demanding on my time. As an Avon Representative I work my own hours. Besides calling on my customers, I can pick my kids up from school every day. I don't know of any other work that would give me such freedom.

Avon means a lot to me in other ways. For one thing, I get to meet so many different people. My customers know Avon cosmetics mean quality, and I'm proud that Avon is the largest cosmetics company in America.

After three years, I can honestly say Avon has given me a wonderful opportunity. I'm earning good money and my husband Chris feels very proud of my accomplishments. I think when a woman can make a go of a business without neglecting her family, she's got it made!"

Find out how you can become an Avon Representative.
Call: 800-325-6400* toll free
or fill in the coupon below. Avon will call you as soon as possible to answer your questions. Of course, there is no obligation.
*(In Missouri call: 800-342-6600)

Hattie Williams' story interested me in filling out this coupon.

NAME_____

ADDRESS_____

CITY_____STATE_____ZIP_____

MY TELEPHONE NO._____

BEST TIME TO CALL_____

Mail to: Avon Products, Inc., P.O. Box 1330, Great Neck, N.Y. 11023

© 1976 Avon Products, Inc., New York, N.Y.

1976

Part
TWO

Advertising and Material Civilization

Brains vs Muscle!

BRAINS HAVE WON!

MUSCLE AT A DISCOUNT!

A Desperate Race for Life of over One Hundred Years.
At last a Washer is made that women can use.

IT IS CALLED

"THE LITTLE JOKER."

MOTHERS, WIVES, DAUGHTERS,

and all the great army of Washers, take courage. There is a
NEW washer made, and it will wash CLEAN. It will wash QUICK.
It will wash EASY. It is CHEAP, SIMPLE, DURABLE. TRY IT. A
trial will convince the most skeptical.

1870

*The brochure that accompanied this advertisement extolled the advantages of
the washing machine to "Mothers, Wives, Daughters and all the great army of
Washers," promising to save them "labor, doctor's bills, soap, fuel, cross babies,
blue Mondays, cold dinners, cross women, sour men, weary aching limbs, sick-
ness, suffering, and death caused by over-work, exposure and colds."*

INVENTIONS

Invention has always been indigenous to American experience. From the earliest promotional brochures extolling the virtues of the New World to the latest advertisements for the innumerable gadgets of a technological society, America's commerce and culture have been funded with an unprecedented investment in invention. Modern cultural commentators, surrounded by the intrusive artifacts of American technology and its planned obsolescence, may well need to be reminded of the nineteenth-century humorist Josh Billings's observation that "the history of man's necessities is the history of his inventions."

The following advertisements trace the development of a consumer society and display the impact of inventions on nearly every dimension of American life. In fact, one way to view the changes in America's economy, culture, and social relations is through the history of inventions. And the advertisements for these inventions reveal how ingenuity and enterprise helped assemble a loosely confederated republic into an enormously powerful industrial democracy. These ads document the historic shift in the late nineteenth century from individual attempts to improve methods of production to corporate preoccupation with product technology. American corporations pooled the intelligence of inventors with advertising and their own managerial skills to create new versions of society dominated by a wealth of material goods. These inventions often raised the standard of living but also occasionally trivialized experience. By the end of the first few decades of the twentieth century, mass production itself had become one of the principal causes of invention. In 1932, two General Motors executives called this the "New Necessity": "We cannot reasonably expect to continue to make the same thing over and over. The simplest way . . . is to

keep changing the product—the market for new things is infinitely elastic
. . . The whole object of research is to keep everyone dissatisfied with what
he has in order to keep the factory busy making new things." This relentless
search for new products has caused American corporate enterprise to depend for its profit incentive on a reversal of the old saying, it is invention
that is the mother of necessity; or, as Ralph Waldo Emerson put it, "Invention breeds invention."

While the personalities of American inventors have frequently been
flamboyant and their expectations extravagant, the advertising that promoted their products has been, for the most part, surprisingly understated.
Over the years, unembellished graphics and simple language have consistently seemed the most appropriate format for expressing the significance
and marketability of each new device, many of which helped transform this
nation into what historian Daniel Boorstin calls a "democracy of things," a
society dependent on a mass of readily purchasable goods. The impact that
the reaper, sewing machine, phonograph, telephone, camera, radio, television, and computer would have on American everyday life could hardly be
predicted from the first modest promotional announcements for these
enormously significant inventions. These advertisements often reveal a dis-
arming mixture of soft-spoken pride and a persistent attention to detail.
Their generally reticent tone suggests that an interest in establishing recognition for the invention of a product was as important as the urge to
monopolize its profits. For several generations of American inventors, this
concern erupted into costly legal battles over patent claims.

By the mid-nineteenth century, it was clear that the inventors who pros-
pered were those who could protect their work from patent infringements.
Establishing the unequivocal right to a patent was conducted with the kind
of aggressiveness with which gold miners staked their claims. Those who
didn't—like Elias Howe and Isaac Singer, Cyrus McCormick and Obed
Hussey, George Baldwin Selden and Henry Ford—spent much of their
time in court haggling over the technicalities of the law. While Howe,
impoverished by the appreciable costs of developing his machine and establishing his claim to it, spent nearly five years struggling to certify his
right to be recognized as the inventor of the sewing machine, Singer point-
edly announced a different ambition: "I don't care a damn for the invention. The dimes are what I'm after." By the end of the nineteenth century,
Singer's promotional expertise had irrevocably identified his name with the
sewing machine.

Inventions helped lay, bit by bit, the foundation of a modern consumer
society by producing an array of purchasable goods, contributing to a growing consumer consciousness, and making mass production possible. Labor
shortages and widespread dependence on household manufacturing left the
United States product-starved in its early decades until new methods of

production could be geared up to satisfy basic needs for adequate food, clothing, and shelter. Samuel Slater's design for America's first factory (1793) and Oliver Evans's system of automated production (1789) strengthened an economy in which advertising would gradually have more products to promote. And when Evans described the product of his grist-mill as "untouched by human hands," he inadvertently added to the language a phrase that has become synonymous with fast, clean production and modern advertising idiom.

In a "democracy of things," Eli Whitney's theory of interchangeable parts eventually became the dominant metaphor of everyday life. When Whitney responded to a late-eighteenth-century advertisement for what was then the nation's largest contract for weapons—ten thousand muskets to be delivered to the federal government over two years—he had never manufactured a single gun. But he had developed a disarmingly new method of production, one that substituted, as he noted, "correct and effective operations of machinery for that skill of the artist which is acquired only by long practice and experience; a species of skill which is not possessed in this country to any considerable extent." Whitney's plan broke down production into a series of separate processes, each turning out a particular component in large, uniform quantities. The final product was then assembled from the aggregate of standardized and interchangeable parts.

Whitney's ingenuity had an indelible, although not immediate, impact on the development of American manufacturing and on the advertising which secured and eventually managed its growth. Along with increases in efficiency and specialization came various adaptations of Whitney's principles to any number of standardized goods. Products would henceforth be designed to look alike.

Long before Henry Ford converted Whitney's principle into the stark realities of the twentieth-century assembly line, advertisers had learned to cultivate new markets to absorb the mass production of standardized products. Throughout the nineteenth century, advertising helped to keep consumer demand far ahead of technical advances in refining metals, developing precision tools, harnessing commercial energy, and transporting perishable goods by capitalizing on the inventions that increased communication with consumers. The successive invention of the steam, rotary, and cylinder presses, as well as advances in paper-making, made it possible by the mid-nineteenth century for nearly everyone to afford a daily copy of what came to be known as the "penny press." The advertisements that filled these urban newspapers traded on improvements in printing and engraving to make the products of American technology more visually appealing.

A wealth of American inventions drew a rush of visitors to London's Crystal Palace Exhibit in 1851, where they saw Morse's telegraph, Colt's repeating pistol, Bigelow's carpets, Goodyear's vulcanized rubber, Singer's sewing machine, and McCormick's reaper. Each invention in its own way provided advertising with opportunities to establish for Americans new relations with their land, commodities, and neighbors, as well as to take on new self-identities. McCormick's reaper, for example, enabled farmers to push deeper into the American frontier, and its advertising pioneered marketing strategies that are now standard features of most campaigns for nationally distributed products, especially automobiles: the use of testimonials, free trials, money-back guarantees, a network of reliable sales and repair agents, as well as "field-tested" equipment.

The sewing machine enabled the textile industry to adapt Whitney's theory of interchangeable parts to the large-scale production of ready-made clothing in the 1850s, which in turn enabled advertising to instill in all social classes a willingness to buy similar products and to assume the interchangeable identities of a community of consumers. When the first "family sewing machine" was offered for home use in 1856, its inventors wisely instituted America's first installment purchase plan as well as the first liberal trade-in policy. (The machine cost $125; the average annual family income at the time was $500.) Henry Ford later made such "easy terms" the center of his advertising appeals.

The sewing machine, in fact, set a paradigm for American invention. Singer and Howe, like most other inventors, formed their own companies, wrote their own ads, and addressed them to the business world, where their inventions had their first appreciable impact. But as refinements were made, each invention was adapted into a mass-produced item for home use. In effect, the sewing machine became the first heavily advertised machine to enter the American home and, ironically, also the first to encourage Americans to be nostalgic about something "homemade."

Once cost-effective methods of mass production and distribution had been established, American inventors shifted their focus to product technology. In the decades following the Civil War, inventors gradually created more new products than the economy could absorb. By the late nineteenth century, more money was being spent on developing and advertising new products than on improving methods of production. Annual advertising expenditures climbed from $50 million in 1867 to $500 million in 1900. (The figure soared to $28 billion in 1977.) Advertisers directed a considerable portion of these outlays toward developing distinctive packages for products. Such inventions as sealed tin cans, glass bottles, cardboard boxes, and paper bags provided new spaces for advertising messages and helped transform the local general store into a supermarket of trademarks and competitive brand names. The American public had to contend with packaging and perhaps for the first time began to confuse what was on the outside of a package with what was on the inside.

As the number of products mounted and sales rose, retail outlets had to be found for the sale of standardized goods. A. T. Stewart, R. H. Macy, John Wanamaker, and Jordan Marsh, among others, set up large retail shops—"department stores"—to accommodate the volume and range of new merchandise. Although not an American innovation, these consumer "palaces," as they came to be called, used expensive plate glass windows, high ceilings, open spaces, and the first of Elisha Otis's novel passenger elevators as a backdrop to the sale of the latest styles in ready-made clothing, dry goods, and home furnishings. As the French novelist Emile Zola observed, American department stores "democratized luxury." These elegantly decorated showrooms turned shopping into a communal activity and pointed the way toward those twentieth-century sprawling suburban consumer kingdoms less elegantly known as shopping centers.

When President Millard Fillmore ordered the first bath and toilet for the White House in 1851, he was roundly criticized in the press for wasting public funds on inventions which were "unsanitary and undemocratic." Yet what was obviously regarded then as an extravagance became—with the support of advertising—an indoor necessity by the early twentieth century. At the same time that hotel entrepreneur Ellsworth M. Statler advertised "a room with a bath for a dollar and a half," large numbers of Americans enjoyed running water and sewerage disposal in "the privacy of their own homes." The status attached to these enamel-walled, mirrored "bathrooms" was financed by an increase in per capita income from $237 in 1870 to $480 in 1900. As a 1915 advertisement for Western Electric reveals, average American housewives, who had once considered such labor-saving devices as the washing machine, dishwasher, carpet sweeper, and lawn mower far beyond their means, now spent considerably more time on their newly installed telephones debating the "costs" of progress once these inventions came within the reach of their family's earnings.

Once Thomas Edison had designed an inexpensive power system to carry electricity from a central dynamo to outlying homes lit by incandescent lamps, advertising converted household inventions into "appliances" and American homes into self-enclosed technological units. Advertisers promoted electrical pumps, heaters, fans, refrigerators, stoves, irons, and vacuum cleaners as convenient, labor-saving instruments designed to give the "modern woman" more leisure time. Hitting hard on status and upward mobility, advertisements portrayed the new electrical appliances as solutions to the "servant problem." Liberated by electricity, Edison's woman of the future would be "neither a slave to servants nor herself a drudge. . . . She will be rather a domestic engineer than a domestic laborer."

The dynamo and the industries it generated drew millions of restless Americans to cities. The urban congestion that resulted from the redistribution of the American population in the late nineteenth century led to numerous adaptations of inventions to the problems of sanitation, fire and police protection, transportation, housing, work space, and communication. For example, the telephone, which had initially allowed the population to remain dispersed by ending rural isolation, now became one of the principal instruments of urbanization. As reports of city life circulated through "party lines," pressure to gain access to the conveniences of city life intensified. At the same time, the telephone quickened the pace of the business world by shortening the time and distance between seller and buyer. And like the typewriter, the telephone helped redefine the work force by providing new job prospects for women, this time in a new setting—skyscrapers with elevators, central plumbing, and heating, and so many windows that the distinction between the inside and the outside could hardly be felt.

By the twentieth century, everything in America seemed to be in motion —and in the service of commerce. The recently invented electric trolleys and elevated trains of the period featured, in contrast to today's overhead advertising displays, revolving panoramas of advertisements beneath the passengers' seats. The worlds depicted in such ads as Sapolio's "Spotless Town" and Phoebe Snow's sootless parlor cars must have seemed far removed from the grim actualities of the lives of so many workers who read these ads on their way to dingy factories where they stood at assembly lines in " 'round the clock" shifts as row after row of interchangeable parts passed uninterruptedly before them in the artificial light. Electricity could keep production rolling day and night.

Edison's own method of invention evolved into a similar adaptation of Whitney's theory of interchangeable parts. Edison eventually abandoned solitary inventiveness in favor of collective enterprise—what he called "the invention business." At his laboratory in Menlo Park, he organized specialists in an assembly line format to turn out "a minor invention every ten days and a big thing every six months or so." Alfred North Whitehead may well have had Edison in mind when he remarked in *Science and the Modern World* (1925) that

> *The greatest invention of the nineteenth century was the invention of the method of invention. . . . In order to understand our epoch we can neglect all the details of change, such as railways, telegraphs, radios, spinning machines, synthetic dyes. We must concentrate on the method itself; that is the real novelty, which has broken up the foundations of the old civilisation.*

Edison's method serves as the prototype for twentieth-century corporate invention. Teams of specialists now assemble in research "parks" to invent, apparently with equal enthusiasm, alternate sources of energy and food as well as more efficient popcorn machines, faster microwave ovens, and yet another line of "revolutionary" counter-top gadgets. Patent statistics confirm this shift from individual to corporate invention. None of the thirty-three patents registered in 1791, the patent office's first year, was granted to a corporation. By 1900, nearly 19 percent of the 28,000 patents were registered in the names of business. In 1976, 80 percent of the 70,236 patents were taken out by corporations.

Twentieth-century corporate invention has taken Whitney's theory of interchangeable parts and enlarged its focus to include the standardization of both the item produced and the individual's relation to it. Given such circumstances, modern inventions have enabled us to duplicate experience in unprecedented ways. For years after his invention of the phonograph in 1877, Edison insisted that its widest application would be in "letter writing, and all kinds of dictation without the aid of a stenographer." Entertainment fell far down on his list of priorities. Nonetheless, the phonograph soon became a favorite pastime, and its changing music trumpeted the arrival of each new era of American culture. All the while technicians worked on perfecting the sound of recording discs. The quality of reproduction is now so fine that many musicians are somewhat reluctant to perform "live" on stage lest they disappoint their audiences with inexact acoustics. Precisely engineered recorded music has become so sophisticated that subliminal sales pitches can now be embedded in the upbeat tunes of chain-store Muzak.

George Eastman's invention of a simple fixed-focus camera enabled anyone to duplicate and relive an experience through its image. His Kodak—first promoted as "the smallest, lightest and simplest of all Detective Cameras"—allowed everyone to have fun snapping pictures spontaneously, without having to master the intricacies of film processing. Advertisers needed only to say "You press the button, we do the rest." Kodak used "picture shows" to promote its cameras and enabled advertising graphics to take on more realistic dimensions. As if to confirm the notion that invention breeds invention, Edison took the next steps when he added motion and then sound to pictures to produce the "talkies" of the late 1920s. Within forty years Edwin H. Land, the inventor of Polaroid products, could proudly announce that his latest camera had made it possible for the consumer to reproduce experience instantaneously. "The photographer," the ads proclaim, could now "observe his work and his subject simultaneously."

Much American inventiveness in the twentieth century has been directed toward facilitating instant relationships—with people, products, places, and events. Although Guglielmo Marconi's patented "wireless" (1896) enabled people to communicate instantaneously over vast distances, it was not until a youthful David Sarnoff, later the president of RCA, recorded the sinking of the *Titanic* in 1912 that radio-telegraphy penetrated the every-day lives of Americans. By the end of World War I, technical knowledge, corporate financing, audience demand, and national prosperity converged to deliver the radio and a new captive audience for advertisers. The air was soon alive with the sound of entertainment, news, weather reports, and "commercials." Herbert Hoover's solemn warning in 1924 that "if a speech by the President is to be used as the meat in a sandwich of two patent medicine advertisements, there will be no radio left" went unheeded by business and the general public. By 1935, fifteen years after the first commercial station went on the air, advertisers were spending $112 million to appeal to the listeners of 31 million radio sets. By 1977, the radio, reinvented from a bulky piece of living room furniture into a compact, portable "transistor," attracted more than $2 billion in advertising revenue for mass appeals to well over 400 million receivers.

Television added dramatic demonstration to advertising and "live" pictures to entertainment and news. More than 700 million people watched Neil Armstrong set foot on the moon. Television allows one, as the early advertisements claimed, to be an "eyewitness to history," and it also breaks down the distinction between being "here" and "there." Instant replays of such events as Jack Ruby's shooting Lee Harvey Oswald, the nightly reports on the carnage in Vietnam in "living color," and the latest "shots" of a terrorist attack have conditioned Americans to regard television as a corroboration of what remains a defenselessness in the sweep of current events and in the bureaucratic routines of daily life. Yet addiction to television also reminds many of us that it is our only form of escape, as the commercials tell us, from the "ordinary."

Inventions have become one important way for Americans to discover their own desires or the problems they want solved. Advertisements for inventions, if prepared carefully, are read not as motive but as response. The product discussed seems naturally to be the solution to the predicament unveiled. Ads for inventions are presented, then, as though they established a causal relationship between problems and products. The safety razor, for example, was designed not only to prevent infection and save the time needed to trek to a barbershop, but also, in the words of one early ad, to avoid "that annoying tonsorial form of blackmail—tips." By 1931, when the thin sheet of steel used to scrape the whiskers off the American chin could stretch halfway around the world, Jacob Schick's invention of an electric "dry shaver" quickened the pace of what had become a habit for the man on the move. Advertisers create the impression, often through the use of engaging first-person narrative, that they understand the particular problems of each consumer—surely one of the ironies of modern corporate invention geared to mass production. Once this intimate relationship has been established, advertisers can then offer their product as a means of rectifying the problem imagined, and, ultimately, as a response to our desires to be someone or somewhere else.

Merchandising inventions became increasingly important as American inventors gradually turned from exploring and domesticating their physical environment to cultivating leisure time and social relationships. Invention and advertising have reduced the anxiety of having to choose between the simultaneity of seemingly contradictory desires—to watch, for example, a late-night movie on television and to get to sleep early or to watch basketball on one channel and football on another. Videotape recorders now allow us to record one program while viewing another. Some models even offer portable camera equipment to enable people to star in their own shows. As Andy Warhol predicted, "The day will come when everyone will be famous for fifteen minutes." Such simultaneous participation and observation may well eventually collapse the distinctions between the two.

Not all Americans can make the necessary social adjustments quickly enough to keep pace with technological change. Prefabricated houses and nuclear weapons can expeditiously change the face of a nation; the "finger lickin' goodness" of fast-food chains and hamburger havens can severely alter the American diet; the whirling discs of computer tape can reduce identities to the interface of digital "bits." Such inventions can serve as instruments of consolidation, reflecting common needs, but they can also intensify feelings of alienation and make us a more private people.

The climate of American experience has always been one of rapid change. From the simple metal plow to the most complex durable plastics, American technical ingenuity has combined with corporate profit incentive to create mass-marketed gadgets and giant machines that have altered the patterns of everyday life. Social change may be occurring so quickly that invention may well be losing much of its meaning. The current reign of gadgets seems to be producing novelty for its own sake. And in the world of gadgets, the more trivial the invention, the more extravagant the language used to advertise it. In contrast to the understatement of early ads for significant inventions, today's floor wax becomes a nationally advertised "wonder"; a bottle opener, a "miracle"; an electric pencil sharpener, a "marvel." And so it goes. Last year's crock pot is this year's doughnut maker. It is the corporate version of the theory of interchangeable parts applied to the "new necessity" of production.

During the next few years, American corporations will launch advertising campaigns for a sewing machine that uses adhesive bond instead of thread, an ultrasonic dishwasher that shakes food from plates, a 180-pound personal robot programmed with your choice of an English or French accent, and individual microcomputers to replace the home computers already in use. Most of the next generation of inventions will depend on the miniature world of interchangeable transistors. Advertising undoubtedly will play the principal role in "educating" the American public to the instantaneous satisfactions of inventions that will alter patterns of everyday life and introduce new terms for social and personal definition.

McCORMICK'S
PATENT
VIRGINIA REAPER.

The above cut represents one of M'CORMICK's PATENT VIRGINIA REAPERS, as built for the harvest of 1848. It has been greatly improved since that time, by the addition of a seat for the driver ; by a change in the position of the crank, so as to effect a direct connection between it and the sickle, (thereby very much lessening the friction and wear of the machinery, by dispensing altogether with the lever and its fixtures ;) by board ribs on the reel, (which operates more gently on the grain than the round ones ;) by a sheet of zinc on the platform, (which very much lessens the labor of raking ;) by an increase of the size, weight and strength of the wheels of the machine, and by improvement made on the cutting apparatus

D. W. BROWN,
OF ASHLAND, OHIO,

Having been duly appointed Agent for the sale of the above valuable labor-saving machine (manufactured by C. H. McCormick & Co., in Chicago, Ill.,) for the Counties of Seneca, Sandusky, Erie, Huron, Richland, Ashland and Wayne, would respectfully inform the farmers of those counties, that he is prepared to furnish them with the above Reapers on very liberal terms.

The Wheat portions of the above territory will be visited, and the Agent will be ready to give any information relative to said Reaper, by addressing him at Ashland, Ashland County, Ohio.

Ashland, March, 1850.

1850

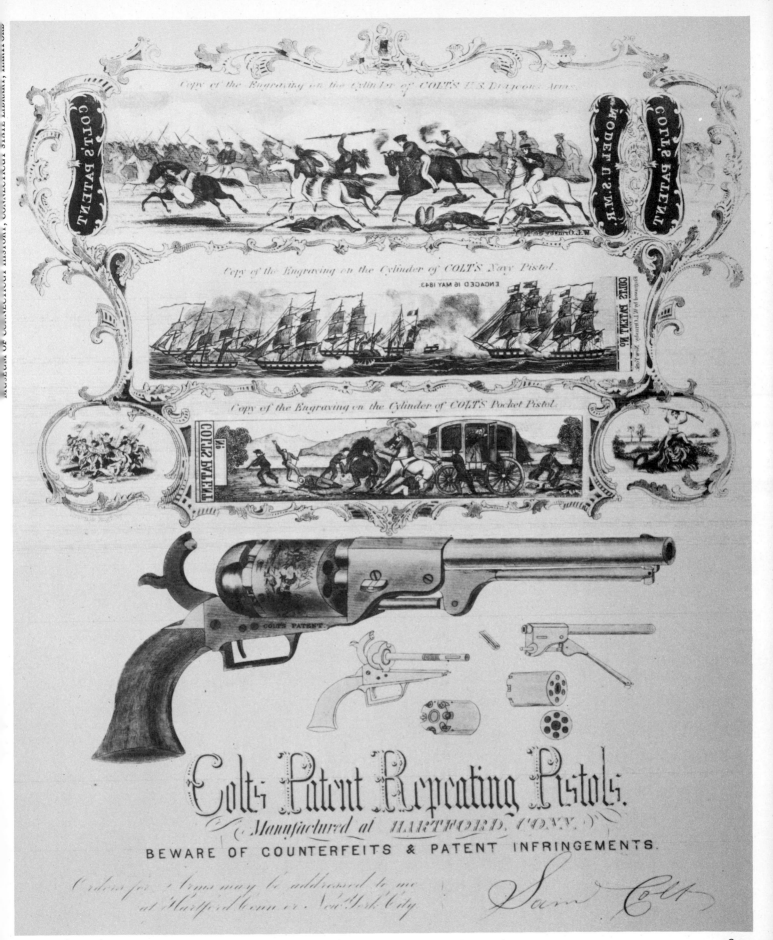

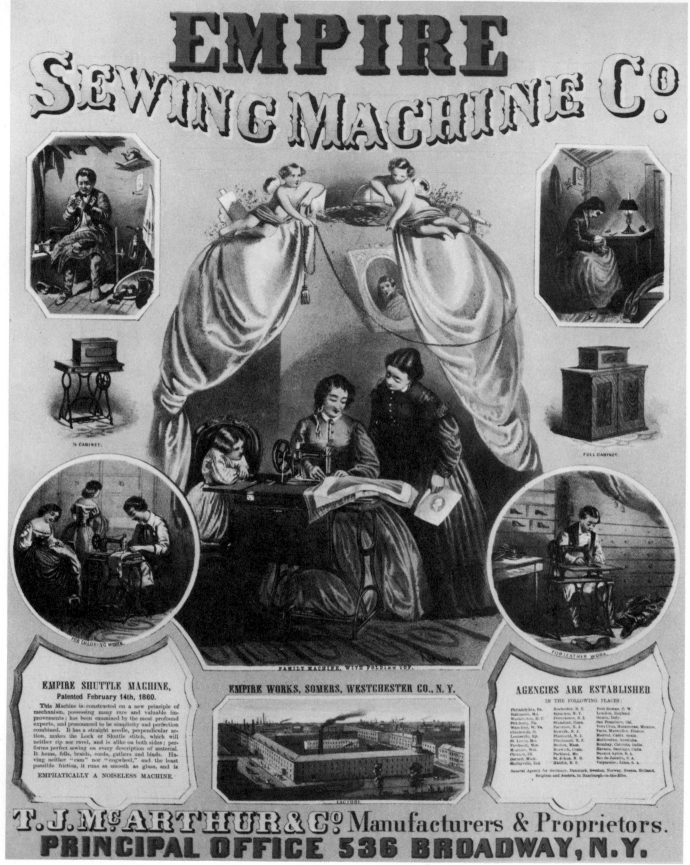

Hills Archimedean
LAWN-MOWER.

In placing this LAWN-MOWER before the public for the season of 1872 it needs no recommendation, as it has acquired a world-wide celebrity. With the improvements recently added to this favorite Mower, we are fully warranted in saying IT HAS NO EQUAL IN THE WORLD! And its immense sale for the last 30 days throughout the United States is sufficient proof of the above assertion and of its great superiority. This LAWN-MOWER is constructed upon truly scientific principles, and is the only perfectly balanced Lawn-Mower ever made; operated by a Ball and ADJUSTABLE HANDLE, points that are indispensable, securing ease of operating and a perfect, beautiful, level cut. The Hills "Archimedean" was the first (and original) balanced Lawn-Mower invented in this country, or any other; was patented in the United States and Great Britain, and its invention brought into general use a machine that is now a necessity, and almost an indispensable article. All others now made are copies of this Machine, and the public are cautioned against them. For sale by all the leading Seedsmen and Agricultural Implement Dealers throughout the United States and Canada. Illustrated catalogues and testimonials, post free, upon application to us or any of our agents. Manufactured by the

HILLS "ARCHIMEDEAN" LAWN-MOWER CO., HARTFORD, CONN.
(Works at Colt's Armory.)

1872

HOUSEKEEPING MADE EASY
BY THE USE OF
RICHARDS & ALEXANDER'S
PATENT DISH WASHER!
Patented October 13, 1863.
The most Unique and important Household Appendage ever invented.

The ordinary table dishes of a family of twelve persons can be washed, drained, and dried by this Machine in TEN minutes; doing away entirely with wiping, preserving the original brilliancy of the crockery, and doing the work more thoroughly than it is done by hand.

This wonderful machine has met with the highest commendations, and is respectfully dedicated to the Housekeepers of America, for whose aid and convenience it has been especially provided. Ladies and Gentlemen, please call and see its operation at

No. 3 MILK STREET, (Up Stairs,) BOSTON.
Great Bargains offered to those wishing to purchase Rights.
GEO. COOLIDGE, Agent, 3 Milk St.

1865

THE TYPE-WRITER!

A REVOLUTION IN WRITING!

This Machine is to the Pen what the Sewing Machine is to the Needle. It is manufactured by E. Remington & Sons, Ilion, N.Y. Hundreds are already in use, giving great satisfaction. The Type-Writer is used in the Departments at Washington; by J. M. Bradstreet & Sons; Dun, Barlow & Co., New York, and by many short-hand reporters, Commercial Agencies, Business Companies, Lawyers, Bankers, Merchants, Editors, Authors, Ministers, Copyists and others throughout the country. It is rapidly coming into general use.
Read the following:

BROOKLYN, N.Y., Dec. 24, 1874.

GENTLEMEN:—In reply to your communication, I willingly state your type-writer furnishes me most splendid aid, and has, from the hour I received it, entirely superseded the pen in official and professional work, and, in fact, in correspondence, memoranda, and all matters of record.

Reporting at short-hand all day is enough for the good right hand without its being drawn on for long-hand copying—a conclusion that had been costing me from three to fifteen dollars a week in the luxury of a copyist. This money I now save, as the working of the machine is only play. I rank it next to my wife; am enthusiastic over it, and regard it as an invention that is to be as universally adopted as the sewing machine, the steam engine, or the printing press.

The judges and the lawyers are delighted with the law work it produces.
Respectfully, etc.,
WILLIAM HEMSTREET, Stenographer.

GENERAL AGENTS,   FOR SALE BY
DENSMORE, YOST & CO.   BARBER & BARRON,
Offices and Salesrooms, 751 BROADWAY, N. Y.
PRICE $125. SEND FOR CIRCULAR. **AGENTS WANTED.**

1875

"B'Gosh! I wish I had one of them over to the treasury."

1883

"The cash register . . . helped make a revolution in accounting among small merchants and in service occupations, and promoted efficiency in department stores, chain stores, and supermarkets by the new data of multi-totals, by the classification of transactions according to size, sales person, and department. For the first time, reliable statistics about an individual business enabled the merchant to figure precisely his annual profit or loss."

Daniel Boorstin, *The Decline of Radicalism* (1969)

1895

The telephone not only created networks of communication that accelerated the nation's economic growth but also engineered the psychological need for immediate results, whether in business or personal affairs.

128

Drawn for Eastman Kodak Co. by A. B. Frost.

There are no Game Laws for those who

HUNT WITH A KODAK

The rod or the gun may be left out, but no nature lover omits a Kodak from his camp outfit.

EASTMAN KODAK CO.

1905 Catalogue free at the dealers, or by mail

Rochester, N. Y.

1905

According to corporate accounts, the brand name "Kodak" had no derivation: "It was simply invented—made up from letters of the alphabet to meet our trade-mark requirements. It was short and euphonious and likely to stick in the public mind, and therefore seemed to us to be admirably adapted to use in exploiting our new product." In 1977, Kodak spent over $50 million on advertising aimed at keeping its name before the public eye.

The problem of shaving has always been a troublesome one with most men. Those who depend on the barber find it expensive—a waste of time and disagreeable in many ways—without taking into account the danger of infection from unsanitary conditions.

My little razor, the "GILLETTE," has solved the problem for all time. There is no reason why every man should not shave himself, because the difficulties have all been overcome by the "GILLETTE."

It requires *No Stropping, No Honing*—is always sharp and in perfect condition—its adjustment is positive and its work is perfect.

Blades so inexpensive, when dull may be thrown away as you would an old pen.

Ask your dealer for the "GILLETTE" today and shave yourself with ease, comfort and economy for the rest of your life.

King C Gillette

The Gillette Safety Razor set consists of triple silver plated holder, 12 double-edged blades (24 keen edges), packed in a velvet lined leather case and the price is $5.00 at all Jewelry, Drug, Cutlery, Hardware and Sporting Goods dealers

An Ideal Holiday Gift

Combination Sets from $6.50 to $50.00

Refuse all substitutes and write us today for our free trial offer.

GILLETTE SALES COMPANY

286 Times Building, New York City

Gillette Safety Razor
NO STROPPING NO HONING

1907

King Gillette patented his newfangled safety razor in 1895, sold fifty-one of them in 1903, but by 1906 he returned well over $100,000 to investors. What had started as a luxury item eventually became a daily ritual for most men. By the time of World War I, the razor had made whiskers an obsolete sign of effeminacy.

Down where Nature cannot send her cooling breezes
Science sends the Electric Fan

Down in the caverns of steel and stone where armies of office workers are meeting the strenuous problems of a business day—where excessive heat tends to retard the productive power of human energy—there electrical science carries the refreshing help Nature finds it so difficult to give.

The G-E ELECTRIC FAN, the result of twenty years' experience in the great factories and laboratories of the General Electric Company, is one of Electricity's most effective means of increasing man-power by increasing man-comfort—of raising the standard marked by that magic word Efficiency. In the home, as in the office and factory, the G-E Electric Fan is efficiency's "first aid"—summer comfort's best assurance.

And it gives both with a truly modern economy. It can be operated four hours for a cent—is readily attached to any lamp socket—gives a lifetime of satisfactory service.

The Guarantee of Excellence on Goods Electrical

GE

Trade *Mark*

The EDISON MAZDA LAMP is another proof of Electricity's great service to efficiency and to comfort. This wonderful lamp has scratched electricity from the luxury list by giving more light for less money. In fact, it uses but *one-third the current* required by the old-style carbon lamps.

With the *current you save* by using Edison Mazdas, you can run your G-E FAN or any of the many G-E devices for increasing the comfort of the home. With the G-E ELECTRIC FLATIRON, for example, you can do the family ironing, indoors or out, in less time, with less labor, and less physical discomfort than ever was possible with the old-fashioned stove-heated irons.

Any electrical dealer or lighting company will gladly show you the various styles and sizes of G-E Fans, Flatirons and Edison Mazda Lamps.

GENERAL ELECTRIC COMPANY

Sales Offices in all Large Cities   The largest Electrical Manufacturer in the world   Agencies Everywhere

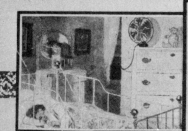

Cool bedrooms on breathless nights by means of G-E Fans.

Make your porch your living room this summer with Edison Mazda Lamps and G-E Fans.

An average family ironing for 15 cents with the G-E Flatiron, $4.25.

1913

The Victrola illustrated here is the $200 style.

Dancing to the music of the Victrola is the favorite pastime

With a Victrola and Victor Dance Records it is easy to learn all the new dances.

The maxixe, hesitation, tango, one-step—you can enjoy all the modern dances in your own home with the Victrola.

Mr. and Mrs. Vernon Castle, teachers and greatest exponents of the modern dances, not only use the Victor and Victor Records exclusively at Castle House, but personally superintend the making of Victor Dance Records.

"How to Dance the One-Step, Hesitation, and Tango" is a new Victor booklet just issued—illustrated with photos of Mr. and Mrs. Vernon Castle and 288 motion-picture photographs. Ask any Victor dealer for a copy, or write to us.

There are Victors and Victrolas in great variety of styles from $10 to $200, and there are Victor dealers in every city in the world who will gladly play any music you wish to hear.

Victor Talking Machine Co., Camden, N. J., U.S.A.

Berliner Gramophone Co., Montreal, Canadian Distributors

Always use Victor Machines with Victor Records and Victor Needles— *the combination.* There is no other way to get the unequaled Victor tone.

Victor Steel Needles, 5 cents per 100, 50 cents per 1000
Victor Fibre Needles, 50 cents per 100 (can be repointed and used eight times)

New Victor Records demonstrated at all dealers on the 28th of each month

1915

"The housewife of the future will be neither a slave to servants nor herself a drudge. She will give less attention to the home, because the home will need less; she will be rather a domestic engineer than a domestic laborer, with the greatest of all handmaidens, electricity, at her service. This and other mechanical forces will so revolutionize the woman's world that a large portion of the aggregate of woman's energy will be conserved for use in broader, more constructive fields."

Thomas A. Edison, "The Woman of the Future" (1912)

Two years after Edison's historic incandescent lamp was patented (1880), Popular Science Monthly cleared the invention of charges that it would damage the user's eyes: "Dr. Javal has recently declared, in a communication to the Société de Médecine Publique et d'Hygiène Professionelle, that the electric light, in the degree of division to which it has been brought, is absolutely harmless, and without danger to the sight."

134

*—and
for the
Traveling
Man*

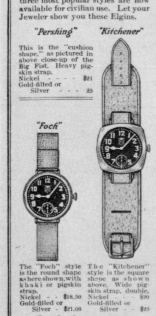

Released by the Armistice, the three most popular styles are now available for civilian use. Let your Jeweler show you these Elgins.

"Pershing"   **"Kitchener"**

This is the "cushion shape," as pictured in above close-up of the Big Fist. Heavy pigskin strap.
Nickel - - - $21
Gold-filled or
Silver - - - 25

"Foch"

The "Foch" style is the round shape as here shown, with khaki or pigskin strap.
Nickel - - $18.50
Gold-filled or
Silver - $21.00

The "Kitchener" style is the square shape as shown above. Wide pigskin strap, double.
Nickel - - $20
Gold-filled or
Silver - - $25

Remember, these strap watches are but three of the many Elgin styles

Elgin Strap Watch

"Life," says the traveling man, "is just catching one train after another. Like any other successful business, mine has to run on schedule, and my Elgin strap watch is the answer. With the time always before me, I know exactly where I'm at.

"Yes, and it's a satisfaction to own a watch that's never dropped, never left under my pillow—as plainly visible in my berth at midnight as at high noon. For a handy *extra* watch for a man on the road —or for any other active man—there's nothing like the Elgin strap watch with the black dial."

Genuine black-dial full-luminous Elgins,

in your choice of the three styles of case and strap here pictured—now ready at your Jeweler's. The Armistice releases them for civilian use.

Handy in winter, when gloves and overcoat make fumbling in your pocket clumsy and unsafe.

Handy in summer, when you wear no vest and half the time no coat.

Buy one while you can get it.

All three styles have genuine Elgin movements—American through and through. Specially constructed for hard outdoor use. Wear one a week and you'd feel lost without—

"The Handy Extra Watch for Men"

1919

At the turn of the century, men regarded wristwatches as effeminate. But World War I demonstrated the watch's convenience, and within twenty years the industry had moved to inexpensive, "disposable" versions. One special feature of early wristwatches proved deadly. Over a period of thirty years, forty people who had routinely come in contact with the radium used in the luminous paint died of cancer and radiation poisoning.

KOTEX

At stores and shops
that cater to women

NEW but tried and proved, Kotex enters universal service from a romantic background. For, although a woman's article, it started as Cellucotton—a wonderful sanitary absorbent which science perfected for use of our men and allied soldiers wounded in France.

With peace came an idea suggested in letters from nurses in France, regarding a new use for this wonderful absorbent, and early in 1919 our laboratory made the first sanitary pads of Cellucotton enclosed in gauze and placed them on sale in various cities. Requests for more followed every sale, and we devoted two years to perfecting the new article—named KOTEX from "cotton-like texture"—and to the building of machinery which makes and seals it hygienically without contact of human hands. Kotex are now ready for every woman's use.

The gauze envelope is 22 inches long, thus leaving generous tabs for pinning. The filler, forty layers of finest Cellucotton, is 3½ inches wide by 9 inches long. Kotex are cool, more absorbent, and of lasting softness. Kotex are cheap in price and easy to throw away.

If KOTEX are not yet on sale in your neighborhood, write us for the names of nearest stores and shops that have them. Or send us sixty-five cents and we will mail you one box of a dozen Kotex in plain wrapper, charges prepaid.

CELLUCOTTON PRODUCTS CO.
208 South La Salle Street, Chicago, Illinois

5c Each 12 for 60c

INEXPENSIVE, COMFORTABLE, HYGIENIC and SAFE — KOTEX

The Radio Magnavox, Type R-2, with 18" horn. The original loud speaker, and now the world's standard. The most attractive and most efficient piece of apparatus of its kind manufactured. Beautiful black enamel finish, nickel plated trimmings, and solid mahogany base with piano finish. Indispensable to those who take pride in their set and the results achieved.

The Radio Magnavox, Type R-3, with 14" horn. Beautiful and durable as it is efficient. Reproduces wireless music and messages in volume without distortion. Anyone can operate it, every one can enjoy it. No adjustments or extras required. No radio set complete without one. There is no substitute for the Radio Magnavox.

Wireless music for home entertainments

ENTERTAIN your friends with radio concerts, enjoy the fascination of radio as a hobby, make wireless a profitable part of your business, get news and market reports before they are published, take public speeches off the air. With a simple receiving set and a Radio MAGNAVOX you can do all this, and more, too, in your own home or office. The front cover of this magazine shows how easy it is, with a Radio MAGNAVOX.

Practically every variety of vocal and instrumental music from jazz to grand opera, news reports in plain English, and many other special features are radio broadcasted daily, *free* to anyone with the simple equipment to receive and reproduce them. Read the article in this issue.

The Radio MAGNAVOX will reproduce them for many people at the same time. Without the MAGNAVOX only the operator wearing a head set can hear. Simply substitute the MAGNAVOX for the head set, hook up with a Magnavox Power Amplifier, and an audience of one or one thousand may hear perfectly. This MAGNAVOX equipment enables everything received by radio to be swelled in volume to the full sound intensity required for any occasion, without losing even the most delicate tone modulations or a single bit of the original clearness and distinctness. It makes a radio set adaptable for office, store or factory use, and the use of radio music practical for home entertainment, concerts and dances. It adds to any set the final touch of up-to-the-minute completeness and multiplies its scope and usefulness many times over.

You yourself can operate the MAGNAVOX the very first day without any previous training or experience. The hook-up is easy, and there are no adjustments. The few instructions necessary furnished free with each outfit. The entire cost no more than the price of a good phonograph.

Any first class radio dealer will install it for you, and give you any further assistance required.

The Magnavox Company are world pioneers in the development of sound amplifying apparatus. It was MAGNAVOX apparatus used by the U. S. Navy and the U. S. Signal Corps to perfect their communication during the Great War. It is MAGNAVOX apparatus now being used by the majority of prominent speakers for addressing large audiences. The facilities and experience which developed this apparatus are back of each piece of equipment bearing the MAGNAVOX trade mark, and are available to you now in making radio simpler, more useful and more enjoyable. Write us a letter or mail the coupon below to our nearest office for FREE *Magnavox* folder.

RADIO MAGNAVOX

Magnavox 3-Stage Power Amplifier. Same as 2-Stage, type, except larger and more powerful. Designed to energize MAGNAVOX where particularly large volume is required for hospitals, public buildings, outdoor entertainment, etc. The final touch of completeness to any set. Solid mahogany finish.

This trade mark on all MAGNAVOX apparatus. Look for it. Accept no substitute.

Magnavox 2-Stage Power Amplifier. Designed to furnish power for the Radio MAGNAVOX, and minimize the possibility of sound distortion where maximum results are necessary. All binding posts plainly lettered. Simply throw the switches to operate. Solid mahogany case.

Make your Ice Box a Frigidaire

How Your Ice Box Is Quickly Converted Into a Frigidaire

1. *The frost coil is placed in the ice compartment of your refrigerator as shown above.*

2. *The compressor (shown below) is placed in the basement or other convenient location.*

3. *The frost coil and the compressor are connected by two small copper tubes, and a connection made to your electric wires.*

That's all. Your refrigerator becomes cold and stays cold. You have Frigidaire electric refrigeration.

IT'S EASY. The cake of ice now in your refrigerator is replaced by the Frigidaire "frost coil," which is *colder than ice and never melts.* You enjoy, immediately, the full convenience of Frigidaire *electric* refrigeration.

Frigidaire maintains a constant, *dry cold*—keeps food fresh and wholesome in any weather—makes dainty ice cubes and delicious desserts for your table— saves the possible annoyance of outside ice supply—adds greatly to the convenience of housekeeping. And Frigidaire is *not* expensive. In many localities its operation costs less than ice.

There are thirty-two household models of Frigidaire—twelve complete with cabinet, and twenty designed for installation in the standard makes of refrigerators. One of these models will exactly fit your needs. There are also Frigidaire models for stores, factories, hospitals, schools and apartments.

Frigidaire—pioneer electric refrigeration—is backed by the General Motors Corporation and by a nation-wide organization of over 2,500 trained sales and service representatives.

Write for the Frigidaire book, "Colder Than Ice." It gives complete information.

Prices
(f o b Dayton)
For converting present refrigerators into Frigidaire $190 up
Frigidaire complete with Cabinet $245 up

DELCO-LIGHT COMPANY, *Subsidiary of General Motors Corporation,* Dept. C-21, DAYTON, OHIO

Makers of Delco-Light Farm Electric Plants, Electric Pumps, Electric Washing Machines and Frigidaire Electric Refrigeration

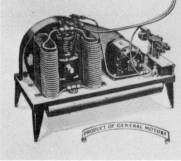

PRODUCT OF GENERAL MOTORS

Frigidaire
ELECTRIC REFRIGERATION

Quiet in the Studio! Not even an undesired whisper may enter the sensitive microphones!

SOUND PICTURES
...*a product of the telephone*

OUT of a half century's experience, the Bell Telephone Laboratories developed for Western Electric the first successful system of sound pictures.

This system (embracing Vitaphone and Movietone) makes possible a great new art in entertainment. Now, in theatres all over the country—Western Electric equipped—you can hear stars of motion pictures, opera and stage in lifelike renderings from the screen.

Producers who use the Western Electric sound system exclusively:
WARNER BROS.
FOX FILMS
VICTOR TALKING MACHINE
PARAMOUNT FAMOUS LASKY
METRO-GOLDWYN-MAYER
UNITED ARTISTS
FIRST NATIONAL
UNIVERSAL
HAL ROACH
CHRISTIE
COLUMBIA PICTURES
HAROLD LLOYD

Hear and see the world's greatest personalities as they talk from the screen.

Hear orchestral accompaniment played from the screen . . . the actual roar of an airplane . . . the thunder of galloping hoofs!

Yesterday's dream is today's fact. And tomorrow? Here is an art now in the early stages of its development which is revolutionizing the field of motion picture entertainment.

Watch—and *listen!*

Western *Electric* SOUND SYSTEM

The VOICE of ACTION

1929

Chaplin recalls Warner Brothers' first talking sequence: "It was a costume picture, showing a very lovely actress . . . emoting silently over some great sorrow, her big soulful eyes imparting anguish beyond the eloquence of Shakespeare. Then suddenly a new element entered the film—the noise that one hears when putting a seashell to one's ear. Then the lovely princess spoke as if talking through sand: 'I shall marry Gregory, even at the cost of giving up the throne.' It was a terrible shock. . . . When the handle of the boudoir door turned I thought someone had cranked up a farm tractor, and when the door closed it sounded like the collision of two lumber trucks. At the beginning they knew nothing about controlling sound: a knight-errant in armor clanged like the noise in a steel factory, a simple family dinner sounded like the rush hour in a cheap restaurant. . . . I came away from the theatre believing the days of sound were numbered."

Charlie Chaplin, *Autobiography* (1964)

DON'T BE A CAVE MAN!

From beginning of time until a few years ago, the only way a man could remove his whiskers was with a sharp instrument. Cave men used stones, shells, bones. Medieval men used steel. Even you have used steel. Then came electric shaving . . . the greatest single contribution to man's comfort in the history of science. And with electric shaving has come today's perfected shaver, the Packard Lektro-Shaver.

Shave the modern way with the . . . PACKARD LEKTRO-SHAVER

We urge any man who is about to buy an electric shaver to compare Packard Lektro-Shaver with all other leading brands. We're convinced you'll choose Packard's smooth, round head that whisks whiskers off cleaner, quicker, smoother. Its action is like miniature scissors, held in the hands of an expert. Only Packard Lektro-Shaver has the cutter that rotates from left to right as well as back and forth. With Packard Lektro-Shaver you never need water, lather, brush, blades or lotion. Never again will you be cut, nicked, scraped. You'll buy shaving perfection with Packard Lektro-Shaver some day . . . why delay? AC or DC, $15.

PROGRESS CORPORATION, 521 Fifth Avenue, New York City

HAIR WITH SKIN—*Razor cuts both whiskers and skin. Photomicrograph (original enlargement 500 times) shows loose particles of skin on whittled whiskers.*

SHAVE YOUR WHISKERS BUT SAVE YOUR SKIN!

HAIR WITHOUT SKIN—*Packard Lektro-Shaver cuts hair off cleanly, squarely, by cutter that oscillates 10,000 to 15,000 times a minute. Photomicrograph, original enlargement 1000 times. Packard spares your skin!*

Some day! why delay!

IF YOUR DEALER CANNOT SUPPLY YOU, USE THIS:

Progress Corp., 521 Fifth Ave., New York City
Enclosed find $15. Please send Packard Lektro-Shaver. Send C.O.D.

Name_____

Address_____ City_____

1937

Although Jacob Schick marketed the first electric shaver in 1931, Packard's raucous, two-fisted advertisements for its Lektro-Shaver helped, in the judgment of Fortune, "to change shaving from a monopoly into an industry."

140

NO CAP! NEW REYNOLDS "400" BALL PEN

Improved, Perfected, and Guaranteed to
Write at least **4 YEARS** WITHOUT REFILLING!

NO CAP TO LOSE OR FUSS WITH

CLICK IT—WRITE

Exclusive Click-It Ball Point Guard ends cap nuisance forever. Click —and pen is ready to write on the tiny, miracle-precision ball point.

CLICK—PARK IT

A flick of the thumb and the Reynolds is ready for pocket or purse. One hand does it all.

QUICK CHANGE

to woman's model! Extra top comes with each Reynolds "400" Pen — no extra cost — extra smart—a hit with the ladies!

CHOICE OF COLORS:
RICH GOLD, SILVER, BLACK

$**12**^{50} NO 20% LUXURY TAX

Covered by U. S. Patents Nos. 2,192,479 and D-143-505. Other patents applied for. Copr. Reynolds Pen Co. 1946. *Reg. U. S. Pat. Off.

FAIR TRADE PRICE! O. P. A. Ceiling. Includes desk stand and modern streamlined gift package.

Reynolds Pen Co., 1550 North Fremont Street, Chicago 22, Illinois
Canadian Plant: Oshawa, Ontario, Canada

NO OTHER PEN CAN MAKE THIS
4-Way Guarantee

1.

GUARANTEED to write *at least* 4 years without refilling—regardless of *how* much you write! No refills to mess with—*ever!*

2.

GUARANTEED to contain—for average users' needs —up to *15 years supply* of new "Satinflo Blue" ink for easy, instant writing!

3.

GUARANTEED—pen itself lasts a lifetime! Service guaranteed for life whenever pen is returned with 35 cents to the factory!

4.

GUARANTEED—each Reynolds "400" Pen goes through a series of the most exacting tests in *actual writing performance*, before it leaves the factory!

★

YOU GET ALSO these other sensational Reynolds advantages: 1. Writes on cloth, wet surfaces, even under water! 2. No blotter needed—ink dries as you write, no smearing! 3. Makes from 6 to 8 clear carbon copies—saves you time and effort! 4. Writes instantly, even high in the sky—no balking, no starving—ever!

NEVER BEFORE
A GRADUATION GIFT LIKE THIS

On sale at all leading stores...

in attractive gift package

1946

Enchanted Evening by Zenith

The Setting: You..Your guests..**1951 Black Magic TV**
with Reflection-Proof Screen

Your guests arrive...You try not to look too obviously proud as you switch on your new Zenith... Conversation ripples to a whisper...

Then—a flood of excited comment..."I can scarcely believe what I'm seeing!"..."I had no idea television could be so big and real"..."It's so wonderfully clear and steady"...

Then comes the magic moment! Never leaving your easy chair, you change programs with Zenith's "Lazy Bones," the amazing remote control that fits in your palm. Click...click...click...you change one program after another, no knob to touch or re-tune!

"It's sheer Black Magic" someone exclaims. And it is...Your magic passport to enchanted evenings from now on, is this incredibly fine, in-

credibly beautiful new Zenith for 1951. Your Zenith dealer invites you to a pre-view...now!

* * *

"Must see" before you buy any TV: Zenith's new 2-in-1 screen with Reflection-Proof Blaxide Tube. Bans room reflections as well as glare, even in fully lighted surroundings, as doctors recommend viewing. Gives you two picture shapes in one set (Giant Circle or rectangular type) at the touch of a switch! New "Super-Range" Chassis gets programs far clearer in outlying locations. Pre-tuned Picturemagnet built-in antenna needs no adjusting. All this plus built-in provision for tuner strips to receive proposed Ultra-High Frequencies on present standards. Glorious new cabinets of lifetime beauty and quality.

(Above) Zenith® TV Combination, the "Kilmer". New 165 sq. in. 2-in-1 screen. New "Cobra-Matic" Record Changer—simplest all-speed changer ever invented! FM-AM radio with new, more powerful speaker. Exquisite Regency cabinet, genuine Mahogany veneers. Your choice of a wide variety of new Zenith TV consoles, table sets, combinations.

New Zenith "Zephyr"® Table radio for Long-Distance AM reception. New Giant Dial-Speaker combines larger, extra-powerful Alnico-5 speaker with easy-tuning dial. "Flexo-Grip" handle. Walnut, Ebony or White plastic cabinet.

New Zenith "Universal"® Super-powered standard broadcast portable — with tone richness comparable to big consoles. Smart luggage-type case in buffalo-grained black or brown. Works on battery, AC, DC.

Over 30 Years of "Know-How" in Radionics® Exclusively • Zenith Radio Corp., Chicago 39, Ill. • Also Makers of America's Finest Hearing Aids

1951

POLAROID PROUDLY PRESENTS

The Land picture-in-a-minute *Camera*

SNAP your picture...   One minute later   LIFT OUT your finished print

ACTUAL SIZE

SEE HOW SIMPLE IT IS TO USE

Easy to load. Film simply drops *into place!* You don't even have to thread a spool.

A single control sets both shutter and lens. Focusing is quick and sure; no rangefinder, no tape measure.

See the print *sixty seconds later.* Lift out your picture — print is on dry, white-bordered durable stock, ready for frame or album — complete even to deckle edge! *Land* prints pass the life-tests used to check conventional snapshots.

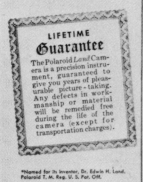

LIFETIME
Guarantee

The Polaroid *Land* Camera is a precision instrument, guaranteed to give you years of pleasurable picture-taking. Any defects in workmanship or material will be remedied free during the life of the camera (except for transportation charges).

*Named for its inventor, Dr. Edwin H. Land. Polaroid T. M. Reg. U. S. Pat. Off.

Here's a new kind of photography, packed with fun and pleasure you've never known before

Now you can enjoy the thrilling new experience of seeing every picture you take the very minute you snap it! No waiting for developing, no wondering "How will the roll come out?"

HERE'S HOW IT WORKS

You snap the picture. After only sixty seconds, you open the camera, lift out your picture — a beautiful, big, lasting print, *in the lifelike sepia tone long favored by leading photographers!*

Film and camera do it all. A roll of inexpensive Polaroid film gives you eight 3¼" by 4¼" pictures. The developer is ingeniously stored right in the film itself. There are no tanks, no liquids. The camera is *dry* — there is nothing to refill!

You'll take better pictures. With your very first roll of Polaroid film, you'll learn to take the best pictures you have ever made — for you'll see *at once* how to make improvements in composition, lighting or pose. You can take professional quality pictures indoors or out, portraits or landscapes, in winter or summer.

More fun, too. More than a million pictures have already been made by Polaroid Camera owners. Professionals and amateurs alike already are finding that the Polaroid Camera opens up a whole new field of photography. It's the house party hit of the year! You can snap arriving dinner guests, then use their pictures as place cards. You can mail those vacation shots to friends while they are still news. And you'll never again miss a once-in-a-lifetime picture — baby's first steps, the graduation, the wedding — for you have the print at once. See this new miracle of photography in action today — and you'll want one to enjoy for years to come.

For free booklet that tells how you can take better pictures and enjoy the new thrill of picture-in-a-minute photography — write Polaroid Corporation, Dept. L-1, Cambridge 39, Massachusetts.

See a demonstration of the new
POLAROID *Land* CAMERA
at camera stores everywhere

1949

Edwin H. Land, Polaroid's inventor, offered the following description of the camera's special advantages: "The process must be concealed from—non-existent for—the photographer, who by definition need think of the art in the taking and not in making photographs. . . . In short, all that should be necessary to get a good picture is to take a good picture, and our task is to make that possible." Polaroid advertisements have repeatedly stressed that the camera does all the work; all consumers need do is choose subjects to photograph.

You are looking inside the world's most remarkable business machine . . . the IBM Electronic Calculator. It solves accounting and research problems faster than any other commercial calculator in general use.

GETTING YOUR ANSWERS

...at electronic speed!

IBM's vast engineering know-how is helping American business, industry and the Armed Forces get the answers . . . fast. Through its leadership in applying electronic principles to calculators and other types of punched card business machines, IBM has given greater speed, accuracy and economy to the nation's vital processes of calculating and accounting.

Already thousands of IBM Electronic Business Machines are in everyday use. We are continuing to manufacture them in quantity . . . as fast as quality production will permit.

IBM INTERNATIONAL BUSINESS MACHINES
590 MADISON AVENUE · NEW YORK 22, N. Y.

1951

The first completely electronic computer of 1945 contained 18,000 vacuum tubes. The invention of the transistor (1947) and the development of integrated circuits in the late 1950s have been superseded in the 1970s by a technology in which, according to Scientific American, "virtually all the logic elements of a digital computer can be fitted onto a chip of silicon no more than a quarter of an inch on a side."

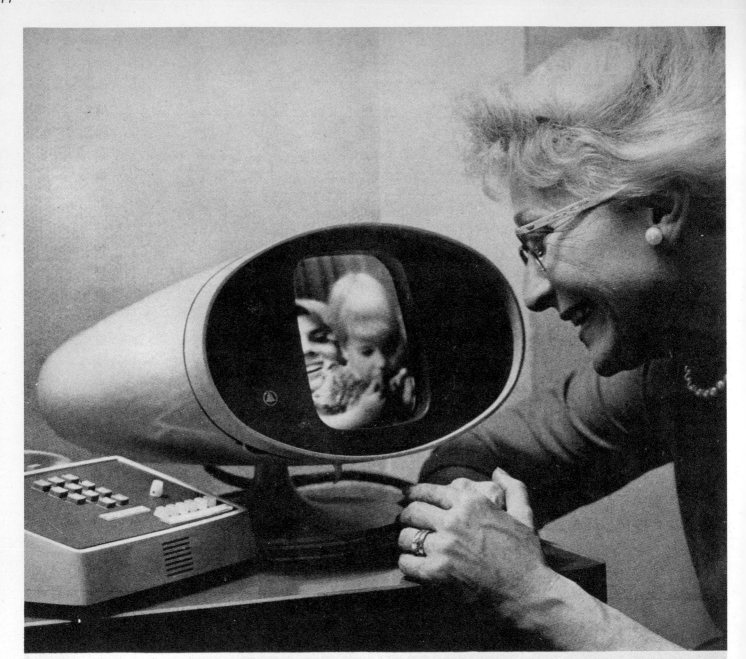

A logical extension of today's telephone service...

Bell System introduces PICTUREPHONE service

Both ends of telephone conversations are pictured; people phone by appointment from family-type booths in attended centers.

■

New York (Grand Central Station), Chicago (Prudential Building), Washington (National Geographic Society Building) have service.

Bell System PICTUREPHONE service now lets callers *see* as well as talk on the telephone. And "hands-free" if they wish.

For the first time, people can make a visual telephone call to another city — the latest example of the research, invention and development that are constantly improving the communications we provide.

The new service is being offered in the cities listed at the left. Bell System attendants at each local center help callers enjoy prearranged face-to-face visits with friends or relatives in either of the other cities.

Further development of PICTUREPHONE service is still in the future. But the service is another step toward our goal of providing you with better, warmer, more nearly complete communication by telephone.

Bell System *Serving you*
American Telephone & Telegraph Co. and Associated Companies

Introducing the Xerox 9400.
Will miracles never cease?

When people saw all the incredible things our Xerox 9200 could do, they called it a miracle. But, at Xerox, we never rest on our miracles.

Introducing the Xerox 9400 Duplicator.

It does everything the 9200 does and more. With its automatic document handler you can feed and cycle up to 200 originals at a time. (Even difficult originals like paste-ups.)

With our density control dial, you can make copies lighter or darker without having to interrupt the job.

You can even correct most problems

yourself with the help of our new self-diagnostic system which constantly monitors the machine.

And if all this wasn't enough, the Xerox 9400 can automatically copy on both sides of a sheet of paper at the same incredible speed of two pages a second.

You see, we believe that one good miracle deserves another.

XEROX

The 9400 and our other new products will be on display at the OMNI Convention Center on November 7, 8 and 9th.
To arrange for a demonstration, call (404) 351-7900.

Now there's a better way.

We've all been in the situation where there were two things that we wanted to watch on at the same time. And as exaggerated as it may seem, some people have been known to actually plop one TV set on top of another in order to watch both.

Well, we've come up with a more practical answer to this problem. Sony's Betamax videotape deck. Betamax, which plugs into any TV set, can videotape something off one channel while you're watching another channel. So you can play it back later.

The SL-8200 Betamax also has an optional automatic timer that you can set to automatically videotape anything up to two hours long while you're doing something else or when you're out of the house.

And our videotape cassettes are reusable—just rerecord right over them.

Sony's Betamax: Now you can watch two things that are on at the same time without having to watch them at the same time.

BETAMAX "IT'S A SONY."
THE LEADER IN VIDEO RECORDING

How to buy a personal computer.

Suddenly everyone is talking about personal computers. Are you ready for one? The best way to find out is to read Apple Computer's "Consumer Guide to Personal Computing." It will answer your unanswered questions and show you how useful and how much fun personal computers can be. And it will help you choose a computer that meets your personal needs.

Who uses personal computers.

Thousands of people have already discovered the Apple computer—businessmen, students, hobbyists. They're using their Apples for financial management, complex problem solving—and just plain fun.

You can use your Apple to analyze the stock market, manage your personal finances, control your home environment, and to invent an unlimited number of sound and action video games. That's just the beginning.

What to look for.

Once you've unlocked the power of the personal computer, you'll be using your Apple in ways you never dreamed of. That's when the capabilities of the computer you buy will really count. You don't want to be limited by the availability of pre-programmed cartridges. You'll want a computer, like Apple, that you can also program yourself. You don't want to settle for a black and white display. You'll want a computer, like Apple, that can turn any color tv into a dazzling array of color graphics.* The more you learn about computers, the more your imagination will demand. So you'll want a computer that can grow with you as your skill and experience with computers grows. Apple's the one.

How to get one.

The quickest way is to get a free copy of the Consumer Guide to Personal Computing. Get yours by calling 800/538-9696. Or by writing us. Then visit your local Apple dealer. We'll give you his name and address when you call.

*Apple II plugs into any standard TV using an inexpensive modulator (not included).

apple computer™
10260 Bandley Dr., Cupertino, CA 95014

1978

Home computers have been selling at a furious pace since their introduction to the general public in 1977. What started as a limited hobby market is expected to grow into a $2 billion industry by 1985, when, according to marketing forecasts, "most middle income homes will have a computer." One industry leader, Dr. David Chung, reports that "the home will eventually be automated. We will use the computer for all our financial work. For printouts of recipes, letters, medical records, self-improvement classes, shopping at home. We'll be able to interrogate it about our stocks and brew the coffee with it."

THE CELEBRATED
AMERICAN IMPROVED VELOCIPEDE.
Patented January 26, 1869.

Many EXPERT RIDERS in New York have given it a trial, and pronounce it *The Strongest, Best Constructed, and Most Perfect Velocipede yet produced.*

The art of riding is very easily acquired. It has been mastered, in many instances, in one day by parties who rode easy and gracefully.

ITS ADVANTAGES OVER OTHER VELOCIPEDES:

1st. The DRIVING WHEEL is from five to ten inches higher, and still the saddle is so low that the rider can touch the floor with both feet.

2d. We balance the machine on the BACK WHEEL instead of the front. In doing this the balance is more perfectly acquired, and the rider can not be thrown from his saddle. Experts pronounce this the true principle of balancing and riding a Velocipede.

3d. The saddle is placed back of the front wheel, thereby giving the rider greater power on the cranks to drive the Velocipede at great speed, or up steep grades.

4th. We apply the BREAK and LEG RESTS to the STANDARD, over front wheel, so that they operate on the wheel in any position.

5th. By inclining the STANDARD, over the front wheel, back at an angle of forty degrees, in turning we TIP THE WHEEL and turn a perfect circle without the WHEEL TOUCHING THE LEG. We also avoid the jar to the guiding arms in going over rough ground or pavement.

6th. You will notice, from cut, the easy and graceful position of the rider.

As all are ambitious to get as large a DRIVING WHEEL as they can use, we give the sizes below, in proportion to a man's height:

Men from 4 ft. 10 in. to 5 ft. 2 in. high, can use a 38 in. wheel and touch the floor with both feet. Men from 5 ft. 3 in. to 5 ft. 6 in. high can use a 41 in. wheel and touch the floor with both feet. Men from 5 ft. 7 in. to 5 ft. 9 in. high can use a 45 in. wheel and touch the floor with both feet. Men from 5 ft. 10 in. to 6 ft. can use a 48 in. wheel and touch the floor with both feet. As all will be desirous of getting the Velocipede that will run the easiest, go the fastest, and turn the shortest, we invite all to send for Circular giving full description.

TOMLINSON, DEMAREST, & CO., FINE CARRIAGE BUILDERS, 620 BROADWAY, NEW YORK.

TRANSPORTATION

Americans like to think of themselves as a highly mobile people—both on the road and in society—and no popular art confirms this national characteristic more dramatically than advertisements for transportation and travel. In the American idiom, "going places" has long meant a geographic as well as a social destination.

America owes its existence to travelers and the exploring spirit. The origins of American popular expression can be found in the enormous body of travel literature that records the discoveries and colonization of the New World. Often composed during the rigors of transit and in a spirit of wide-eyed wonder, these early travel accounts helped skew American writing toward its experiential, first-person, "on-the-road" tradition. They were not always truthful, however, having as an immediate purpose the luring of additional colonists and investment to some region invariably described as another Eden, a new Promised Land. In fact, so promotional were these "true reports" that American historian Richard Hofstadter regards them collectively as "one of the first concerted and sustained advertising campaigns in the history of the modern world."

Getting to the New World was usually easier than getting around in it. Horses were expensive, coaches a conspicuous luxury, roads nonexistent. It took the intrepid Bostonian Sarah Kemble Knight five months to make a round-trip business excursion to New York City on horseback in 1704. Intercity stagecoaches (really stage "wagons") were introduced in 1756, but given their limited passenger capacity and cost, they remained a luxury service. Even private coaches were extremely rare: only twenty-six could be seen in New York as late as 1770. But as carriage-makers perfected their craft and as an affluent class increasingly demanded Cinderella trappings of wealth, fine equipage became one of the chief status symbols of the new American society. By the 1830s, carriage advertisements like the following appeared regularly in American newspapers:

The carriage's prestige value can still be seen in the well-known General Motors's "Body by Fisher" logo, which trades on the preeminent worth of handcrafted goods in an industrial age.

As a prestige item, the horse-drawn carriage had nothing to fear from the Steam Age, though as a practical vehicle it barely survived the roads of that turbulent era. With technological efforts being concentrated on steamboats, railroads, and canals, few states seemed to worry about the primitive condition of roadways outside the city limits. Travel reports, full of grumblings about the frequency of potholes and mud, nevertheless express repeated surprise over the raw accomplishments of steamboats and railroads. By the 1820s steamboats had grown to be a common sight on American waterways, and racing evolved into a dangerous game as captains risked fatal boiler explosions by pushing full steam ahead to beat a river rival. Yet as one experienced European traveler observed, "The life of an American is, indeed, only a constant *racing*, and why should he fear it so much on board the steamboats?" When railroads came into their own in the 1830s and 1840s, steam transportation rapidly began to shape the schedules of everyday life, and the mighty locomotive quickly assumed a prominent role in the mythology of an industrialized democracy.

The earliest railroad passenger cars were simply conventional carriages adapted to rails. But in no time mechanics had designed larger coaches, and by the 1840s a travel-weary Charles Dickens sourly observed that an American train was "a great deal of jolting, a great deal of noise, a great deal of wall, not much window, a locomotive engine, a shriek, and a bell." But these barbaric conditions disappeared a generation after Dickens's celebrated American visit.

In the 1860s the Pullman Company introduced its famous compartment cars and immediately set the standards for American mass luxury. Sailing over the same midwestern roadbeds that Conestoga wagons had lumbered over only a few decades earlier, the Pullman "moving hotels" offered the ordinary citizen the opportunity to travel in what was advertised as "palatial" style. The cars soon found their way into folklore as masculine sanctuaries where businessmen could, with perfect impunity, drink, smoke, spit, and exchange with instantly acquired friends another "didja hear the one about."

Nineteenth-century advertisements for railroads, steamships, clipper ships, and riverboats—with their dual emphasis on luxury and speed—convincingly document a growing national preoccupation with mobility and status. The advertisements made effective use of the artistic poster techniques then being developed in France. But unlike today's popular travel posters they were designed to sell the vehicle rather than the destination. Among the most colorful depictions of post-Civil War culture, these early travel posters were soon overshadowed by a blitz of stunning advertisements for what was to be the first mechanical means of private transportation offered for mass consumption—the bicycle.

Clumsy high-wheelers and velocipedes had been on the American market since the middle of the century. But not until the invention of the modern two-wheel safety bicycle in the late 1880s did cycling become a national fad and a big business. In 1882, the year the word "bike" entered the language, there were an estimated 20,000 cycles in use; by 1895 the number had climbed astonishingly to 10 million. Bicycle posters appeared everywhere, their bold art nouveau styles lending a swirly air of elegance and effortlessness to the ordinary strains of bike-riding. Most of the advertisements featured etherealized women riders who seemed to be ecstatic with their liberation as they glided along with consummate ease.

Skeptics and moralists at once found cause for alarm. Because of cycling, women were beginning to dress more casually, more sportily. Conservative Victorian physicians argued that things had gone far enough. First, the sewing machine—that "woman-killer"—had introduced a peddling craze that reputedly caused a number of serious gynecological side effects. And now, according to an article in the *Georgia Journal of Medicine and Surgery* (March, 1899), a new peddling machine was producing dangerous female disorders, especially at exhilarating speeds when "the body is thrown forward, causing the clothing to press against the clitoris, thereby eliciting and arousing feelings hitherto unknown and unrealized by the young maiden."

By the end of the Gay Nineties the bicycle fad petered out, leaving behind it a trail of popular songs and expressions, personalities, fashions, and romantic images. But by then the advertising profession was dreaming up campaigns to introduce the public to a far stranger vehicle—the horseless carriage. The chief consumption object of modern American society, the automobile was first manufactured for the likes of the affluent Grosse Pointers who crowded to watch former champion cyclist Barney Oldfield take his red Ford 999 up to 75 miles per hour. In Europe, where most of the major technical automotive advances were implemented, the motor car would remain a plaything of the upper classes for decades. On the other hand, American engineers and manufacturers began to notice quite early that Eli Whitney's munitions plant based on "interchangeable parts" could be combined with the new bottling industry's assembly-line operations to produce relatively inexpensive automobiles. A persistent experimenter, Henry Ford finally knew less about machinery than he did about mechanization: Out of the industrial principles that produced the Colt and the Coke the Model T was born.

The means of production affect social roles as significantly as do the objects manufactured. Clearly, the automobile assembly line created a new type of industrial worker—one tooled like an interchangeable part to fit perfectly into a uniform system of production. Not all commentators were as sanguine about the automobile industry's methods of "progressive assembling" as the following writer for *Collier's Weekly*:

> *Although a single plant will employ 10,000 men (more than the population of many a country town) very few skilled mechanics are engaged in the making of a modern automobile. Benches and vises are as extinct as dinosaurs and dodos. In three days, a Pole, a Hungarian, a Chinaman, any immigrant who may not speak a word of English, can learn to perform any one of the hundreds of tasks in an automobile plant. Indeed, he is considered hopeless if he cannot. No two men, no dozen men, no hundred men, are absolutely necessary. Any group may drop out of the organization, but in a few hours their places will be filled by men who never in their lives have been in an assembling plant, and who, nevertheless, meet all requirements. Those who make the parts do not know what functions they perform in a car; those who assemble the engines cannot adjust them.*

This was written in 1917, three years after Henry Ford had startled American industry by nearly doubling current wages to a $5.00 per day minimum. Although sensitive to the needs of labor, Ford was also shrewdly aware that workers required higher wages if they were to join the swelling ranks of automobile consumers. Surely one of the most astounding feats of modern salesmanship has been the successful promotion of skillfully "crafted" automobile "masterpieces" to the very workers who monotonously assembled them.

By disabling European competitors, World War I served as a terrific boon to the American automobile industry. To stimulate business even further, Congress passed in 1916 the first Federal Aid Road Act to construct a nationwide network of highways. By the late 1920s, the new Duco-lacquered, annually remodeled automobile had become the most impressive symbol of material civilization. Its manufacture tied together a huge number of separate industries and sales forces. It affected practically every aspect of daily life, creating new jobs and destroying old ones, radically changing everyday notions of distance and time, rearranging the boundaries of city, country, and suburb, relocating shopping areas, rescheduling family routines, and offering young people an unprecedented mobility as well as an entirely new and exciting kind of privacy.

Economists exaggerate when they attribute the famous prosperity of the 1920s almost exclusively to the automobile, yet the car did, as Stuart Chase observes, suffuse "the country with the visible *appearance* of a prosperity in which everybody seemed to share." The mass consumption of automobiles in the 1920s represents one of the most profound changes in American social history. In 1919 there were nearly 7 million automobiles on American roads; by 1928 the number had grown to well over 21 million. Robert and Helen Lynd, in *Middletown*, their celebrated 1929 study of an average American community, demonstrated the social impact of the passenger car by using a more modest statistical scale: of 26 Middletown working-class families without bathroom facilities, 21 nevertheless proudly owned automobiles. Nobody was paying any attention to Will Rogers's suggestion that the traffic problem could best be solved by "keeping unpaid-for cars off the road."

Advertisers quickly learned that nuts-and-bolts copy and "affordability" claims alone would not sell cars. In its time the Model T represented the "better idea" (the free-floating comparative is quite at home in automobile copy), but who wanted the box-like bare essentials of a car once other motorists had begun to rule the roads with sleek Overlands and smart Buicks, not to mention Pierce Arrows, Marmon 34's, and Rubay Carrosseries? Most people, advertisers correctly guessed, had little desire to own a "people's car"; they wanted instead to "move up" in class to a luxury car, which itself was often a people's car designed to look expensive. From a commercial standpoint, the early history of the automobile falls into three fairly distinct marketing periods. As former General Motors president Alfred P. Sloan, Jr., describes it in *My Years with General Motors* (1963), there was the period before 1908, which with its expensive cars was entirely that of a *class* market; then the period from 1908 to the mid-twenties, which was dominantly that of a *mass* market, ruled by Ford and his concept of basic transportation at a low dollar price; and, after that, the period of the mass market served by better and better cars, or what might be thought of as the *mass-class* market, with increasing diversity." According to Sloan, the "mass-class" market (a "General Motors concept") was made possible by the interaction of four factors: installment-buying plans, used-car trade-ins, the closed-body car, and, most important for advertising ceremony, the annual model.

Since the 1920s, advertising has played an integral role in determining the over-all design of automobiles and has contributed proportionately to the additional expenses that luxurious "appointments" and tempting "options" ultimately mean to the consumer. It has done this—as it has performed so many everyday "miracles"—by persistently wrapping the commodity in so many layers of sociocultural abstractions that it becomes nearly impossible to use or merely look at the object without participating in the collective fiction. Nobody simply buys a car; rather, one purchases a Buick, a Cadillac, a Volkswagen, along with the entire range of values each "package" has, through heavy advertising, come to embody. Because it deals with an extremely vital cultural phenomenon, automobile promotion offers an excellent record of how modern advertising eventually made the use-value theory of classical economics as obsolete as the Model T. As Thorstein Veblen recognized, advertising created an additional economic dimension for everyday goods—their symbolic value.

Automobile advertising accomplished this by consistently promoting the car as the fulfillment of a modern desire for style, status, sex, and speed. The car idling near a fashionably dressed model; the car parked in front of a stately home; the car caressed by a theatrically aroused woman; the car easily outdistancing its rivals at a performance rally. Infinite variations on these themes have established over the years a predictable set of automobile advertising conventions. So routinely did copywriters during the 1920s associate their products with fashion, sexuality, social status, and speed that, during the 1930s, advertisements (notably those for the Dusenberg) started to feature only the symbolic props, confident that these in themselves would fully suggest the vehicle's reputed virtues. Not all went so far as to eliminate the car entirely, but many advertisers were content to show only a few automotive details, relying on a hood ornament, a radiator grill, or a spare-tire rack to spark a series of fruitful associations. But exceptions prove the conventions. The professionally iconoclastic Volkswagen campaigns of the 1960s—ads that seemed to knock their product by truthfully showing "real" folks and modest homes, no cheesecake and down-to-earth stinginess—worked effectively only because the copy could take for granted the hackneyed selling strategies consumers had been conditioned to expect from Detroit manufacturers. The Volkswagen copywriters had mastered a fundamental law of selling: Truth in advertising is usually advertising that doesn't quite sound like advertising.

Transportation and travel advertisements habitually play off one another. The first railroad cars not only resembled private coaches, but in order to stay economically competitive they eventually began to advertise all the comforts of a "first-class steamer." Years later the earliest airline ads would nervously borrow the language and imagery of luxury liners to assure novice passengers that their flight experience would be one of smooth sailing. By the 1970s the airlines could even get the ocean liner's piano bar tinkling at 33,000 feet. The automobile has used the airplane symbolically ever since the earliest days of aviation, and illustrators still like to picture cars standing at airports or speeding down runways. The introduction of commercial jet travel in the late 1950s—with its new packaging of status (the jetsetter), style ("When you've got it, flaunt it"), sex ("Fly me!"), and speed—led to striking changes in automobile design and copy. Cars were engineered to reflect "aerodynamic" features, and advertising followed suit by loading copy with jet jargon, even to the point of sending wheelless vehicles into the stratosphere. More recently, in keeping with the sci-fi imagery of the Space Age, advertisements have begun to showcase automobiles in odd-looking landscapes illuminated by eerie lights: "A dramatic combination of styling and technology for 1978 . . . and beyond," headlines a Ford Futura ad in which the car is nearly overshadowed by a bizarre creation of the Ford aerospace unit.

In 1952, while aircraft manufacturers paraded fighter jets in the popular magazines, the Ford Motor Company ran a series of Norman Rockwell illustrated advertisements depicting the history of the American automobile. The lead-off ad piously portrayed a young Henry Ford busily engaged in the construction of his 1896 buggy-like car. The copy read in part:

> *The revolution of those wheels on that May night started one of the great revolutions in history. A dream of mankind had come true—transportation for everyone. The first little Ford helped build the American Road. The American Road is more than a slow river of rustling traffic. It symbolizes the power of our way of life, endlessly working in the service of all mankind.*

A few years later, President Eisenhower and Senator Albert Gore marshaled through Congress the Interstate Highway Act of 1956 and novelist Jack Kerouac completed his macadam odyssey, *On the Road*. Suburbs and shopping centers started up on land that a few years earlier had harbored deer and quail. Detroit designed a new type of automobile for the American superhighway, one engineered to give a maximum "ride" over long, straight, fast stretches with a minimum of driving requirements. As a countermeasure to the new mass-market big cars, independent manufacturers attempted to promote a number of small cars—the euphemisms "compact" and "subcompact" had not yet gained currency—but these had little chance of making a hit with a status-conscious American public. Spurning the appearance of the toylike Henry J's, Willys Aero's, and Crosley station wagons, Henry Ford II confidently expressed the automotive industry's concept of the upwardly-mobile consumer: "To the average American, our present car and its size represents an outward symbol of prestige and well-being."

By the mid-1960s, however, automobile consumption had become a political issue—a matter of an individual's prestige versus the public's well-being. Municipal public transit was dying; the number of riders declined 25 percent between 1955 and 1965. The railroads were rapidly going bankrupt, losing short passenger hauls to bus lines, long hauls to airlines, and a whopping percentage of freight to the powerful new truck companies. The car was still king, but sociologists, urban planners, and Ralph Nader had begun to speak of it as a mixed blessing. The private automobile bore a major responsibility for air pollution, congestion, noise, and the vast depletion of what used to be called "fuel" but was now spoken of as "energy." The alluring democratic vistas celebrated in the 1952 Ford "American Road" copy were quickly turning into demographic horrors. Congress passed the Motor Vehicle Air Pollution Control Act in 1965. In 1967 a New York City transportation administrator reported to a Senate subcommittee that "in 1907 it was found that the average speed of horse-drawn vehicles through the city's streets was 11.5 miles per hour. In 1966 the average speed of motor vehicles through the central business district was 8.5 miles per hour—and during the mid-day crushes slower still." Some relief came in the form of imports promising, among other more economical things, a cultural alternative to the aggressively antisocial American car. The Big Three reacted to the challenge of foreign competitors by maintaining a holding pattern of strategic compromise: They advertised smaller automobiles that would happily be everything to everybody—compacts with plenty of room, luxury with no sacrifice of economy, safety with no forfeiture of power.

Contemporary automobile manufacturers have not been alone in their struggle with environmentalists and citizens' groups, as the highly publicized grass-roots demonstration against the Concorde jet has shown. In fact, throughout the 1970s airlines have come under a number of federal and local attacks, ranging from monopolistic price control and safety standards to airport sites and noise levels. If the automobile and the aircraft have had a long-standing symbolic companionship in advertising imagery, part of the reason is symbiotic: Located miles outside of city limits, airports depend heavily on highway access and passenger car commutation. Both automotive and aircraft profits dropped severely during the energy crunch of the early 1970s, mainly because of heady overexpansion. The airlines buoyantly contracted for jumbo jets and airbuses, only to find that the new gargantuan carriers taxied into their oversized hangars just about the time that the 1970s slump wrecked vacation plans, squelched businessmen's first-class habits, and dramatically escalated fuel costs. Unlike automobiles, air transportation had never reached down to Henry Ford's "ordinary folks." A 1977 Gallup poll study shows that 37 percent of Americans over eighteen have never flown. Recent advertisements, however, with their "super-saver" fares, "no-frills" flights, and "discover your roots" appeals show the once glamorous airlines finally acknowledging jet travel as just another form of mass transportation.

TROY, BALLSTON
AND
SARATOGA,

DAILY LINE OF
COACHES.

This line will commence running on the first day of July, leaving each place at half past 8 A. M. every day. Passengers wishing to travel from Saratoga to Lebanon Springs, will find this line not only the most expeditious but cheapest.

Passengers for Pittsfield, Northampton and Hartford by taking this line will dine at Troy, lodge at Pittsfield, and arrive at Hartford early the next day. The road is now put in the best order, and all that is now wanting is that liberality which the establishment merits.

☞ *Seats taken at G. W. Wilcox's,* York House, *Saratoga,* and at all the Principal Houses in Troy.

L. V. & J. B. REED, Proprietors.

J. S. KEELER, *Agent,* Troy.
S. DEXTER, *Agent,* Saratoga.

TROY, JUNE 25, 1834.

N. B. On the arrival of the **ERIE** or **CHAMPLAIN**, Parties can be accommodated with coaches to Saratoga or Ballston the same evening.

1895

"Miss M., a strong, healthy country girl, to be 'in the swim,' purchased a bicycle, exercised freely upon it. The bloom of youth soon faded from her former rosy cheeks, her health failed, menstruation became painful and irregular. The family physician could find no cause for this state of facts. Visit after visit was made. The usual course of tonics was tried without appreciative results. At last he questioned her about her daily bicycle rides, and after much coaxing ascertained from her that, in her rides on the wheel, it was no uncommon thing for her to experience a sexual orgasm three or four times on a ride of one hour."

W. E. Fitch, M.D., *Georgia Journal of Medicine and Surgery* (March 1899)

SAXON $395

SAXON
Strength Economy Service

These thoroughbred Kentuckians, Misses Florence Hess and Eleanora Bosworth of Middlesboro, Kentucky, endorse the Saxon Roadster as a thoroughbred car.

More and more women are buying Saxon Roadsters

The American woman of today is the most keenly critical motor car buyer in the world.

To the selection of a car she brings all the careful shrewdness she employs in making household investments.

Her daily contact with many different sales-people has taught her the purchasing power of the dollar. And she has a wonderful intuitive sense of values—a sense that is largely lacking in men.

Consider then—for a moment—the significance that invests the fact that more and more women are buying Saxon Roadsters as their personal cars. Consider the belief it implies on their part in the supreme value of Saxon Roadster.

Reduced to simplest terms it means that, after

careful comparisons, they have concluded that Saxon Roadster is the best investment in its price class.

They believe it is better looking, that it is better built, that it will go farther, more safely, more comfortably, at less cost than any other car in its price class.

And the judgment of these women buyers is amply vindicated by the remarkable records for low upkeep and long service that Saxon Roadster owners are daily reporting.

Your nearest Saxon dealer will be glad to point out to you the various fine car features of Saxon Roadster and give you an interesting demonstration so that you may judge its abilities for yourself. Write us for his name. Address Dept. 33.

SAXON MOTOR CAR CORPORATION

DETROIT   (500)

The Saxon Motor Car Corp. does not announce yearly models

"A Quick Getaway"

IN these progressive days there are divers
means of transportation, but when in
urgent haste, aircraft is first choice.

Straight and *swift* are the words and
both are exemplified in Curtiss Flying Craft
with a maximum of safety besides.

CURTISS AEROPLANE & MOTOR CORPORATION
Sales Offices: 52 VANDERBILT AVENUE, NEW YORK
CURTISS ENGINEERING CORP., Garden City, Long Island
THE BURGESS CO., Marblehead, Mass.

Member Manufacturers'   *Aircraft Association*

Save Money—Save Time—Save Temper

MAKE your trips to and from work a pleasure instead of a mean ride on a crowded car. Ride a bicycle. Don't wait on uncertain car schedules. Go when you're ready. Go by the shortest route. You can leave home later and get back sooner.

Think of the convenience. Think of the money saved. You will pay for your bicycle in a few months. Is it any wonder that more people are riding bicycles today than ever before?

How good it makes you feel! The red blood sings thru your veins, driving away those morning headaches and that old sluggish feeling! You get to work feeling like taking that old job and fairly "eating it up!" Health and a clear brain go a long way towards making a successful man. A bicycle goes nearly all the way towards making a healthy man!

The bicycle is the most economical mode of transportation. It is the most healthful. It is a pleasant benefit for every member of your family.

CYCLE TRADES OF AMERICA, Inc., 35 Warren Street, New York, U. S. A.

See Your Dealer Today

Ride a Bicycle

I've Always Wanted a Playboy

Well—I've always been frank with my parents.

I might as well be candid now.

I am tired of walking—that's sure—tired of borrowing father's car—tired of riding in the other fellow's car.

The truth is—I have always wanted a Playboy.

There are only a few months of school left.

Right now nothing could be finer than the Playboy for a friendly foursome—four cat-fur coats—a zip and zest in the swanky seat behind and a French horn to herald our coming.

One year ago I hardly dared to ask.

Now the price is $1695. And it's an eight, of course.

Father, I think, wants to do it. Mother, I am sure, will be pleased if he does.

There is nothing like independence.

I have got to go somewhere every day.

As I said above, I am tired of walking—street cars are just incubators for automobile prospects.

I have always wanted a Playboy.

I hope it's red—I hope it's soon.

JORDAN MOTOR CAR COMPANY, *Inc.,* CLEVELAND, OHIO

Price quoted, f. o. b. Cleveland. Add Federal Tax.

JORDAN

You can't blame me—much. I am not sick or anything—I love the out of doors—the thrilling swoop of the flying toboggan—a wonderful day—someone you like.

1926

"They [the Babbitt family] went, with ardor and some thoroughness, into the matters of streamline bodies, hill-climbing power, wire wheels, chrome steel, ignition systems, and body colors. It was an aspiration for knightly rank. In the city of Zenith, in the barbarous twentieth century, a family's motor indicated its social rank as precisely as the grades of the peerage determined the rank of an English family."

Sinclair Lewis, *Babbitt* (1922)

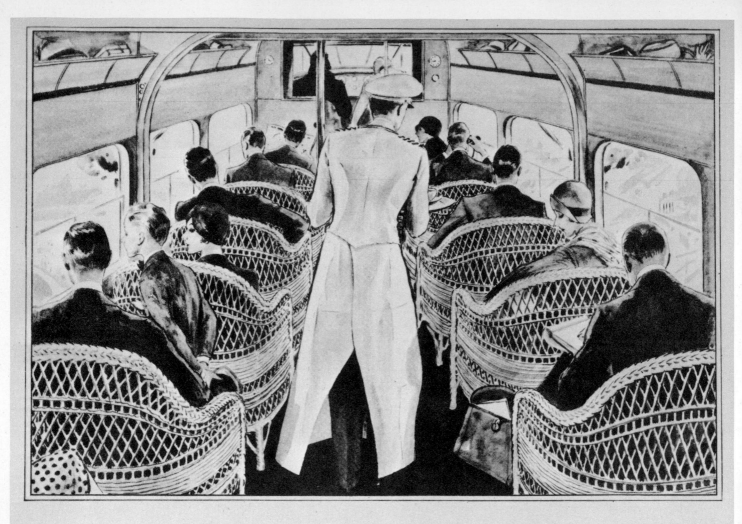

FIRST TIME UP!

You settle back in your wicker chair a little nervously as the engines roar. Then a burst of speed across the flying-field! Forty miles an hour . . . fifty-five! Someone shouts:

"Watch the wheels!"

Unless your eyes are fixed on the great balloon tires no sense perception tells when you have left the earth. There is only an astonishing feeling of stability; then comfortable relaxation as the motors are throttled down. The giant, tri-motored car moves upward on a cushioning ramp of air. . . .

Gradually you experience a sensation that is certainly one of the most extraordinary man has ever felt. You are transcending human nature. You feel immeasurably superior to the crawling beings in the miniature world immersed in silence two thousand feet below. Though ordinarily you may suffer from fear of heights, this fear does not touch you now, *for there are no lines of perspective drawing you earthward!*

Streets, monuments, buildings, vehicles and living creatures, are fractions of inches in size. Hedgerows, fences, and symmetrically plowed fields of red and brown earth form rug-like patterns, while distance gives the raw surfaces a velvety texture.

Boats, moving along a river the color of green onyx, push threads of cotton from their bows. Trains wind through the hills with lazy deliberation. Automobiles creep along ribboned roads. Sheep, cattle, horses graze heads downward in the fields, unaware that you are watching from the sky.

The air of other-worldliness that hangs over the earth below is emphasized by the fact that you are hardly aware of forward motion, *though moving twice as fast as the fastest express trains,* and it is as easy to stand poised on one foot in the cabin as on the floor of your own bedroom. Your fellow passengers move freely about, shifting the ten wicker chairs companionably, to play cards, to typewrite, to make sketches, or, gathering in groups, first on one side of the plane then on the other, to study the panorama below.

You soon accept the truth of the reported safety of these giant commercial planes. What if a motor fails? With two, the plane can continue to its destination! If two fail—the remaining motor can extend the angle of descent to cover an area almost half the size of Delaware. And if all three fail the plane has a gliding range of miles.

Ford tri-motored, all-metal planes have demonstrated railroad efficiency for over a million miles of flight, carrying mail, freight and passengers . . . in tropical regions, in arctic regions, at sea level and over the highest mountain ranges on this continent.

Events of the last twelve months have put commercial flying in America on the level of stable industries. Great businesses have accepted it as a dependable means of swift transport, cutting two-thirds off railroad time. Business men no longer think of the mere thrill of "going up"; they think rather in terms of profitable service.

In the modern business world, the dawn of each new day presents a different scene . . . new products, new competition, new markets. To meet its challenge, you must be prepared.

When the occasion comes for your first time up, it will not be to "joy-ride" in an antiquated and hazardous machine; but far more probably it will be to reach some distant meeting-place in advance of business competition!

FORD MOTOR COMPANY

1928

She drives a Duesenberg

1934

Mile-stone on a road that has no end

ON a downtown corner in a well-known Eastern city is a new and significant building.

It is a service station—one of the most complete and luxurious that may be found anywhere in America. Its beauty is unusual. Yet its significance lies in the fact that here, in stone and steel, is a prediction.

For this service station is an indication of what tomorrow may bring to the highways of America. It offers new and thoughtful conveniences to the travelling public. It is a milestone on the road toward the day when major service stations may be, in effect, depots of travel rather than ports of call.

Gulf believes that motoring is still in a stage of comparative infancy. It believes in its increasing importance in the American scene. And as this form of transportation grows in magnitude, the scope, comforts and facilities of service stations must broaden with it.

With this in mind, Gulf is constantly studying traffic flow and traffic trends, to the end of offering still other small but important comforts to road-weary motorists.

For Gulf believes that good service is only the beginning of better service. It is an evolutionary process which, because of the very nature of the industry we serve, can have no end. © 1935. GULF REFINING CO., PITTSBURGH, PA.

GULF REFINING COMPANY

1935

The Equatorial Heart
of Darkest Africa

INTERNATIONAL TRUCKS chosen
for COMMANDER GATTI'S
"Jungle Yachts"

Commander and Mrs. Gatti on their 9th expedition,
which is described in "Great Mother Forest"
published by Chas. Scribner's Sons.

The trailers and the fleet of International Trucks
are loaded on the freighter bound for Africa.

Two streamlined trailers make five-room home
on base-camp location.

Three more International Trucks in the
Gatti expedition fleet.

THE celebrated explorer, Commander Attilio Gatti, who has spent thirteen years of his life in the African wilderness, is again at the border of the Belgian Congo, outfitted and equipped for the greatest adventure of his career. During the next year, while the Commander and his wife roam over the immense heart of the equatorial jungle, they will center their operations around their "Jungle Yachts."

The nucleus of the Tenth Gatti African Expedition is a de luxe apartment on wheels—two streamlined trailer units designed by Count Alexis de Sakhnoffsky and powered by International Trucks. Other Internationals will serve the complex needs of the project over an area one-third as large as the United States, and largely unexplored.

Commander Gatti says about his fleet of International Trucks:

". . . . On our automotive power hangs the success of our venture in the jungle trails and mountains of Africa. We had to have as power cars the very, very best on the market. And we had to have other reliable trucks to carry our great stock of supplies and provisions, our precious movie and photo equipment, our camp, etc. We could not risk the irreplaceable results of months of hard work.

"For this, however, we did not have to make any new research. The many years I have spent in Africa and the 100,000 miles I have already made there with trucks and cars of a dozen different makes have taught me enough. Without hesitation I let experience decide and I took all International Trucks. I know they will give us great service for the major transport and as liaison units for the various parts of our caravan."

International Harvester will be glad to mail you, on request, an illustrated booklet completely describing this modern expedition into Africa.

INTERNATIONAL HARVESTER COMPANY
(INCORPORATED)
180 North Michigan Avenue   Chicago, Illinois

International Truck sizes range from ½-ton to powerful 6-wheelers.

Observation-living room, showing library, bar, and the Commander's desk.

One of two luxurious bedrooms. Electric
lighting is indirect throughout.

Electric kitchen that would do justice to
the Gatti penthouse on Park Avenue.

Bathroom in black tile. Full-length tub
and fittings in superb color harmony.

INTERNATIONAL TRUCKS

THE *Scarab*

A CHALLENGE and A PROPHECY · ·

THE CHALLENGE: Created after a decade of aircraft and automotive research, the Scarab rear-engine motor car comes as a friendly but direct challenge to the necessary conservatism of the big-production motor car manufacturers. The Scarab expresses Vision vs. Conservatism; Functional Design vs. Traditional Design; Individuality vs. Standardization; Fine Craftsmanship vs. Mass Production. Produced by a group whose soundness of experience and engineering finesse is thoroughly established, the obvious "rightness" of the Scarab design is its greatest challenge.

THE PROPHECY: The new Scarab will set all future styles in motor cars. The following features now exclusive to the Scarab, will be adopted by all makers of fine cars within three years. These features mark the final departure of motor car engineering from all horse-and-buggy tradition:

Engine in the rear • Unit body—no chassis • Inside floor area—7'6" x 5'7" • Running board and hood space usable inside body • Loose chairs, adjustable to all positions • Rear davenport seat convertible to full-length couch • Card and dining table • New, full-vision driver's position • Thermostatically controlled heat • Forced, draftless ventilation, with rain, dust and insect filter • Fully insulated against sound and temperature • Smooth body lines minimizing wind noises • Concealed, recessed rear window • Grill-enclosed headlights • Electric door locks—no projecting handles • Flush-type hinges • Exceptionally long wheelbase for overall length (no overhang) • Minimum unsprung weight • Soft, individual springing of all wheels • Less weight on front axle—for easier steering • Maximum brakes at rear—not front—for safe, rapid deceleration • Slanted windows, no reflections.

Production for 1936 will be limited to 100 cars • Priced from five thousand dollars, f. o. b. Dearborn, Michigan. Demonstration upon invitation only.

Wm B. Stout

STOUT MOTOR CAR CORPORATION
DEARBORN, MICHIGAN

"Hi, Fifteen-Footer, You're THE LONGEST of the LOT
...the very longest of all lowest-priced cars!"

The Special De Luxe Sport Sedan, $802

Chevrolet believes that the car that fills the starring role—the car that gives the most brilliant performance in the whole field of low-cost motoring—should *look* as well as act the part.

So Chevrolet for '40 is a big, strapping fifteen-footer—*the very longest of all lowest-priced cars*—measuring a full 181 inches from front of grille to rear of body!

Every one of those inches is streamlined to breath-taking beauty. Every one of them adds up to make this big "Royal Clipper" model the most comfortable car in its price range. And every one belongs to a car that cleaves the air like an arrow when you step on the throttle!

Because, as you know, Chevrolet for '40 is the liveliest of all low-priced cars . . . powered by a super-

silent Valve-in-Head Engine which places it first in acceleration, first in hill-climbing, first in all-round action . . . and yet it's so economical that everybody envies the Chevrolet owner its extremely low cost of operation and upkeep.

You're in line for a new motor car this year and you know where the *value* is. People say—and the popularity polls prove—"Chevrolet's FIRST Again!"

CHEVROLET MOTOR DIVISION
General Motors Sales Corporation. DETROIT, MICHIGAN

It measures a thrilling fifteen feet plus—181 inches from front of grille to rear of body—and it's "every inch the king" of lowest-priced cars!

FIRST IN QUALITY CHEVROLET FIRST IN VALUE

$659

AND UP, "at Flint, Michigan. Transportation based on rail rates, state and local taxes (if any), optional equipment and accessories—extra. Prices subject to change without notice.

"Chevrolet's FIRST Again"

EYE IT·· TRY IT·· BUY IT!

"CHEVROLET'S FIRST AGAIN!"

A year's vacation! Prof. Robert J. Niess has won an overseas fellowship for outstanding research. As a good research man should, Prof. Niess got all the facts on American and European cars before he selected the Henry J for his European trip.

The professor knows! The Professor needs a smart, sturdy car for use at the University of Michigan —with unusual economy for European gas prices! At nearby Willow Run, he follows a Henry J through the production line.

Shopping on campus! His wife, Martha, is delighted with the shorter turning radius and triple-tooth steering that make the Henry J so easy to park. And it can save them up to $600 the first year, on initial cost, upkeep and other expenses!

The adventure begins! The whole family including daughters Martha and Barbara, drive to New York, where they'll embark for France. On the trip, the Henry J averaged a cent-a-mile for gasoline!

Up the gangplank! No sign of weariness after their drive from Michigan...for the Henry J's airplane-type shock absorbers afford the smoothest ride in the low price field! Martha and Barbara slept most of the way in quiet comfort.

The Henry J's aboard! The Niess family want a really *dependable* car for foreign travel. Hence the Henry J. They feel the low-price foreign cars aren't big enough for comfort—and they like the Henry J's 58-inch front seat and big-car roominess!

Michigan Miles or Paris Kilometers...

Henry J **Costs Less to Drive!**

Vive Paris! Professor Niess has a whole year to devote to study and research. Then it's back to Michigan for the whole family and their smart, tough, thrifty Henry J. Instead of spending extra money getting your present car ready for winter, why not trade for a brand new, dependable Henry J! Let your Kaiser-Frazer dealer give you the facts today!

$1362
Delivered at Willow Run with Federal taxes paid and local tax (if any) additional. Prices subject to change without notice.

Kaiser•Frazer's *Henry J*
the Fashion Academy Car for today!

1951

Fewer than 130,000 Henry J's were sold before the thrifty car was put out to pasture. The reason for its failure was probably best summed up by a Georgian farmer who claimed that his 1951 model was "like an unsavory gal ah once knew. She was really pretty great—but ah wouldn't associate mahself in public with 'er."

Full color was first introduced to American magazines by Mellin's Food in 1893. The following advertisements depict some of the ways it has been used strategically since then to make a variety of products visually appealing. These color advertisements, representing the work of some of America's outstanding illustrators, have been selected from the most competitive areas of selling—automobiles, cigarettes, cosmetics, fashion, and food. Taken in sequence, from late nineteenth-century poster art to contemporary color photography, the illustrations vividly portray the changing uses of full-color techniques through eighty years of American advertising.

PHOENIX SILK HOSE

for lasting service and style unsurpassed

Men's 50¢ to $1.50 per pair
Women's 75¢ to $2. per pair

Misses' 75¢ per pair
Infants 25¢ & 50¢ per pair

AT THE BEST SHOPS

Made in the "U.S.A." by the
PHOENIX KNITTING WORKS
234 Broadway, Milwaukee

A "SIGHT DRAFT"—WITH INTEREST

1915

POMPEIAN
BEAUTY POWDER

"LOVE AT FIRST SIGHT"

Her beauty instantly captivates him. His glances linger at first delightedly, then lovingly, upon the dainty texture of her skin. For nearly every woman can find the secret of "Instant Beauty" in the "Complete Pompeian Beauty Toilette."

First a touch of fragrant Pompeian DAY Cream. Work this softening, vanishing cream well into the skin, so that the powder will not stick in spots. Now the Pompeian BEAUTY Powder, with its pearly touch and captivating perfume. Then a bit of Pompeian BLOOM on the cheeks. This touch of color adds the bloom of youthful beauty and makes your eyes seem darker and more lustrous. Presto! What a change in a few moments.

"Don't envy beauty—use Pompeian and have it."

Pompeian DAY Cream—(Vanishing). Keeps the skin smooth and velvety. Removes face shine. Has an exquisite perfume. All druggists, 50c.

Pompeian BEAUTY Powder — Adds a lovely clearness to the skin. Stays on unusually long. Its fragrance captivates. Pure and harmless. Shades: white, brunette, and flesh. All druggists, 50c.

Pompeian BLOOM—A rouge that is imperceptible when properly applied. In three shades—light, dark, and medium (the popular shade). All druggists, 50c.

SPECIAL HALF-BOX OFFER
(Positively only one to a family)

To one person only in a family, we will send a box of Pompeian BEAUTY Powder (containing exactly one-half regular 50c package) and samples of DAY Cream and BLOOM for only two dimes. With the samples you can make many interesting beauty experiments.

The Pompeian Mfg. Co., 2001 Superior Ave., Cleveland, Ohio

POMPEIAN CO., 2001 Superior Ave., Cleveland, O.

Gentlemen : Enclosed please find two dimes, for which send me your special *powder* offer. No member of my family has accepted this offer before.

Name

Address

City

State

Flesh shade sent unless white or brunette requested

1919

Looking Pleasant this Time

FOR the first time in months the young housewife looks at the figures without scowling *awfully,* and she has Jell-O to thank for the pleasure she derives from inspecting them now.

Any woman who wants to know how Jell-O can help her out in the matter of her monthly bills, or in other particulars, will find the information in the new Jell-O Book, just out, which is more beautiful and complete than any other ever issued, and it will be sent free to any woman furnishing her name and address.

THE GENESEE PURE FOOD COMPANY. Le Roy, N. Y., and Bridgeburg, Ont.

1920

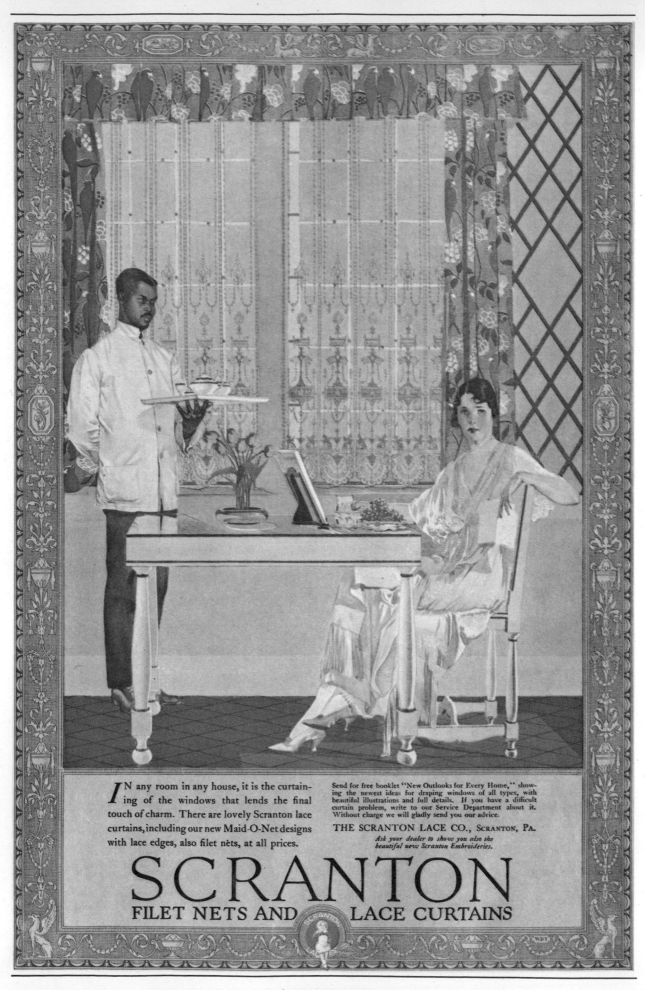

IN any room in any house, it is the curtaining of the windows that lends the final touch of charm. There are lovely Scranton lace curtains, including our new Maid-O-Net designs with lace edges, also filet nets, at all prices.

Send for free booklet "New Outlooks for Every Home," showing the newest ideas for draping windows of all types, with beautiful illustrations and full details. If you have a difficult curtain problem, write to our Service Department about it. Without charge we will gladly send you our advice.

THE SCRANTON LACE CO., SCRANTON, PA.

Ask your dealer to show you also the beautiful new Scranton Embroideries.

SCRANTON
FILET NETS AND LACE CURTAINS

COLES PHILLIPS

© H. H. Co.

Holeproof Hosiery

TRIM ankles, demurely alluring. How they fascinate, captivate. And well she knows glove-fitting Holeproof Hosiery makes them so.

In this short-skirted era, Holeproof is becoming as famous for its sheerness, shapeliness and lustrous beauty, as it is for wonderful wearing qualities.

Leading stores are now showing the newest ideas for Spring in staple and fancy styles in Pure Silk, in Silk Faced and in Lisles for men, women and children.

HOLEPROOF HOSIERY COMPANY, MILWAUKEE, WISCONSIN

Holeproof Hosiery Company of Canada, Limited, London, Ont.

1921.

DO YOU INHALE?

Certainly...

7 out of 10 smokers inhale knowingly... the other 3 inhale unknowingly

DO you inhale? Seven out of ten smokers *know* they do. The other three inhale without realizing it. *Every* smoker breathes in some part of the smoke he or she draws out of a cigarette.

Think, then, how important it is to be certain that your cigarette smoke is pure and clean —to be sure you don't inhale certain impurities!

Do you inhale? Lucky Strike has dared to raise this much-avoided subject...because cer-tain impurities concealed in even the finest, mildest tobacco leaves are removed by Luckies' famous purifying process. Luckies created that process. Only Luckies have it!

Do you inhale? More than 20,000 physicians, after Luckies had been furnished them for tests, *basing their opinions on their smoking experience,* stated that Luckies are less irritating to the throat than other cigarettes.

"It's toasted"

Your Protection - against irritation - against cough

LUCKY STRIKE "IT'S TOASTED" **CIGARETTES**

O. K. AMERICA

TUNE IN ON LUCKY STRIKE — 60 modern minutes with the world's finest dance orchestras, and famous Lucky Strike features, every Tuesday, Thursday and Saturday evening over N. B. C. networks.

1932

When he starts to read you the story of his life, "From Bootblack to Butterfly," don't weep, don't scream. Just relax, with a sunny-smooth Old Gold. You'll find its mild and mellow tobaccos as soothing as a lullaby.

STYMIED BY A STUPID?

... light an Old Gold

AT TRYING TIMES ... TRY A *SMOOTH* OLD GOLD

1935

As smart and as modern as youth itself

As Paris couturiers set the style with new creations, so Franklin with its latest achievement, sets the style in motor cars. Franklin the originator of low bodies, of enclosed sport types and dozens of other style features, has become a symbol of the progressive mode. Franklin open models suggest the airplane fuselage in their streamline contour, rolled belt panels and graceful air-wing fenders.

Like modern airplanes, the Franklin is powered with an air-cooled engine. And like a zooming take-off, Franklin's newest sensation is its fast getaway in second—quiet as high, even up to 55 miles an hour.

As you drive the car, you thrill to its great power—you praise its incomparable comfort —you instantly sense its soaring smoothness. It is different from any other car you have ever driven. If you've flown, you instantly sense the driving feel of an airplane.

Drive a Franklin! It's the one different motoring thrill you can experience today.

FRANKLIN AUTOMOBILE COMPANY, SYRACUSE, N. Y.

The new Franklin prices begin at $2160 F.O.B. Factory

FRANKLIN

REST

YOU leave your office at the end of the day, wearied by a hard day's work.

● Ahead of you wait the responsibilities of the evening. If only there could be a little relaxation sandwiched in between!

● There is—for the man who owns a Packard. He steps from his office into his car, and instantly he is cradled in quiet and comfort. The worries of the day are forgotten in the pleasure of driving a car that almost drives itself. He enjoys a bodily peace, a mental solace. He arrives home refreshed.

● For of all the cars man has ever designed, the most restful, we believe, is the new Packard. There's not a sound from its body, barely a whisper from its motor. The cushions, contoured by experts, *make you relax*. The brakes that stop you so quickly work with such a velvety softness you scarcely know you're stopping. Shock absorbers and spring action are so perfected that ruts and bumps go unnoticed. Instead of riding, you *float!* You *rest!*

● We believe that you, as a business man, deserve the restfulness that a new Packard can bring you. We believe you want and need this car. Why not buy it—*now?* See the new Packards at your Packard dealer's. Or simply phone him—he will arrange for you to ride home from your office in one of these new cars. Very soon after that, we feel confident, you will be making the homeward trip each evening in your own Packard.

PACKARD

ASK THE MAN WHO OWNS ONE

1934

SECURE AND PRACTICAL FOR RECREATION AND UTILITY

Open areas surrounding almost any country club offer room for the owner of a Pitcairn Autogiro to fly directly to his golf game. Requiring little room to take off and even less to land, the pilot owner can fly directly to the scene of almost any sporting event. The practicality of such use has long ago been demonstrated by those owners of the Pitcairn Autogiro who have flown to football games, race tracks, hunt meets and other social gatherings in many locations. The ability to land on and take off from any reasonably sized open ground with security frees the pilot from the necessity of seeking a safe landing only at the large airport. The 1932 Pitcairn Tandem has been refined in design for greater speed and pleasure. Improved streamlining and more engine power add to speed. Tandem cockpits that afford the full visibility so desirable to the amateur flyer, have dual controls to permit sharing the sport of flying. A demonstration can be arranged at the point where you would use your own Autogiro. Write for descriptive literature.

PITCAIRN AIRCRAFT, INC., PITCAIRN FIELD, WILLOW GROVE, PA.

CAR OF THE TIMES — YOUR DE SOTO

HERE IT IS—the car that brings the future right down to today—your new *De Soto!*

Only De Soto, backed by Chrysler Corporation, could have conceived this superb car.

Notice that running boards are concealed... and new Airfoil Lights (concealed headlamps) are *invisible* by day.

You can express your own taste in fabrics and colors...De Soto's interiors are *personalized.*

And talk about performance! The new Powermaster Engine packs *115 horsepower!* And this extra power-margin is not all!

New *Fluid Drive and Simpli-Matic Transmission give No-Shift Driving that tops all previous

"bests"...with better-than-ever economy!

See this De Soto...see how it's styled to *stand out*—built to *stand up.* Your De Soto dealer will be glad to give you a demonstration.

Call or phone *now.* De Soto Division of Chrysler Corporation, Detroit, Mich. *Prices and specifications subject to change without notice.*

Hear Major Bowes' Hour, C.B.S., Thursdays, 9-10 P.M., E.S.T.

DEFENSE PRODUCTS OF CHRYSLER CORPORATION.

Tanks • Anti-Aircraft Cannon • Reconnaissance Cars • Command Cars • Weapon Carriers • Troop Transports • Ambulances • Tent Heaters • Field Kitchens • Cantonment Furnaces • Marine Engines • Industrial Engines.

*AVAILABLE AT MODERATE ADDITIONAL COST

6N 40-99

NEW AIRFOIL LIGHTS
OUT OF SIGHT EXCEPT AT NIGHT

PERSONALIZED **INTERIORS**
COLOR-MATCHED TO YOUR TASTE

***FLUID DRIVE** WITH
SIMPLI-MATIC TRANSMISSION
NEW 115-H.P. PERFORMANCE

TOMORROW'S STYLE TODAY

I dreamed
I took the bull
by the horns...
in my
maidenform bra

New Variette* bra by Maidenform* is made with sensational new Vyrene spandex — the non-rubber wonder that lasts <u>ages</u> longer than ordinary elastics. Spiral-stitched or embroidered cups for rounder, <u>naturally</u> <u>curved</u> curves! All sizes in white, from 2.50.

P. S. You'll find this very same Variette bra <u>built</u> <u>into</u> the dreamy new collection of 1962 *maidenform* swimsuits!

For the man who expects the extraordinary—Manhattan® English Viyella® sport shirts.
Faultless tailoring in a remarkable fabric of 55% pedigreed lambs' wool and 45% cotton that
actually becomes softer, mellower with every washing. Never shrinks. Never loses shape.
In rich solids or classic tartans and patterns. At fine stores in the U.S.A.

Manhattan® VIYELLA REGD.

The Manhattan Shirt Company, a Division of Manhattan Industries, Inc., 1271 Avenue of the Americas, New York, N.Y. 10020.

Favori S89

1976

Dear Ma: This is ME— in a PULLMAN!

1. Well, Ma . . . here I am taking my first trip in a Pullman. And every time I take one of my lazy six-foot stretches I sure am glad I'm riding by Pullman. Riding most ways is just riding. But riding by Pullman is *living!* And the service, Ma —just look at all I get on a Pullman . . .

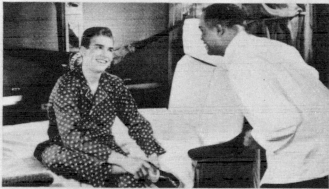

2. Take the porter . . . He calls me "sir" and treats me like a king. (I bet he thinks I'm much older than 19.) He takes my bags and shows me my berth. He makes my bed. He shines my shoes. He brushes my clothes. He brings extra blankets, extra pillows, even a drink of water at the press of a button! And, last thing at night, he asks what time I want to be called in the morning! (Gosh!)

3. And the bed, Ma! With *two* pillows, and fresh, snuggly sheets, and a nice soft, comfortable mattress, like the kind we have at home. All mine, Ma! Plenty of room to stretch and turn. Class, Ma? Listen! Two bed lamps, coat hangers, a little hammock to put my clothes in. And even a private air cooler *in my berth!* (What won't they think of next!)

4. I saw a big league pitcher in the lounge! We got acquainted, talked baseball to bedtime. (Gee, you meet nice people in a lounge car.) The lounge car, you know, is just like a private club for everybody with a Pullman ticket. It's a friendly place, with big, lazy chairs, free magazines to read, and a porter ready to jump the minute you clap your hands!

5. A washroom you can swing a cat in! You might think, Ma, that a washroom in a Pullman is a hole-in-the-wall affair. But it isn't. It's big and roomy, with hot and cold running water, and a special bowl with a goose-neck faucet for cleaning my teeth. It even has an outlet for my electric razor. And Ma, you can use a million towels if you want! (It's wonderful!)

FOR COMFORT AND SAFETY— GO PULLMAN

6. And what do you think it cost? Only $2.65 to ride *Pullman* the whole 300 miles; plus my first class railroad ticket. And this'll please *you*, Ma. It's the *safest* way to travel there is. So it's Pullman for my money. For you, too, Ma. From now on we travel in *style!*

"You Walk In The Same Thing You Fly In"

FATHER: "Wonder if there are other fathers of Army pilots who have never been up in a plane?"

SON: *"Why don't you try it, Dad?"*

FATHER: "Still afraid, I guess."

SON: *"But you walk in the* SAME *thing you fly in."*

FATHER: "Meaning what?"

SON: *"Simply that* EVERY *vehicle travels* THROUGH AIR — *be it train, ship, or automobile."*

FATHER: "But THEY travel on the earth's surface."

SON: *"So do our planes, when they begin and end every journey."*

FATHER: "But they don't stay there."

SON: *"That's an exclusive advantage of aviation. The boat out there can only go where the river goes; the train is rooted to the rails. But an airplane is free to go* EVERYWHERE *because air is everywhere."*

FATHER: "OK son, I'll do it sometime when the need is urgent enough."

When—
"The Need Is Urgent Enough!"

Many who never traveled by air before Pearl Harbor have learned that *War* constitutes an urgent enough need to do so now. As a result, they save priceless time and expedite their war-work. They are learning, not only from the Army and Navy communiques, but from *personal* experience, that the *use* of air is indispensable today.

AMERICAN AIRLINES *Inc.*
ROUTE OF THE FLAGSHIPS UNITING CANADA, U. S. A. AND MEXICO

LUXURY ALOFT IN THE *Martin Mars* FLYING HOTEL

1 Off to Europe, via Martin Mars. When Victory is finally won, you'll be taking that trip of your dreams . . . a two-week holiday abroad!

2 So step aboard the Mars and look about. Two full decks. Spacious, air-conditioned rooms. Courteous service. A flying hotel!

3 Note the size, smartness and comfort of the Mars' lounge! No cramped seats, or narrow aisles. Plenty of room for walking about!

4 A full-course dinner, from the Mars' galley, served by smiling stewards. Soft lights . . . gay laughter . . . music! De luxe transportation!

5 After dinner you'll want to explore the big ship. Here, for example, is the ultra-modern Skytop Room, a favorite rendezvous.

6 Your snug cabin is waiting when you're ready for bed. Nothing to disturb your slumber as the great ship speeds toward Europe and vacation.

7 Morning . . . and you're there! Only a few hours have passed. Ahead lie days of sight-seeing, adventure . . . thanks to the Martin Mars!

Fantasy? Long-range prediction? Not at all! The plane shown here is flying today! It's a Martin Mars transport! True, today's Mars contains no luxurious furnishings. Every inch of space is needed for war supplies. But commercial versions of these huge Navy transports will offer every comfort to tomorrow's trans-ocean travelers. So when you plan that trip abroad . . . plan to fly via Martin Mars!

THE GLENN L. MARTIN COMPANY, BALTIMORE 3, MD.
THE GLENN L. MARTIN-NEBRASKA CO., OMAHA

Martin AIRCRAFT
Builders of Dependable Aircraft Since 1909

Scenes like this are typical of the Lincoln Highway and Pike's Peak Highway

GREYHOUND ROUTES THAT REVEAL
"*This Amazing America*"

ONLY BY HIGHWAY

...You Meet the *Real America*!

● There's just one way to know and enjoy the magnificent Country in which you live. That's to see it close up, face to face, within hand-clasp range of its friendly and interesting people —in the very shadow of its trees and mountains—along its lively and pleasant residential streets.

That way is the *Highway*. Which is the same as saying, "By Greyhound"— because Greyhound alone serves nearly all the famous-name National Highways of the U. S. A. and Canada, plus thousands of miles of other equally interesting highroads that reach to every corner of This Amazing America.

Greyhound unlocks the magic of American Highways to millions who do not drive their own cars . . . and it offers much more than private car travel. Its cost-per-mile is less—there's relaxation as a skilled operator handles the wheel—there is no parking bother—you can sit back and fully enjoy the passing scene.

It's true that nearly as many people ride these comfortable Greyhound coaches for business trips as for holidays, visits, vacations. But all of these millions get an *extra* bonus of scenic travel—the experience of meeting the real America close up . . . for these are pleasures you'll find *Only by Highway.*

GREYHOUND

aboard the lovely *Andrea Doria*

Mural by world-famous Pietro Zuffi: "Neptune's Banquet" in the Grand Ballroom

The exciting NEW ship...
with a heritage of centuries

Into this lovely ship has gone all the proud craftsmanship born of centuries of tradition . . . every modern device for your pleasure and convenience. From the glistening mosaics of her three magnificent outdoor swimming pools to radar; from gleaming Venetian crystal to air conditioning; from breath-taking tapestries to modern turbines that drive her sleek hull at 23 express-speed knots. . . . She is the glory of yesterday . . . the newest of today. She is the *Andrea Doria*.

Italian Line
"ITALIA" – Società di Navigazione – Genova
See your Travel Agent or
AMERICAN EXPORT LINES (General Agents)
39 Broadway, New York 6, N. Y.

ANDREA DORIA express service on the Sunny Southern Route • 6 days to GIBRALTAR • 8 days to NAPLES • 9 days to CANNES and GENOA
SATURNIA • VULCANIA • CONTE BIANCAMANO to AZORES • LISBON • GIBRALTAR • BARCELONA • MAJORCA • PALERMO • NAPLES • CANNES • GENOA

178

This is your reward for the great Dodge advance—the daring new, dramatic new '56 Dodge.

The Magic Touch of Tomorrow!

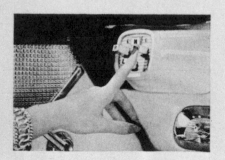

The *look* of success! The *feel* of success! The *power* of success!

They come to you in a dramatically beautiful, dynamically powered new Dodge that introduces the ease and safety of push-button driving —the Magic Touch of Tomorrow! It is a truly great value.

New '56 DODGE

VALUE LEADER OF THE FORWARD LOOK

1955

LOOK UP TO THE DC-8!

The DC-8, now in flight, will soon carry you to new heights of luxurious air travel.

DC-8 introduces you to Her Serene Highness–the Stratosphere

Beneath the outstretched wings of the DC-8, the world falls swiftly below. The sky you climb into turns from blue to purple, and as you reach new heights, there comes over you a sense of serenity you've never known before.

Cradled in your pressurized cabin in the Douglas Jetliner eight miles high, with the sun and moon your neighbors, you gaze down on the toylike towns and peaks and waters of the world. Tranquilly suspend-ed in the clear quiet of the stratosphere, you experience no sense of speed, no vibration, no engine's roar . . . nothing but a beautiful peace of mind and body.

But the DC-8 offers you more than speed and serenity. It brings you a family history of experience, dependability and comfort un-matched in the annals of flight. It is this — *and more*—which makes passengers and pilots look up to Douglas. You'll sense it all when you take your first flight in the fabulous . . .

DOUGLAS DC-8 JETLINER

Built by the most respected name in aviation

These famous air lines already have purchased the DC-8: ALITALIA-Linee Aeree Italiane • DELTA AIR LINES • EASTERN AIR LINES • JAPAN AIR LINES • KLM ROYAL DUTCH AIR LINES
NATIONAL AIRLINES • OLYMPIC AIRWAYS • PANAGRA • PANAIR DO BRASIL • PAN AMERICAN WORLD AIRWAYS • SCANDINAVIAN AIRLINES SYSTEM • SWISSAIR
TRANS-CANADA AIR LINES • TRANS CARIBBEAN AIRWAYS • TRANSPORTS AERIENS INTERCONTINENTAUX • UNION AEROMARITIME DE TRANSPORT • UNITED AIR LINES

1958

A dramatic portrayal of the Body by Fisher in the B-58 Buick SPECIAL Two-Door Riviera.

Passport to a silent world—
THE NEW "SOUND BARRIER" BODY BY FISHER

Before you buy any new car, *listen* to how well it's built!

In a new "Sound Barrier" Body by Fisher, the absence of rattles—the freedom from road and engine noise—tells you plenty:

It tells you this body is built to shrug off the bumps, built to stay tight—for years.

The secret is Life-Span Build—a rigid, integrally joined, bridge-type construction that provides extra body strength—more "living room" inside.

The new "Sound Barrier" body is another Fisher Body exclusive—the latest in 50 years of "firsts."

* * *

Another Fisher Body Bonus: ripple-free Safety Plate glass, front, rear *and side!*

SHAKEDOWN CRUISE FOR A TAUT SHIP. Two days on this torture rack are the equivalent of years of ruts and potholes. But even twists and jolts like these can't loosen up the tight build of a "Sound Barrier" Body by Fisher.

Only the "GM Five" give you the Bonus of BODY BY FISHER

58 YEARS OF BODY BUILDING LEADERSHIP

CHEVROLET · PONTIAC · OLDSMOBILE · BUICK · CADILLAC

1958

They'll know you've *arrived*

when you drive up in an Edsel

Step into an Edsel and you'll learn where the excitement is this year.

Other drivers spot that classic vertical grille a block away—and never fail to take a long look at this year's most exciting car.

On the open road, your Edsel is watched eagerly for its already-famous performance.

And parked in front of your home, your Edsel always gets even more attention—because it always says a lot about you. It says you chose elegant styling, luxurious comfort and such exclusive features as Edsel's famous Teletouch Drive—only shift that puts the buttons where they belong, on the steering-wheel hub.

Your Edsel also means you made a wonderful buy. For of all medium-priced cars, this one really new car is actually priced the lowest.* See your Edsel Dealer this week.

Based on comparison of suggested retail delivered prices of the Edsel Ranger and similarly equipped cars in the medium-price field.

Above: Edsel Citation 2-door Hardtop. Engine: the E-475, with 10.5 to one compression ratio, 345 hp, 475 ft.-lb. torque. Transmission: Automatic with Teletouch Drive. Suspension: Ball-joint with optional air suspension. Brakes: self-adjusting.

EDSEL DIVISION · FORD MOTOR COMPANY

1958 EDSEL

Of all medium-priced cars, the one that's really new is the lowest-priced, too!

1958

By 1960 the name "Edsel" had become synonymous with "flop," "bomb," and "fiasco." The Ford Motor Company had originally asked the well-known American poet Marianne Moore to come up with a compelling name for its new product. She suggested such things as: Hurricane Hirundo, The Resilient Bullet, Anticipator, Mongoose Civique, Pastelogram, Varsity Stroke, Astranaut, Pluma Piluma, and Utopian Turtle Top. The company finally settled on a name it felt had "personal dignity and meaning to many of us"—Edsel.

Ugly is only skin-deep.

It may not be much to look at. But beneath that humble exterior beats an air-cooled engine. It won't boil over and ruin your piston rings. It won't freeze over and ruin your life. It's in the back of the car, where the weight on the rear wheels makes the traction very good in snow and sand. And it will give you about 29 miles to a gallon of gas.

After a while you get to like so much about the VW, you even get to like what it looks like.

You find that there's enough legroom for almost anybody's legs. Enough headroom for almost anybody's head. With a hat on it. Snug-fitting bucket seats. Doors that close so well you can hardly close them. (They're so airtight, it's better to open the window a crack first.)

Those plain, unglamorous wheels are each suspended independently. So when a bump makes one wheel bounce, the bounce doesn't make the other wheel bump. It's things like that you pay the $1663* for, when you buy a VW. The ugliness doesn't add a thing to the cost of the car.

That's the beauty of it.

Pontiac Motor Division • General Motors Corporation

There's a live one under the hood.

(Have you priced a tiger lately?)

Purrs if you're nice. Snarls when you prod it. Trophy V-8, standard in Pontiac GTO. 389 cubic inches. 335 horsepower. 431 lb-ft of torque. Also standard: bucket seats, heavy-duty suspension, real walnut dash, Hurst floor shifter, dual exhausts, even special tires—redlines! (You don't build a GTO with options, you personalize it.) Want something wilder? Got it: 3-2bbl, 360 hp. Want something tamer? Got that, too—Pontiac Le Mans. Take our 140-hp six or order up the V-8 you like: 250 hp, 285 hp. Try something. Drive a "sporty" car. Then prowl around in a Wide-Track a while. You'll know who's a tiger.

**Quick Wide-Track Tigers
Pontiac Le Mans & GTO**

Tired of compacts that put you too close for comfort? Arms too close to the door . . . legs too close to the floor? Think big, think smart. Get fired up with the new '66 Dodge Dart GT. With Dart GT, you can insist on size and still economize. Check the price. Check the interior: foam-padded seats, wall-to-wall carpeting, door-to-

door luxury. Demand more comfort in your compact—more spirit, more for your money. Step into '66 Dart. Take it on the road. Which way do you want to go, Six or V8? '66 Dodge Dart goes both ways without attacking your budget. If you're fed up with compacts that don't make it in size, styling, and spunk, you've got it made

with '66 Dart. The Dodge-sized compact. It's got what you want. The Dodge Rebellion wants you.

'66 Dodge Dart

DODGE DIVISION  CHRYSLER MOTORS CORPORATION

JOIN THE DODGE REBELLION

Avoid the cramped compact squeeze.

Stretch out in '66 Dodge Dart.

1966

All of us come from someplace else.

Just once, you should walk down the same street your great-grandfather walked.

Picture this if you will.

A man who's spent all his life in the United States gets on a plane, crosses a great ocean, lands.

He walks the same streets his family walked centuries ago.

He sees his name, which is rare in America, filling three pages in a phone book.

He speaks haltingly the language he wishes he had learned better as a child.

As America's airline to the world, Pan Am does a lot of things.

We help business travelers make meetings on the other side of the world. Our planes take goods to and from six continents. We take vacationers just about anywhere they want to go.

But nothing we do seems to have as much meaning as when we help somebody discover the second heritage that every American has.

PAN AM
America's airline to the world.

See your travel agent.

1977

THE AMERICAN DIET

Food and beverages did not become major advertised products in America until a decade or so after the Civil War, when new farm machinery, refrigerated railroad cars, safe and attractive methods of packaging, discoveries in food chemistry, and changes in family behavior all began to exert powerful influences on American eating habits.

For all practical purposes, the history of the modern American diet begins with the invention of the can opener in 1858. Edible canned food had been successfully processed in Europe a few decades earlier, but mainly for soldiers, sailors, and explorers—bulky cans of veal accompanied Sir William Parry's 1824 Arctic expedition. In 1825 the first patent for a canning process in America was applied for, and by the 1840s canned corn, tomatoes, and seafood had found limited markets in the Northeast. The Gold Rush helped stimulate demand for canned food, and in the same year the can opener was introduced, Gail Borden opened the first canning plant for his condensed milk. The Civil War gave new momentum to the canning industry and made the tin can a familiar part of the American landscape. But general public acceptance came slowly, and it was not until big business began to weave together a number of technological and industrial innovations (most importantly, the modern "open top" seamed container) in the late 1890s that canned convenience food became a staple of the American diet.

As industrial engineers learned to mass-produce containers, advertising agents learned the promotional value of the brand-name package. The idea of the convenient, sanitary "package"—can, bottle, jar, or box—was a marketing development that would in time totally transform selling strategies by proving that raw goods could be profitably turned into readily identifiable, standardized products. What is obvious now was not so obvious in an era when both manufacturers and retailers had very little experience with advertising and no knowledge of national markets. The earliest food advertisements (Baker's Chocolate being a notable exception) rarely mentioned goods by a specific brand name. A retailer would simply announce in local papers the cost per quantity of crackers, vinegar, lard, or flour. Grocers dealt almost exclusively with staples in bulk, doled out to customers from barrels, crates, and hogsheads. "Shelf goods" were virtually unknown. Then in 1878 a crucial change in foodstuff-marketing occurred when the American Cereal Company designed a distinctive package for a new product, launched an intense sales campaign, and within a few years had molded public opinion enough to inspire customers to ask their grocers for a box of Quaker Oats rather than the usual oatmeal.

The mass-produced food package, surely one of the most significant innovations to come out of the Gilded Age, depended on two related phenomena for its sales effectiveness: (1) the enactment of tough trademark protection laws, and (2) a power shift throughout the entire commercial structure that enabled the manufacturer, rather than the retailer, jobber, or wholesaler, to determine the where, what, and when of mass consumption. Such critical changes in American business history did not happen overnight, but by the opening of the twentieth century it was becoming clear that the most important economic contribution of advertising had been its discovery that the repeatedly promoted, trademarked, packaged product could stimulate direct contact between manufacturer and consumer.

As advertising grew indispensable to American business enterprise, control shifted from the middle to the extremes of the production-distribution-consumption relationship. Many ads reflected retailing's loss of prestige by depicting haughty women shoppers snootily rejecting an unnamed product and insisting that their grocers supply them only with the trusted advertised brand they requested, thank you. By tying together trademark and package with a tight string of favorable and memorable associations, advertisers found they could sell the manufacturing firm along with its goods, so that in the public mind Campbell's would be eternally synonymous with soup or Van Camp's with pork and beans. But the most profound sociocultural results of advertising's shake-up of the product-distribution chain was its remarkable transformation of the nineteenth-century customer into the twentieth-century consumer.

By 1900 a number of brand-name food manufacturers had managed through insistent advertising to secure favored positions in the American marketplace. Swift and Armour were packing and shipping meat to every major city in the country. Van Camp had been inspired with the ingenious idea of preparing his "delicious and appetizing" Boston baked beans in tomato sauce. Royal Baking Powder, a pioneer of magazine advertising, repeatedly used the single slogan "Absolutely Pure." Jos. Schlitz Brewers hammered home with the "Beer That Made Milwaukee Famous" to promote its new "food" product. The Genesee Pure Food Company from LeRoy, New York, touted Jell-O, almost from the day of its invention, as "America's Most Famous Dessert." Aunt Jemima popped out of a gigantic flour barrel at the 1893 Chicago World's Columbian Exposition to demonstrate her down-home pancake recipe. "Eventually? Why Not Now," coyly asked Gold Medal Flour girls. Nabisco convinced the nation to buy Uneeda Biscuits (thinking British usage would upgrade their native "crackers") in what was at the time the single most concentrated campaign in advertising history. A giant "57" dominated the Heinz exhibit at Atlantic City's popular Ocean Pier, where the Pittsburgh Pickle King continued to parade his belief that for the best food advertising you couldn't beat the free sample. At their sanitarium-factories in Battle Creek, C. W. Post and W. K. Kellogg were encouraging inmates to try such peculiar stuff as ready-to-eat cold cereal. In his Camden, New Jersey, laboratory, a twenty-five-year-old chemistry Ph.D. had finally perfected his Campbell's Condensed Tomato Soup. The advertising manager of Nestlé's Baby Food was designing campaigns to predispose mothers to Nestlé's "before the child is born." The Coca-Cola Company of Atlanta, Georgia, was giving away everything from pocket knives to Japanese fans in order to get customers into the habit of ordering a drink that, the firm's advertising director claimed, "Once started, is its own advertisement."

Novelties, posters, newspapers, car cards, and billboards helped the new national brands along, but much of the decisive advertising appeared in the new mass magazines. There, in the fraying back pages, the dramatic growth of food advertising is still visible. Between 1871 and 1900, for example, the number of food and beverage ads in one of the classiest monthlies, *Century*, rose from three and a half to a hundred sixty-nine pages annually. But that was a small beginning compared to what later "big books" with advertising pages fully integrated into the text would do. In *Ladies' Home Journal*, *Collier's*, *Woman's Home Companion*, and *Cosmopolitan*, the sensory impact of glossy food ads (understanding that food sales seem to depend as much upon color as taste, Campbell's reputedly supplied printers with its own tomato-red ink), was enhanced by the surrounding articles and stories that featured the daily triumphs of middle-class housekeeping. In these magazines, even recipes began to assume the dimensions of drama.

By the 1920s, the Lynds observed that the eating habits of Middletown families had changed radically since the 1890s:

These dietary changes have been facilitated also by the development of the modern women's magazines. . . . Through these periodicals, as well as through the daily press, billboards, and other channels, modern advertising pounds away at the habits of the Middletown housewife. Whole industries mobilize to impress a new dietary habit upon her.

Gone were the heavy, season-determined, time-consuming meals of the nineteenth century—the meat-and-potatoes breakfast, the huge formal midday dinner, the evening "tea." Housewives began to spend less time and energy preparing meals, and mealtime occasions became shorter and more fragmented: a light, hurry-up breakfast; an informal, quickly prepared lunch, oriented to schoolchildren's needs and taste; an evening dinner, now the main family event of the day, became the new pattern. These changes naturally developed gradually and were the consequence of a large number of social and economic forces—most significantly, the new schedules placed on daily life by the ordinary business day.

The content of the American diet changed along with the social and marketing context. Recent Department of Agriculture figures reveal a number of significant dietary changes since 1910. Although protein intake remained somewhat constant between 1910 and 1976, annual meat consumption rose from 135 to 170 pounds per person, flour and cereal products slid from 300 to approximately 130 pounds per person, and refined sweeteners (mainly sugar) jumped an alarming 50 percent. Consumption of vegetables climbed from nearly 110 pounds per person in 1920 to over 210 pounds in 1976, with processed vegetables finally surpassing fresh in 1955. A great many overlapping factors contributed to this dietary transformation, but it is safe to say that far fewer changes would have occurred without the day-to-day stimulations of advertising. As a food journal reported in the mid-twenties: "Advertising did not cause the American people to settle on three meals a day as the right number. But advertising does dictate to them largely what they eat at those meals."

In the early 1900s the biggest problem facing the manufacturers and advertisers of convenience foods was not the Pure Food and Drug movement (aggressively supported by leading women's magazines) but the instinctive sales resistance of housewives, who saw one of their primary domestic functions being co-opted. Studying the changing social mores of Middletowners, the Lynds noted that "the preparation of food in the nineties was one of woman's chief glories." And glories, advertisers knew, are not surrendered easily. Prejudice toward cans existed among housewives well into the 1920s, as women's clubs continued to debate such questions as "Shall a Conscientious Housewife Use Canned Foods?" Ready-to-eat cereals, canned soups, sun-belt fruit, and presliced grocer's bread had early won the sales battles over breakfast and lunch. Advertisers expected to have a tougher time persuading women to rely on convenience foods for the all-important dinner time, but by the 1930s even the evening meal was not an inviolable domain. With the disappearance of a servant class and the proliferation of extrafamilial activities centered around the diverse interests of age groups (sports, bridge clubs, and so on), heightened social value was placed on leisure time. And leisure, as Veblen had been the first to note and advertisers the first to exploit, had itself taken on the characteristics of a possession, a commodity that could, like any other acquisition, signal status and prestige. What the housewife might surrender in culinary repute (though advertisements never even hinted this) she gained in the prestige of leisure time.

The profound changes in eating habits which began to shape early-twentieth-century domestic life were paralleled by relentless experimentation in food retailing. So rapidly did new marketing methods replace one another that even as early as 1898 the Chase & Sanborn Company could run a deliberately nostalgic advertisement associating its coffee with the comfy atmosphere of the old-fashioned country store. In 1912 the already venerable A&P inaugurated its system of "economy stores" and, along with a number of other popular chains, began to exert enormous pressure on local retailers everywhere. As the chains expanded aggressively in the early 1920s, food advertisements would frequently document the struggle between the dedicated, community-oriented grocers and the anonymous, nationally organized invaders—a conflict then being duplicated in nearly every sector of American life. But by the 1930s the local grocers, despite some legislative assistance from a sympathetic Congress, found themselves confronted with a new menace, one that made even the streamlined chains look obsolete: the supermarket.

The history of the American diet since the 1930s is largely the history of the supermarket. But, as Daniel Boorstin observes, the supermarket was itself the natural outgrowth of the small, unit-packaged food product. For all of advertising's habitual nostalgia for the old-fashioned, the homemade, and the country store, nationally promoted packaged products, not chains or supermarkets, were ultimately responsible for the demise of the small, local grocer. Independents who constructed their factory-outlet style supermarkets during the Depression years knew that the steady volume of national advertising had made personalized in-store selling a thing of the past. Besides, if persistent advertising had reduced the ancient art of cooking to mere heating, then the complementary art of food shopping could be just as easily reduced to mere reaching: Predictably, some popular early supermarkets had names like "Grab It Here" and "Pay 'n Take It." Yet despite occasional lapses of merchandising taste, the new supermarkets did a booming business (24 percent of total grocery sales by 1940; 70 percent by 1960). The shopper contributed the automobile, the spacious refrigerator, and the disposition to yield to impulse buying; and the supermarket—assisted by newly perfected Du Pont cellophane, chrome, shiny shopping carts, beguiling fluorescent lights, and frozen food—spruced itself up to become the consumer Camelot of the Fabulous Fifties.

By the 1930s the indispensable automobile had also spawned another American institution—roadside food. Throughout the restless Depression years, travelers along Routes 30, 66, or "Rowt One" became addicted to hot dogs, Bar-B-Q sandwiches, ice cream cones, candy bars, popsicles, and the 12 oz. bottle of soda pop—hamburgers and french fries would come to roadside food a bit later. While fast food (i.e., anything that doesn't require a knife and fork) had been around since the early days of railroad lunch counters, roadside service had grown up simultaneously with the automobile. But the Depression created a whole new popular taste for the convenient drive-in eatery, whose marketing strategies often resembled those of the brash new supermarkets. It is no coincidence that the showpiece of standardized fast food, McDonald's, started in the 1940s as a California drive-in/self-service restaurant, and that much of its over-all success stems from its extravagant technological obsession to wrap and package everything. On many 1930s highways the food and packages themselves assumed awesome iconographic proportions as a new breed of roadside architects designed restaurants to look like hot dogs, tamales, and coffee cups. Some drivers may still recall the gigantic overflowing ice cream packages just outside of Hartford, Connecticut—a masterpiece of American vernacular.

Although they may share a common ancestry, the supermarket and fast-food chains compete fiercely today for the same consumer dollar. As increasing numbers of housewives find employment outside the home and as more families agree with the stroking slogan that they "deserve a break today" (the idiom cleverly suggesting both a refreshing pause from domestic routine and a breather from high food prices), fast-food restaurants continue to cut drastically into supermarket profits. Some companies (notably ITT) have attempted to infuse supermarket merchandising with new life by introducing nonfrozen, preservative-free, high-temperature precooked, retort-pouched food that can be prepared so quickly and simply —"No utensils, no cleanup" goes the copy—that "It's even easier than eating out." And the recent popularity of home microwave ovens that can cook hamburgers and frankfurters in less than two minutes may finally put the modern kitchen on a competitive footing with the neighborhood fast-food factory.

Yet for all the publicized highway feuding, supermarkets and fast-food chains taken together represent the marketing culmination of what sociologist Kenneth Kenniston calls our "new technological diet . . . the high-salt, high-fat, high-sugar diet that is becoming more and more the American norm." To Kenniston, conventional arguments about individual choice and "consumer sovereignty" are irrelevant because the dietary problem seems one of total environment:

> *The amount of chemical pollution and additives in the air, the water, and the food supply—in short, in the total diet of the average American child or adult—has markedly increased. Chemical additives in food recently reached an average of four pounds per person per year, double the level of a decade ago. Gross food additive use has also doubled in the past fifteen years—from 400 million pounds in 1960 to more than 800 million today—and it continues to grow. In 1973, about 1,300 chemicals were routinely added to manufactured food; by 1975, the figure had risen to more than 3,000.*
>
> Kenneth Kenniston,
> *All Our Children*
> (1977)

Yet, as the food industry knows, the number of health-conscious, chemical-scared consumers is also growing rapidly. As people begin to worry that the break they deserve today may actually turn out to be the chromosome break of tomorrow, the food industry will be forced to—in safety-belt fashion—mobilize its machinery for the production of less potentially harmful ingredients. For advertising, the issue isn't so much whether the nitrates and nitrites in bacon are cancer-causing carcinogens, but only whether the Surgeon General and a sufficient number of consumers truly believe they are. The major cereal companies are already under heavy attack from the Federal Trade Commission for "shared monopoly" practices as well as for their allegedly exploitative television advertising of highly sugared food for children. Fewer additives may mean less brand addiction; or someone may prove that the inherent chemical composition of food already makes eating dangerous to health. But one thing is certain: At a time when yoghurt and soul food can find marketing identities as fast foods, no one imagines a return to slow food as the dietary foundation of everyday life.

In 1863 James W. Tufts invented and patented his Arctic Soda Fountain apparatus for use in his Somerville, Massachusetts, drug store. Foreign travelers had long noted Americans' passion for ice-cold drinks.

GOOD HEAVENS FRIEND HOW CAN YOU WEAR AN OVERCOAT AND LOOK SO COOL
THIS WARM WEATHER?
I ALWAYS BRING MY OVERCOAT DOWN TOWN, AS I FIND AFTER DRINKING A GLASS
OF "BLAKELY'S BLIZZARD SODA," DRAWN FROM HIS "ARCTIC FOUNTAIN," THAT I AM COLD
THE BALANCE OF THE DAY.

194

TEN MINUTES FOR REFRESHMENTS.

1886

Fast food has a long tradition in America. An early English traveler, Captain Frederick Marryat, observed in 1839: "The cars stop, all the doors are thrown open, and out rush all, the passengers like boys out of school, and crowd round the tables to solace themselves with pies, patties, cakes, hard-boiled eggs, hams, custards and a variety of railroad luxuries too numerous to mention. The bell rings for departure, in they all hurry with their hands and mouths full, and off they go again until the next stopping-place induces them to relieve the monotony of the journey by masticating without being hungry."

"Excuse me—I know what I want, and I want what I asked for—**TOASTED CORN FLAKES** —Good day"

The package of the genuine bears this signature

W. K. Kellogg

A particularly haughty example of how manufacturers pressured grocers into stocking their products by appealing directly to "consumer sovereignty."

The Homes That Never Serve Oatmeal

In the lowliest sections of our largest cities not one home in twelve serves oats. Among the homes of the highest types we breed, seven-eighths are oatmeal homes

Where People Don't Know

We have made a house-to-house canvass of the tenement districts, both of New York and Chicago.

We have gone to the homes where are bred the anemic, the incapable, the undeveloped. Where tuberculosis finds its ready prey. Where the average child is extremely nervous, and it shows at school the lack of concentration.

We have talked with the mothers who know the least about that which contributes to health and growth, to mental and physical power. To the ignorant, the careless, the unadvised.

We find in those sections that not one home in twelve serves oats in any form. Most of the stores supplying those sections scarcely sell oatmeal at all.

Where People Do Know

We have canvassed hundreds of homes of the educated, the prosperous, the competent—the homes of the leaders in every walk of life. We have talked with the mothers who know food values, or who are guided by physicians who know.

We find that oatmeal is a regular diet in seven out of eight of these homes. The percentage is even larger if we leave out the childless homes. We find that four-fifths of all college students come from these oatmeal homes.

We find that eight-tenths of all physicians serve oatmeal at home. We find, in one university, that 48 out of 50 of the leading professors regularly eat oatmeal.

We find that Boston consumes 22 times as much oatmeal per capita as do two certain states with lowest average intelligence.

What Does This Mean?

This doesn't mean that some can afford oats and others cannot. Quaker Oats—the finest oatmeal produced—costs but one-half cent per dish. And a pound of Quaker Oats supplies the nutrition of six loaves of bread.

It means that some know, and others don't know, the food needs of a child. Some know, and some don't know, what the food of youth means in a child's career.

Some know, and some don't know, that the highest authorities on foods for the young give the first rank to oatmeal.

Facts About Oats

Oats are far richer than all other cereals in proteids, organic phosphorus and lecithin.

Proteid is the body-builder, the energy-giving food. The average man at the average work uses up $3\frac{1}{2}$ ounces of proteid per day.

Phosphorus is the most important element in the structure of the brain. Lecithin is the most important in the structure of the nerves and nerve centers.

Oats hold first place as a perfectly balanced food. It is the staple food of the world's hardiest race, famous for brain and brawn.

There is nothing else which compares with oats as a breakfast food for the young. Nothing else so well supplies the needs of the years of growth.

It is also a food of which one never tires—one of the most delicious foods in existence.

Quaker Oats

Just the Rich, Plump, Luscious Oats

By 62 siftings we pick out the richest, plumpest grains that grow for use in Quaker Oats. We get only ten pounds of such oats from a bushel. It is thus we secure that enticing flavor found only in Quaker Oats.

Millions of homes, almost the world over, have found this the best of the oat foods.

It has a larger sale than all others combined because children like it best.

Look for the
Quaker trade-mark
on every package

<u>Regular size package, 10c</u>

Family size package for smaller cities and country trade, 25c.

The prices noted do not apply in the extreme West or South.

The Quaker Oats Company
CHICAGO

(47)

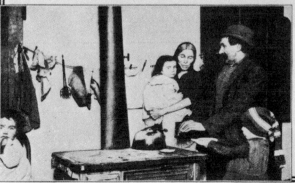

A Home of the Underfed

The Hurry-Up Breakfast

How much of a man's fortune depends on his breakfast?

A good Breakfast, not too big, goes a long way toward making a man feel good.

When a man feels good he can do his best work.

Now it sometimes (not always) takes time to prepare a good breakfast.

The exception is the breakfast with

Post Toasties

Here's a breakfast that's ever ready to serve instantly—that's delicious—that makes a man (or woman or child) feel good—for it *is* good.

The thin crispy wafers of toasted corn with some milk or cream and sugar (if you like it) should be responsible for a whole lot of success.

Post Toasties start off a good many thousands right each morning.

"The Memory Lingers"

Postum Cereal Company, Limited,
Battle Creek, Mich., U. S. A.

Canadian Postum Cereal Co., Ltd.,
Windsor, Ontario, Canada

1912

In pre-World War I America, industrial engineers had begun to examine factory labor from the point of view of Frederick W. Taylor's highly influential Principles of Scientific Management *(1911). This advertisement illustrates how Taylor's new "time study" methods were beginning to insinuate themselves into everyday household affairs.*

"I envy the fortunate buyer
This gem of good taste to acquire!
Such a *chef-d'oeuvre* if hung in the Louvre,
The nations would flock to admire!"

A Masterpiece

To get the full enjoyment of Campbell's Tomato Soup eat it slowly, deliberately. Taste and enjoy every spoonful. Then you realize why so many people of critical tastes pronounce this popular *Campbell* "kind" the standard of perfection in tomato soup.

"The object of art," declared Sir Joshua Reynolds, "is to *carry out Nature's intention.*" And what this famous "philosopher of art," as he is called, said about painting applies aptly to this masterpiece of culinary art—

Campbell's Tomato Soup

Nature, in the red-ripe, vine-matured tomato, provides the "color-scheme" and the keynote of flavor, as you might say; while the accomplished Campbell chefs, by blending the best part of this natural product with the best of other wholesome ingredients, unite the piquant freshness of nature with the nourishing quality demanded in a food product for daily use.

Here you have richness combined with delicacy; a touch of natural sweetness—never cloying; a fine tonic zest which enlivens the appetite and lends added savor to the entire meal. In every sense a *chef-d'oeuvre* to grace the best appointed table.

No wonder that practical housewives order this tempting soup from the grocer by the dozen or the case.

Asparagus	Chicken-Gumbo (Okra)	Mock Turtle	Pepper Pot
Beef	Clam Bouillon	Mulligatawny	Printanier
Bouillon	Clam Chowder	Mutton	Tomato
Celery	Consommé	Ox Tail	Tomato-Okra
Chicken	Julienne	Pea	Vegetable
			Vermicelli-Tomato

Campbell's Soups

LOOK FOR THE RED-AND-WHITE LABEL

Portrait of Andy Warhol as a Campbell Kid?

1919

"Canning gives the American family—especially in cities and factory towns—a kitchen garden where all good things grow, and where it is always harvest time. There are more tomatoes in a ten-cent can than could be bought fresh in city markets for that sum when tomatoes are at their cheapest, and this is true of most other tinned foods. A regular Arabian Nights garden, where raspberries, apricots, olives, and pineapples, always ripe, grow side by side with peas, pumpkins, spinach; a garden with baked beans, vines and spaghetti bushes, and sauerkraut beds, and great cauldrons of hot soup, and through it running a branch of the ocean in which one can catch salmon, lobsters, crabs and shrimp, and dig oysters and clams."

James H. Collins, *The Story of Canned Foods* (1924)

When I drive
Around
In my costly motor car
(as Ring Lardner says)
I always take
A spare tire
An extra tube
And
My Life-Savers.
I can't smoke—
The ashes blow
In my eye
Or my friend's eyes
And the cigar
Burns up one side,
Or goes out.
But I want something
–don't know just why–
To turn over
And twist around
On my tongue
The answer is
Life-Savers,
So snappy
So comforting
So smooth and cool,
They keep my throat
Moist and flexible
And each one
Sort of wears down
Slowly
Giving off that spicy
Honey-fied
Aromatic
Piquant flavor
Until it's just a thin
Brittle
Delicious rim
Of sweetness;
And it breaks
And is gone,
Like a pleasant dream,
But I can dream it
All over again
Whenever I like.

MINT PRODUCTS CO., Inc.
New York—Montreal

6c

PEP·O·MINT
LIFE SAVERS
THE CANDY MINT WITH THE HOLE

THE CANDY MINT WITH THE HOLE

CL·O·VE LIFE SAVERS
The spicy, breath-sweetening snap of Cloves.

WINT·O·GREEN LIFE SAVERS
No flavor was ever more popular than Wintergreen.

CINN·O·MON LIFE SAVERS
Crisp, delicious—like apple pie and cookies—that's Cinnamon.

LIC·O·RICE LIFE SAVERS
The old favorite flavor—Licorice good for a "tickly" throat, too.

1920

The candy with the hole here capitalizes on the Imagist poetry then in vogue.
The connection of Life Savers with American poetry goes deeper than clever
copy, however: The popular mint was developed and marketed by the father of
the well-known American poet Hart Crane. A Cleveland candy manufacturer
more interested in old-fashioned chocolates, Clarence Crane lost interest in his
poorly packaged product and sold in 1913.

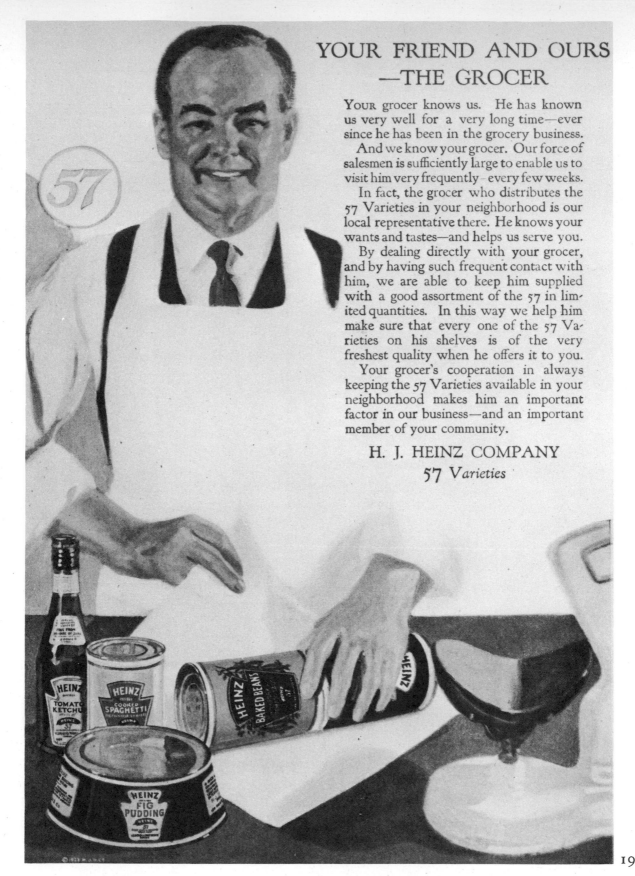

YOUR FRIEND AND OURS —THE GROCER

YOUR grocer knows us. He has known us very well for a very long time—ever since he has been in the grocery business.

And we know your grocer. Our force of salesmen is sufficiently large to enable us to visit him very frequently - every few weeks.

In fact, the grocer who distributes the 57 Varieties in your neighborhood is our local representative there. He knows your wants and tastes—and helps us serve you.

By dealing directly with your grocer, and by having such frequent contact with him, we are able to keep him supplied with a good assortment of the 57 in limited quantities. In this way we help him make sure that every one of the 57 Varieties on his shelves is of the very freshest quality when he offers it to you.

Your grocer's cooperation in always keeping the 57 Varieties available in your neighborhood makes him an important factor in our business—and an important member of your community.

H. J. HEINZ COMPANY
57 Varieties

1923

Like many food processors, the H. J. Heinz Company came out in support of the local grocer during the expansion of chain stores in the early 1920s. But brand-name shelf goods were already helping to make the neighborhood grocer obsolete as the perfunctory wrapping and superfluous scale unintentionally demonstrate.

Just one thing to do
and it's ready to serve

NO cooking; the actual cooking has already been done. No sauce to make. No cheese to add. No seasoning. The only thing left for you is the heating—five minutes of heating.

For the busy homemaker Beech-Nut Spaghetti is a friend at almost any time of the day or week. Quick luncheons at short notice—Beech-Nut Spaghetti. Sunday night suppers—Beech-Nut Spaghetti. As main dish, as side dish, or served with bacon, mushrooms, sausage, chopped meat—Beech-Nut Spaghetti is delicious every time.

Sauced with rich, creamy cheese and sound, juicy tomatoes, Beech-Nut Spaghetti presents a well-balanced dish, with a flavor mellow and rare. A surprising treat to all spaghetti lovers and wonderfully satisfying for specially keen attacks of hunger in the family. Keep a supply at home for everyday use and for emergencies. Beech-Nut Packing Company, Canajoharie, N. Y.

Beech-Nut   Prepared Spaghetti

BEECH-NUT QUALITY   AT EVERYDAY PRICES

1926

The point is made simply and succinctly: Cooking is heating. Later convenience food ads would contain "recipes" or require an extra ingredient so the housewife could feel she was actually creating a meal for her family.

• this little bride
went to a PIGGLY WIGGLY *Store*

. . . and shopped as expertly as her Grandmother!

AND WHY shouldn't she? For in the friendly, orderly aisles of a Piggly Wiggly Store, even the most inexperienced shopper feels right at home. With everything in plain sight—arranged for quick and easy self-serving—you can go through the turnstile without a menu idea in your head, and come out with a well-balanced meal in your basket.

Here you can take *your* pick from the fresh fruits and vegetables that speak of near-by orchards and gardens. Here you can take your time to study the labels on cans and bottles and boxes. Shelf after shelf of names you know and quality you can be sure of. One delightful discovery after another in the way of new and different foods. Visible meal-time suggestions that give you a happy interest in meal-planning. Notice, too, that similar products are grouped together, so you can make comparisons and make your selections, wisely and well. And when you look at the price-tags—above

each item—you'll see that someone has already done your "bargaining" for you. For Piggly Wiggly prices are always consistently low. And what can give you greater satisfaction than knowing you are buying the very best food and still keeping well within your budget?

Tomorrow morning, step into the Piggly Wiggly Store in your neighborhood. Serve yourself and see how much farther your money goes when you are both "salesman" and "customer."

Go through the turnstile without a menu idea in your head

Come out with a well-balanced meal in your basket

PIGGLY WIGGLY *Stores*

© 1932. P.W.A.C.

1932

The supermarkets introduced "impulse buying" and advertising stressed it. This ad for one of the earliest supermarket chains spells out what was to become the guiding philosophy of consumption for future generations of American shoppers.

THE MAN YOU MARRIED WAS ONCE A BOY...

★ *Before he got big he used to shinny up a tree for green apples. He used to dodge a rock-salt gun to steal watermelons. And he never missed supper if he suspected maw was servin' roastin' ears.*

You can bring those days back to the boy in that husband of yours, Mrs. Whatever-Your-Married-Name-Is! ... Bring 'em back with great big golden kernels of corn.... Bring 'em back with fresh corn that comes in a can.... Bring 'em back with corn-on-the-cob-without-the-cob.

★ Niblets is that mealtime magician. *Niblets* is the name—corn-on-the-cob-without-the-cob ... Niblets is unlike all other corn because it is packed from an entirely different *breed* (Del Maiz). Fifteen years of seed culture have produced this exclusive new kind of corn with taller, more luscious kernels. This means that Niblets corn can be cut from the cob deep enough to give you whole, unbroken kernels without the tough cob fibers. Packed in vacuum to keep that fresh, garden flavor. Five generous servings in every can. ... If the boy in every man loves Niblets ... how about boys that are still boys? Sure, everyone and his brother loves Niblets ... serve and see!

There's only one Niblets (Reg. U. S. Pat. Off.)—with the Green Giant on label. Packed exclusively by Minnesota Valley Canning Co., Le Sueur, Minn., and Fine Foods of Canada, Ltd., Tecumseh, Ont.

Niblets FRESH CORN OFF THE COB

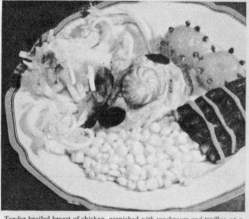

Tender broiled breast of chicken, garnished with mushroom and truffles, on a thin slice of broiled ham. Green asparagus, banded with pimento strips. Crisp curls of young celery. Whole apricots garlanded with cloves. And finally, sweet, tender, golden Niblets, hot and buttered. Isn't that a meal!

206

The Widow and the Flounder

1. What is this strange power I have over widows? Take the Widow Jones. Just to make conversation, I happen to mention how much I love flounder. And what does she do but invite me for supper . . . and dish up as sizzlin' an *ocean-fresh* flounder as I ever tasted since I left the sea!!!

2. Ocean-fresh, did I say! By Judas, you could almost see salt water still on it! "Where in tarnation did you get this wonderful fish?" I says . . . So she told me the wondrous story of Birds Eye Flounder Fillets.

3. Seems Birds Eye fishermen go out in the North Atlantic where the sweetest flounders swim. They take the freshest flounders in the load, and Quick-Freeze the meaty fillets only 4 hours after the boat makes port.

4. This Quick-Freezing miracle, she says, seals in all the ocean-flavor, and brings it a-glowin' in freshness to your dinner table . . . even if you live in Kansas, like us, a thousand miles from the ocean.

5. Now, I say to you . . . if you love flounder (and I'm sorry for you if you don't) . . . but if you love it and haven't yet tried Birds Eye, you've still got a lot to live for . . . especially when you figure out how cheap it is . . .

6. For the Widow says that Birds Eye Flounder Fillets come fuss-free—all washed and trimmed. She says it would take 4 lbs. of whole flounder to give you as much as you get from 1 lb. of Birds Eye. (P.S. She's been specializin' on *all* Birds Eye Foods lately, and says she'll serve them thirty-five times a week if a certain gentleman keeps calling. I wonder could she mean me!)

7. Where you can get these wonderful foods! . . . You may not always find a Birds Eye dealer right around the corner. For all stores do not yet have these marvelous foods. But it will be worth your while to look for one. Finding it, can bring you the food thrill of your life. Remember, Birds Eye is the pioneer in Quick-Frozen foods and *still* represents only the *TOP* QUALITY. Therefore be *sure* to look for the Birds Eye in the window, and the Birds Eye on the package.

Try these wonderful foods today!

Oysters—Yes, in June
Red Perch—sweet and delicious
Lobstermeat—for summer salads
Fancy-Fresh Bay Scallops
Salmon Steaks—center cuts

Baby Green Lima Beans
Peas and Carrots—garden-fresh
Real Country Style Fryers
Tender, Young Broilers
Chopped Steak—never ground!

And there are more than 50 others—all cleaned, trimmed, ready to cook or serve. Get a box today!

FARM-FRESH FOODS—IN PACKAGES

If you don't know where to buy Birds Eye Foods—or want more information about them, just write Frosted Foods Sales Corp., 250 Park Ave., New York, N.Y.

Copyright, 1940, General Foods Corp.

1940

208

MEAT AND THE JOB

The ability to "keep doing" depends largely on well-being . . . Proteins are essential to well-being and to life itself . . . They build and repair body tissues . . . Only your daily foods can supply them . . . The proteins of meat are the right kind—of highest biologic value

When your family asks for meat, isn't it good the flavor they reach for brings them valuable nutrients too . . . nutrients which they need . . . which contribute much to the body's well-being?

Human nature's "yen" for that good meat flavor is one of the most consistent manifestations in the history of food.

In these wartime days, however, we often have to plan more carefully to keep Meat on the Table.

Fortunately, all cuts of meat, from stew to steak, and in between, contain complete, highest-quality proteins. Proteins differ widely in various foods due to the kinds and amounts of amino (a-mee-no) acids which they contain.

The proteins of meat contain all ten of the so-called amino acids* which are considered essential, in quantities that parallel the body's needs and in a form the body readily uses. That's why meat is so often referred to as "the yardstick of protein foods."

Not acids as commonly known, but a name used by science to define certain chemical substances.

AMERICAN MEAT INSTITUTE
Headquarters, Chicago. Members throughout the United States

Smile with "The Life of Riley," featuring William Bendix, every Sunday afternoon at 3:00 — 3:30 EWT. Blue Network. See paper for local station.

A WAR MEAT-MEAL

THE VERSATILE MEAT LOAF—*a grand extender for a little meat—equally nutritious when made from beef, pork, veal or lamb. Vary the meat—vary the sauces—it tastes good hot or cold. Consult your favorite recipe book.*

In addition to complete, highest-quality proteins, all meat contains B vitamins (thiamine, riboflavin, niacin) and minerals (iron, copper, phosphorus). These nutritional essentials are not stored in the body to any appreciable extent—must be supplied in the daily foods you eat.

This Seal means that all nutritional statements made in this advertisement are acceptable to the Council on Foods and Nutrition of the American Medical Association.

1944

Tony and "friend" on the Garry Moore Show

Garry Moore says: **"Won't they tell even _you_, Tony?"**

Tony: No, the Kellogg's folks won't tell me, or anyone, how they make
their special sugar frosting. But I could be persuaded to
reveal . . .

Garry: Go on, go on—tell your old pal, Gare . . .

Tony: Well, O.K. Kellogg's secret sugar frosting makes
these crisp flakes of corn gr-r-reat
for breakfast and . . . here try 'em yourself for a snack.

Garry: Amazing! No wonder so many people enjoy—

Tony: Enjoy Kellogg's Sugar Frosted Flakes? Well,
I should say they do. Confidentially, they're the . . .
here, try some more.

Garry: Very generous of you, Mr. T. M-m-m-man! These
ARE the _GREATEST!_

Kellogg's SUGAR FROSTED FLAKES

1955

_The cast of characters on Kidvid has changed but the products are basically the
same. The illustration also shows an early attempt of print advertising to cash
in on the growing power of television._

Quick frozen—for quick serving

An old-fashioned fried chicken dinner

with fluffy mashed potatoes

Remember how Mom used to get up early every Sunday to fix a scrumptious chicken dinner? *We* do . . . so we've patterned our newest TV Dinner after that good, old-fashioned feast. However, *our* complete chicken dinners are all cooked and ready to pop into the oven on their own individual serving trays. No thawing.

In 25 minutes, you'll be enjoying this irresistible well-balanced meal: Plenty of extra-meaty, extra-tender, golden-fried Swanson Chicken . . . garden-fresh vegetables . . . and fluffy mashed potatoes whipped in milk.

You never cooked so well, so fast before. Do get Swanson TV Chicken Dinners for your family right away. Now available at frozen food counters.

Swanson TV Dinners

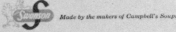

C. A. SWANSON & SONS · OMAHA 8, NEBRASKA

Made by the makers of Campbell's Soups

Introducing a classic phenomenon of the Fabulous Fifties: the TV dinner.

What do steaks sizzle for?

Hunt's of course!

...because Hunt's is rich and thick
and spiced with imagination!

Hunt Foods, Inc., Fullerton, Calif.

NEWEST LOOK!

NEW BOTTLES, NEW LABELS, FOR THESE SIMPLY DELICIOUS KRAFT DRESSINGS

Smooth-pouring bottles so elegant you could put them right on the table! Smart new labels with good food ideas on the back! Inside—America's two favorite Frenches, and a great Oil & Vinegar by Kraft.

All Kraft Dressings are made with liquid vegetable oil, high in poly-unsaturates.

Here's the real man-type dressing that has so many fans. Robust, sparkling Miracle French!

So delightful—Kraft Oil & Vinegar, gently seasoned with herbs. Try Kraft's creamy new Coleslaw Dressing, too.

New look, yes, but the same great dressing— savory Kraft French that the whole family loves.

Salad Hat by Lilly Daché

1962

How many frozen meals can a man eat before icicles form on his heart?

The beauty of a good, home-cooked meal is the good things it tells a man. There's a message.

But frozen meals can be cold, cold all the way.

Naturally, from time to time, you have to serve dinners that don't take a lot of time and trouble.

But they should taste like somebody did.

Schrafft's Frozen Foods do.

We're not going to tell you that Schrafft's Frozen Creamed Chicken whispers of moonlight and magnolias.

But those generous chunks of tender young chicken do say, "I know what it takes to satisfy *your* appetite, sweetheart."

And the delicately seasoned cream sauce *is* kind of delicious.

And if it doesn't win you looks of love as you set it on the table and waltz out the door, at least it won't get you icy stares.

FRANK G. SHATTUCK COMPANY

HURRY-UP MEALS YOU DON'T HAVE TO MAKE EXCUSES FOR.

SCHRAFFT'S

McDonald's introduces Big Mac. A meal disguised as a sandwich.

It's as good as it is big. Under scoops of our own secret sauce are two lean patties of 100% beef.

There's a slice of melty cheddar-blend cheese; some fresh, crisp lettuce; and crunchy dill pickle slices. All wrapped up in a freshly toasted sesame seed bun.

Come now, bring us your bigger than average appetite.

It's all at your kind of place.

McDonald's

1969

"When I want meat, I want a steak. But when I want a hamburger, I want a Big Mac. It has all those disreputable things—cheese made of glue, Russian dressing three generations removed from the steppes, and this very thin patty of something that is close enough to meat. It's an incredibly decadent eating experience."

Gael Greene, New York food critic

What we do to our internal environment shouldn't happen to the Hudson River.

A word on your personal ecology system from Dannon Yogurt.

Most of us are all wrought up over what people have done to our environment. To our air, land and water. And our wildlife.

But some of the stuff we put *inside* our systems shouldn't happen to a dog—or to the Hudson River.

Over-spiced. Over-fat. Over-loaded with additives.

Read the fine print on the back of some yogurt packages.

You may find some strange contents. Chemicals with unpronounceable names. Artificial flavoring. Artificial sweeteners. Things that nature never intended for your ecology.

We don't put anything artificial into Dannon Yogurt. Because we don't have to.

No preservatives, for example. Because we use fresh-cooked fruit preserves and we deliver our yogurt quickly—direct to stores in our own trucks. No hanging around in warehouses. So what do we need preservatives for?

We don't use artificial stabilizers, because our yogurt is naturally thick and smooth.

Artificial flavor? No laboratory could possibly improve on the taste that Dannon gave yogurt.

We just don't use additives period.

Our yogurt is *naturally* quite reasonable in calories. Besides, it's between 98 and 99% fat-free.

What's good enough for nature is good enough for Dannon. And for you.

The fight against pollution begins *inside* you.

The natural yogurt, no artificial anything

FASHION

No account of a society can be complete without a graphic survey of clothing—its gradual adaptation into costume, and its sudden transformation into fashion. The following set of advertisements features some of the major trends in American clothing history, including ordinary, everyday dress as well as the flamboyant and bizarre.

Throughout colonial times, clothing styles adhered pretty closely to British standards and clearly reflected, as did all European apparel, the social rank of its wearer. Deviations could be serious: A seventeenth-century New England law established harsh penalties for people caught dressing above their social station. By the end of the eighteenth century, however, the drive toward political freedom set off a corresponding independence in American dress. Homespun became a kind of radical chic, as well-bred American girls proudly displayed plain, rough dresses as a sign of their liberation from decadent European fashions. Washington appeared at his inauguration not in full regalia, as some arch-conservatives would have liked, but in a Connecticut cloth suit fashioned by a tailor whose advertisement he had seen in a New York newspaper.

Revolutions, of both the hard and soft varieties, can have a profound effect on clothing—at least temporarily. For most Americans, durable versions of homemade and homespun, like butternut cloth or buckskin breeches and frontier fringe, would serve well into the nineteenth century. But with the prosperity of the 1820s and 1830s an emerging affluent urban class gladly abandoned its domestic plain style for the fancier garments of the newly established tailors, dressmakers, and milliners whose tasteful engravings figure as the finest products of early American advertising art.

During this time, Paris, not London, set the style for tailored American apparel, taking a lead which, despite a few flops and falterings, it would always maintain.

In the 1830s expensive magazines like *Godey's Lady's Book* and *Graham's* began imitating European fashion announcements by featuring each month an attractively hand-painted watercolor of the latest styles. Other American magazines soon followed suit, and the fashion plate became a highly persuasive form of publicity as well as an eagerly awaited object of popular art: Scarlett O'Hara found, much to her irritation, that the Civil War rudely interrupted her subscription to *Godey's*. Deriving mainly from the handsome illustrations for late-eighteenth-century novels, the fashion plate, though detached from any text, retained a fictional atmosphere in its groupings, gestures, and drawing-room or pastoral backdrops. Originally, advertisements for tailors and their fashions had focused primarily on shops, skills, and unmodeled garments. With the colorful fashion plate, pioneering advertisers discovered the promotional value of constructing a fictional milieu for the season's latest collections.

Yet the fashion plates of *Godey's* and *Graham's* had very little impact on the lives of most American men and women, who, as the industrial revolution gathered steam, began to shift from homemade to ready-made apparel. A ready-made clothing industry had developed slowly in the early decades of the nineteenth century, producing cheap and unappealing garments and accessories for laborers and sailors. The industry by the 1840s, however, had found a huge market in the South, as plantation owners increasingly relied on coarse factory-produced clothing for their slaves. In addition to all their other sufferings, slaves had to endure the trials and errors of a new insensitive industry. As an ex-slave put it: "We prays for the end of tribulations and the end of beatings and for shoes that fit our feet." At first sold only in socially disreputable "slopshops," ready-mades improved in fit and fashion as the industry improved in technique and marketing. Starting with overcoats, the new industry rapidly altered its own image by producing inexpensive but respectable lines that could easily compete with prestigious tailor-made goods. By 1860, well over 4,000 factories turned out nearly 80 million dollars' worth of clothing.

But it was not until the 1870s, after the unprecedented industrial demands of the Civil War had shown that factories could mass-produce garments to keep pace with the newly invented sewing machine's 125 stitches per minute, that ready-made clothing finally evolved into a big business. The pace of fashion changed, too. Manufacturers learned they could introduce new articles of clothing (like lightweight topcoats) in new shapes and colors and rely on the advertising pages of the big-city dailies and the new mass magazines for effective promotion. As fashion came to be dictated more by the clothier than by the tailor, it assumed a pivotal role in determining the design and duration of ready-made apparel. Fashion itself developed into an industry, and fashionableness, once the privilege and paranoia of a tiny, wealthy class, became a social and cultural possibility for millions.

Fashion had always depended on skillful copying, but the phenomenal success of interchangeable machine-made clothing resulted in a new law of mass culture: Imitation accelerates obsolescence. A new fashion rapidly replaces an old—as Veblen crankily pointed out—not necessarily because the new one is more aesthetically pleasing, but because the more affluent a community grows the more consumption will demand the kind of conspicuous waste inherent in the trivial succession of styles. Veblen's observations in his classic, *The Theory of the Leisure Class*, introduced the subject of fashion to serious socioeconomic analysis and provided a way to understand the vagaries of fashion in a civilization that was beginning to base its hierarchies on economic status rather than social station. Toward the end of the nineteenth century, as consumption became not just a means of satisfying needs but a continual reaffirmation of one's social and economic identity, fashion developed into an intricate index of the minute gradations within a predominantly middle-class culture.

It is impossible today to comprehend all the moral values and social nuances represented by clothing during the Victorian period. The men and especially the women of that age have come down to us as merely looking outrageously overdressed, overprotected in all seasons by layer after layer of decorated apparel. In 1890 a worried physician observed that "the cultured woman of the city dressed in the height of fashion wore an average of 37 pounds of street costume in the winter months, of which 19 pounds suspended from the waist." To be so wrapped up, so "packaged," of course, proclaimed one's property value. The well-dressed, brocaded woman, smothered in fabric and whalebone, was a living advertisement of her husband's capacity to spend exorbitantly—she was a walking embodiment of "conspicuous waist." In their heavy vests, suits, and greatcoats, the men seemed designed by their clothiers to convey an air of stolidity and thickness, to look unshakable in office and home. In the wild and woolly age of industry, a man's worth could almost be gauged by his girth.

But the "horseless" age would be a "hoopless" one. The increase in leisure time, the growing popularity of outdoor sports, the bicycle fads and motor car fantasies, all contributed to a reshaping of American clothing styles. Tight-lacing and stiff apparel gave way to casual, more flexible fashions, and the American clothing industry began to take a leading role in the development of sportswear. The shirtwaist had appeared early in the 1890s and, along with the walking skirt, offered women an exhilarating new freedom of movement that led directly to the corsetless, boyish figures of the 1920s. Men's clothiers also picked up on the athletic image coming into vogue during the Progressive Era by designing jackets and trousers that emphasized rugged physical strength. By the end of the First World War a slimmer style had come to dominate men's fashion, and the stiff collar—long a symbol of masculine starchiness—was made obsolete by the daring introduction of a dress shirt with soft attached collars. From the 1920s on, casual wear plays a steady role in the evolution and convolutions of American fashion. As the eclectic, jock fashions of the 1970s amply reveal, sportswear represents for the latest generation of American designers an exciting repertoire of native attire, a rich source of stylistic permutation and combination.

Until quite recently, the American fashion industry has been noted more for its promotional capability than for its originality. Paris, Rome, and London may vie with each other as fashion centers, but none has the advertising clout of New York City, where, if a style takes, the appearance of American men and women can be totally revamped from head to toe in a few months. In the late 1960s the mini-skirt, a London import, transformed the wardrobes of American women nearly as fast as a new Beatles release reached the top of the charts. Yet not all styles can be promoted so successfully. In its attempts to cash in on the idiosyncratic styles of celebrities, activists, and subcultures, the fashion industry has often bombed. The very early effort to turn bloomers—a feminist costume created in 1850 by a young American woman—into high fashion failed miserably, even after it was recycled in London for some much needed credibility. Short shorts, the sexy 1950s street style generated by American teenagers, failed to make the fashion grade when reintroduced as the "hot pants" of the early 1970s. Certain styles depend on a spontaneous, colloquial sprightliness and wit in order to flourish.

American fashions, as Ernest Hemingway and Louis Armstrong discovered, are often native styles that have been to Paris. Consider the denim look of the last two decades. Blue jeans had been around since 1850, when they were carved out of a tough medieval French fabric (*serge de Nîmes*, hence denim) by a Bavarian immigrant for California prospectors. Cheap and sturdy, dungarees were popularized by farmers and ranch hands long before they made their factory debut during World War II. From there they became even more widespread as the costume of college students and juvenile delinquents. But like a great variety of American sportswear and work gear, jeans did not achieve fashion status until they had been refashioned and refitted by such Paris designers as Givenchy and St. Laurent, who added a touch of chic the House of Levi Strauss had never attempted to give.

One feature of fashion advertising is its sensitivity to practically every area of social and economic change. In 1919 a University of California anthropologist examined minutely thousands of fashion advertisements dating back to the 1860s to prove precisely how styles of clothing exemplify social cycles of stability and change. Though seldom put to such scholarly uses, fashion advertisements nevertheless can condense a great deal of cultural information in a few striking details. And so interdependent is the fashion industry itself with most other forms of enterprise that changes in one sector often have a dramatic impact on another: The heady promotion of underarm deodorants, for example, following the introduction of the 1920s sleeveless frock; the matching accessories and make-up industry following the mod fashions of the 1960s. Virtually every advertisement in this volume shows, directly or indirectly, some degree of cultural or commercial interaction with the all-encompassing world of fashion.

At any given time in most societies a large number of costumes, styles, and fashions compete and interact with each other to form the clothing of the period. But so strongly do some styles of dress seem to embody the collective sensibility of an age, that our visual impressions of past periods (these usually ticked off conveniently by decades) are often inescapably determined by a few stereotypical clothing features: the leg-o'-mutton sleeves of the 1830s, the crinoline of the 1860s, the 1880s bustle, the Coke-bottle look of the Gay Nineties, the broad shoulders of the Progressive Era, the skimpy chemise of the 1920s, the slinky satin of the 1930s, the button-down 1950s, the mini-skirted 1960s, the sweat chic of the 1970s. It hardly matters that a particular costume may have been worn by few or by many, for a season or an entire decade, or that each fashion coexisted with many others. Every period of American history seems branded with its stylistic logo: Who can conjure up the Roaring Twenties without imagining a John Held flapper, all silky legs, pearls, and insouciant slouch? The advertisements included here illustrate some of these outstanding episodes in the annals of American fashion. And to balance the ensemble a few famous flops are featured along the way.

1842

"BLOOMERISM,"
OR THE
NEW FEMALE COSTUME OF 1851,

As it has appeared in the various Cities and Towns.

BOSTON: S. W. WHEELER, 66 Cornhill—1851.

1851

The young women factory-workers at Lowell, Massachusetts, were so taken with bloomers that they organized a Bloomer Institute for: "(1). Mutual improvement—in literature, science and morals; (2) Emancipation from the thralldom of that dictatorial French goddess Fashion, and an exemplary enforcement of the Right and Duty to dress according to the demands and proffers of Nature." The Bloomer was designed by Libby Miller in 1850 and popularized by feminists Elizabeth Cady Stanton and Amelia Bloomer.

MADAME DEAN'S SPINAL SUPPORTING CORSETS.

They support the Spine, relieve the muscles of the back, brace the shoulders in a natural and easy manner, imparting **graceful carriage** to the wearer without discomfort, **expanding the chest,** thereby giving **full action to the lungs,** and **health** and **comfort** to the body. Take the place of the ORDINARY CORSET in every respect, and are made of fine **Coutil,** in the best manner, in various styles and sold by agents everywhere at **popular prices. Mrs. Wm. Papes,** Keota, Iowa, says:—I have been an invalid for six years, have travelled extensively for health, yet never received as much benefit as I have in a few weeks wear, of your MADAME DEAN'S CORSET. I am gaining strength all the time, and could not do without it. It has proven to me a *godsend.*

FREE Our new book entitled: "Dress Reform for Ladies" with elegant wood engraving and Biography of **Worth,** the **King of Fashion,** Paris; also our **New Illustrated Catalogue** sent **free** to any address on receipt of two 2-cent stamps to pay postage and packing.

AGENTS WANTED for these celebrated Corsets. No experience required. Four orders per day give the agent **$150 monthly.** Our agents report from four to twenty sales daily. **$3.00** outfit. Send at once for terms and full particulars. SCHIELE & CO., 390 Broadway, New York.

1894

"The corset is, in economic theory, substantially a mutilation, undergone for the purpose of lowering the subject's vitality and rendering her permanently and obviously unfit for work. It is true, the corset impairs the personal attractions of the wearer, but the loss suffered on that score is offset by the gain in reputability which comes of her visibly increased expensiveness and infirmity."

Thorstein Veblen, *The Theory of the Leisure Class* (1899)

COPYRIGHT 1907, THE HOUSE OF KUPPENHEIMER, CHICAGO

The Beaufort

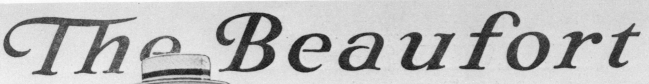

(By the House of Kuppenheimer)

A CRISP and definite new note is struck in the Young Men's BEAUFORT for Spring, 1915.

Take it point by point in its style details:—The original collar and lapel. The natural shoulders, innocent of padding. The shaped body with *military high-waist effect.* The five-button waistcoat, worn with the top button open, giving a decided effect as it rolls back from a rich scarf and a background of neat shirt pattern.

The BEAUFORT registers all the new fashion essentials. More than that—it *is* the fashion. The ensemble is right. The effect is there. Young men with a sense of Dress know how important this is. It means more than the appearance of the clothes in the store or show window. It is the way they look on the man who wears them.

It is this knack of design, quite as much as the niceties of fit and tailoring, that young men recognize in the House of Kuppenheimer—that makes them strong for Kuppenheimer Styles, and go out of their way if necessary to find them.

Young men know what they want and who is producing it. They saw in the work of this House as early as last season the first hint of the new *military* styles—which tells them plainly enough who leads in these fashions this Spring.

Prices—$20 to $40

Kuppenheimer Clothes are sold by a representative store in nearly every Metropolitan center of the United States and Canada. Your name on a post card will bring you our Book of Fashions.

THE HOUSE OF KUPPENHEIMER
CHICAGO

Copyright, 1915, The House of Kuppenheimer

226

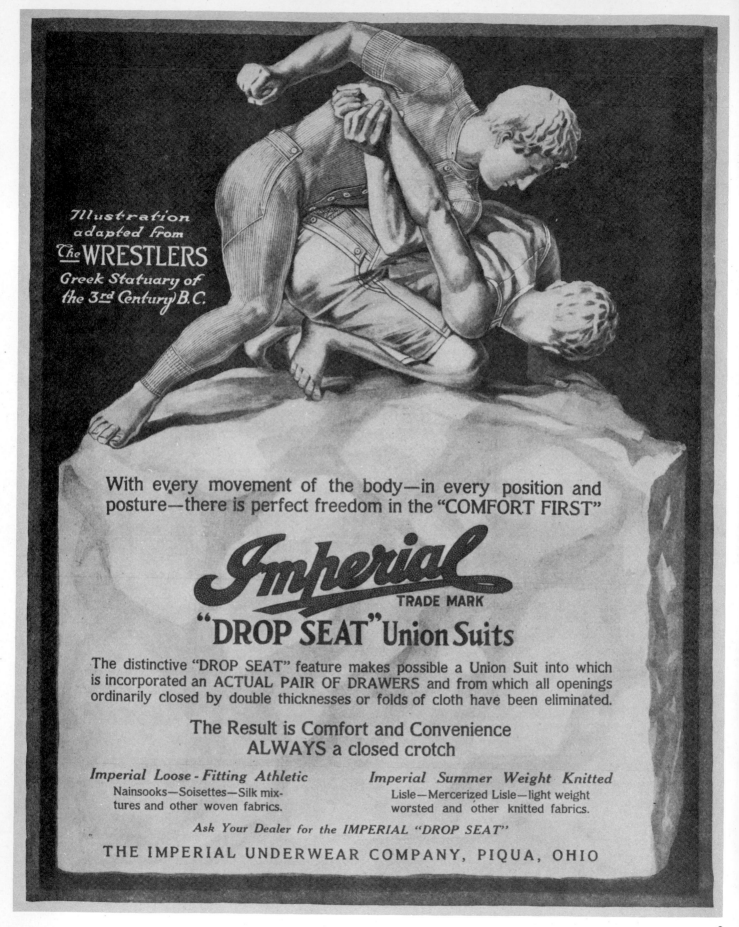

1918

THIS NEW LUXURIOUS FREEDOM!

SCANTIES *by Model*

REG. U.S. PAT. OFF.

JUST ENOUGH—NO MORE! Now flung into Fashion's discard are all excess underthings—along with the petticoat, high boots and the bustle. To be dressed smartly today—one wears less—just enough—no more. *A dress and Scanties—that's all!* How little it takes to banish all bulges! But one pair of shoulder straps. A single garment of silken nothingness—that is on—or off—in one short second—and bobs in and out of the washtub like a pair of sheer stockings. Every smart woman should have at least one Scanties in her wardrobe. . . . . *Haven't you often wished to appear your charming self and yet veil all so subtly . . it's in Scanties, this new luxurious freedom.*

Model Brassière Co.
INCORPORATED

LONDON   200 Fifth Avenue, New York   PARIS
Largest Brassiere Manufacturer in the World

THE SCANTIES illustrated is style 357, fashioned of silk jersey and *Skinners Satin*—Exquisitely practical—Specially priced at $12.50

SCANTIES in pink, white, peach or black are now for sale in the brassiere department of all stores that cater to stylish women . . . . $5 to $25

SCANTIES . . A SCANT EIGHT-OUNCE FIGURE-MOULDING GARMENT combining *the* BRASSIERE . . *the* VEST . . *the* GIRDLE . . *the* PANTIES . . . . . ALL-IN-ONE!

PAINTING BY A. E. MARTY

AUTHORITATIVE as only constant and careful study of style trends at their source can make them, Stehli Silks are woven by an organization of international scope and reputation. They are silks that provide . . . in color, weave and texture . . . a matchless medium for the approved expression of the modern mode . . . From the sheerest chiffon to the richest satin crepe . . . they drape in unwrinkled lines of lan-guorous grace . . . . crepes to mould the fluid, softened lines of the new feminized silhouette. Colors that forecast the note of each approaching season and reach fulfillment in its dominating tones . . . No wonder smart wardrobes make their proudest boast in gowns of Stehli Silks! For your own frocks you will find Stehli Silks at leading department stores . . . also in the season's newest and loveliest of ready-to-wear dresses.

Stehli Silks

Copyright 1928, by Stehli Silks Corporation, 200 Madison Avenue, New York—Paris—London and Zurich

1928

"*An entirely new, completely revolutionary dress gradually appeared. . . . A dress that began to emerge just after the last World War, partly an expression of a deep-set, sweeping upheaval that ran through every phase of civilized living. This dress had no precedent. No such dress had ever been seen before—and the woman it created was a startling innovation. It was almost a chemise. It had no waist line, for its narrowest point came at a woman's widest—her hips. In profile, it made legs seem to start at the neck. It was pure silhouette, cut to the bone and thrown slightly off its stance by the posture its lines demanded—rear in, chest in. The coiffeurs cooperated by cutting hair closer and closer to the skull, and plaster-ing it against the cheeks—a structural detail instead of a crowning glory.*"

Harper's Bazaar, May 1940

MOTOR FLEECE OVERCOATS

HART SCHAFFNER & MARX

"Now, Scientific Housewife, have a look at this coat!"

"It's perfect on you, Bill."

"I don't mean that. You know what they did? Built a machine. To rub the cloth, to test it. It's a new cloth. Motor Fleece. And it had to be rubbed hard 7500 times before it showed the least trace of wear."

"It's terribly becoming, Bill."

"Wait. That's 3000 hours of wear. If I wore it 8 hours a day, that's 375 days!"

"But you don't."

"I might."

"Did it cost much, Bill?"

"It cost me less than a lot worse coat would have cost me sixteen years ago, and whaddye think of *that*?"

"I think it's grand. I honestly think you've had more *sense* since you gave away your depression clothes than you ever had before. And I think that's why we're going through this winter out of the red. Bill, you've found out what I kept telling you—that spending for *good* things is the finest kind of saving. Tell you what—"

"What?"

"Let's take what you saved and see a very swell, very funny show!"

© 1932

LORD AND TAYLOR

VOGUE'S *finds of the fortnight*

THIS fortnight, we set out with the sole idea of finding something that will do for your summer-in-town wardrobe what a bit of chutney does for your summer palate. After a couple of months' exposure to country suns and winds, clothes bought in the spring sadly lack the *esprit* you want for your less casual engagements. So we chose satin. We chose taffeta. We believe in the intrinsic chic of these two materials; we believe in their practicality. You can wear them now with white accessories, and look cool as a julep. You can wear them later with dark accessories, come autumn. They're classics. We believe in their individuality, and in their urbanity. There's nothing about the sleekness of satin or the crisp chic of dark taffeta that suggests "country." So, with this little credo in our hearts, we scoured the New York markets, and present what we feel are *finds*—two taffeta costumes for luncheon; a black satin dress in which to be carried off to cocktails in your Cadillac; and a satin gown for dinner at Chatham Walk.

58

1934

The fashion industry, with its emphasis on stylish silhouettes, should be given credit for engineering the marketing strategies that shaped automobile copy and frequently made the advertising for both products virtually indistinguishable.

LOUISE DAHL-WOLFE

CAN'T·DO·WITHOUTABLES

**HARPER'S BAZAAR'S BASIC COLLEGE
WARDROBE, AVAILABLE IN SIXTY-SIX
SHOPS THROUGHOUT THE COUNTRY**

• So long as corner drugstores sell Coca-Cola and chewing gum, as bells ring in dormitories and girls dress in fireman's time, clothes like these will be around, beloved, faithful to the end. • First on the left, and first as a downright necessity, are the two sweaters and the tweed skirt—in this case, a cardigan and pull-over of natural Shetland wool, worn with a green Harris tweed skirt. (Together, about $33.) The cardigan will be buttoned up the back as often as up the front. Bonwit Teller. • In the center, a plaid skirt has an ascot to match, to be tucked into the neck of a new middy jacket, called a Muddler, of dark blue wool jersey with wide revers and patch pockets. This is about $20. Bonwit Teller. The White House, San Francisco. • On the right, a Harris reversible raincoat is wine-red wool outside, with natural gabardine inside. About $18. Bonwit Teller. Meier and Frank, Portland, Oregon.

54

A DAY IN THE
LIFE OF
REILLY

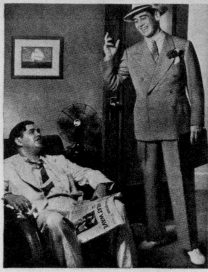

9 A.M. There's a heat wave on. Jim Reilly, Jr. enters his office looking as though he hadn't heard about it. Not so, Sam Smith, insurance broker, who is hot *and* bothered.

9:30 A.M. "You must carry ice cubes in your pockets", says Smith, "and a pressing iron! . . . to keep looking like that!" "Neither", replies Reilly "but I'll let you in on a little secret . . ."

5:30 P.M. Reilly is off to the Thursday night Country Club supper dance with Mrs. Reilly to be. Evidently, neither he nor his suit has yet heard of the heat wave...or the humidity.

9:00 P.M. Wilted, perspiring males cannot be coaxed on to the dance floor in this heat. So Reilly has plenty of room to step. And his suit still looks freshly pressed!

11:30 P.M. Reilly says "Good Night". Certainly this fond farewell should wrinkle his suit completely; cost him the price of a pressing next day. Millions of men have found it so!

NEXT MORNING. But no—Reilly's suit is just as fresh and cool and immaculate as the day before. For he was, and is wearing a CORONADO—*The *Air-Cooled Suit That Resists Wrinkles.* And Sam Smith too, is now living the Life of Reilly!

* IMPORTED
Coronado
THE *AIR COOLED SUIT
THAT RESISTS WRINKLES

Superbly tailored of an amazing British fabric, CORONADO is almost weightless, actually has a "frosty feel", and fights off wrinkles with stubborn persistence. In business and sports models, light and dark shades. Cool *Celanese Rayon trimmed. *Coat and Trousers,* $29.75

*Reg. U. S. Pat. Off.

Coronado is Controlled &
Tailored Exclusively by J. SCHOENEMAN, INC. *Baltimore, Md.*

1939

MUNKACSI

SAKS FIFTH AVENUE

THE AMERICAN GIRL DEFIES A THREAT—

SHE WILL CONTINUE TO DRESS

EXACTLY AS SHE PLEASES

Nazis Warn Berlin Women Against Wearing Trousers

Wireless to THE NEW YORK TIMES.

BERLIN, June 24—A new notice now being conspicuously displayed in the main entrances of apartment houses in Berlin's fashionable West End declares:

"Residents of this apartment house are requested to note the addresses of those women who, in spite of the seriousness of the time, run about in men's trousers. Whoever in these days favors such degenerate, mad excesses of fashion will be the first to be called up when a law is decreed for conscription of female labor."

The notices are signed by the local group headquarters of the National Socialist party, which thereby openly disagrees with the definition of individual freedom proclaimed by Dr. Robert Ley, head of the German Labor Front, on April 29, which was:

"A man is free, among other things, when he can eat, drink, dress and live as and where he or finds necessary."

1940

Martin Munkacsi, a photojournalist turned fashion photographer, was one of the first to bring models out of the studio and into the outdoors. In doing so, he changed the way American women would think about fashion and about themselves as fashionable creatures. Richard Avedon said of his mentor: "Today the world of what is called fashion is peopled with Munkacsi's babies, his heirs."

right this way!

once again Jantzen gives you the perfect short-cut to a perfect summer...wonderful new sun classics, beautifully-tailored... in fine-quality color-fast fabrics that take to sun and fun as naturally as the whole wide world takes to love and song and moments like this. The girl's shorts, Juilliard Zephyroy Sanforized corduroy, pastels and white 3.95... the men's shorts, Bando's water-repellent Crown-tested "Green light" rayon-and-cotton fabric in natural, maize, blue, 3.95...at most stores.

*Jantzen
swim suits · sun clothes

TAN WITH JAN...Jantzen's marvelous sun-cream lotion for a smooth soft skin-tan

*Reg. U. S. Pat. Off.

Windswept Silhouette for Spring . . . in navy and white dotted Silk Taffeta

Lord & Taylor, New York • Gus Mayer Ltd., New Orleans • Makoff, Salt Lake City • Neusteters, Denver • Hutzler Bros., Baltimore
Young Quinlan, Minneapolis • Miller Bros., Chattanooga • Miller's, Knoxville • Frost Bros., San Antonio • The Fair, Fort Worth

1956

Two extremes of the 1950s: the sheath and the sack.

APPLE VALLEY

WESTERN UNION
TELEGRAM

LA137
L LLB140 PD=APPLE VALLEY CALIF 4=
HERMAN BOBO KANE THE THIRD=
    30 FIFTH AVE NEW YORK NY=

BOBO, HERO, I'M HERE. YOUR BUTTERY BIRTHDAY TELEGRAM
AWAITING ME. SMOOTH FLIGHT, SMOOTH PILOT AND CUTEST AIRSTRIP
RIGHT AT DOOR OF APPLE VALLEY INN. MILLY, DREAMY DAY AND
BUGG-EYED CROWD TOOK IN NATHAN-STRONG CHIC CHEMISE AND MY
CLOUD NINE PRANCE. OPENERS CALL FOR A CALTEX CLAD DIP, A
TERRACE COCKTAIL SIP, AND A LONG DRAUGHT OF DELICIOUS AIR
AND HEAVENLY HORIZONS. THE ADDRESS IS APPLE VALLEY INN.
    LOLLY.

Birthday Telegrams . . . the Bestest Way to Remember

Silk linen chemise by Nathan-Strong, about $70. All Nathan-Strong fashions lined with Kabat fabric. • Josef Milan straw satchel, about $24 plus tax

1957

"Did you say 'Sports Shirts'?"

A 1912 model sportsman exchanges stares with his 1951 counterpart! BOTH are the best-dressed men of their day. BOTH wear Arrow. But what a difference! The early Arrow Collar Man had *Style*. Ditto today's Arrow Sports Shirt Man—with *easy, casual* COMFORT added!

Bali Cay! Beautiful, colorful "Island Prints"!

When the sun is high, men turn to Arrow sports shirts! Here are the coolest, most comfortable, most colorful on the horizon. New leafy patterns ...Hawaiian prints... brilliant flower designs ...and many others inspired by tropical isles.

You'll look your best, FEEL your best in these style-packed Bali Cays—cut free for action and comfort! All completely washable—won't shrink out of fit.

ALL ARROW sports shirts have the revolutionary new Arafold collar. *See* it! *Wear* it! Cluett, Peabody & Co., Inc.

ARROW
Bali Cay
SPORTS SHIRTS

Starting our second 100 years of Style Leadership

1951

Blue Bell, Inc., Empire State Building, New York

FAIR 'N' FANCY DENIMS in the long, lean pants you love—those wonderfully flattering **BLUE BELL WRANGLERS.** They've that tapered Western fit, are easy to wash, and so long-wearing. Made of AVONDALE vat-dyed Sanforized denim in six sunny colors: wheat, turquoise, red, light blue, light gray or charcoal. Sizes 10 to 18, $3.98. In dark blue, 10 to 20, $3.49.

1957

240

DRIES NEAT— STAYS NEAT

This wash 'n' wear suit made
with "Dacron" keeps its press
wearing after wearing
...needs little, if any, ironing

This cool, light suit made with "Dacron"* polyester
fiber keeps you looking your best even on the hottest,
steamiest days. Wear it—it'll stay neat. Wash it—
it'll dry neat, needing little, if any, ironing. This neat-
ness and convenience last the life of this remarkable
suit, because it is made with a high percentage of
"Dacron". Select your wash 'n' wear suit made with
"Dacron" today. Choose from many handsome
styles, colors, and patterns.

DACRON
REG. U. S. PAT. OFF.

DU PONT
REG. U. S. PAT. OFF.

BETTER THINGS FOR BETTER LIVING...THROUGH CHEMISTRY

A FIBER CONTENT
NATIONALLY ADVERTISED
BY DU PONT
This fabric contains
68% or MORE
DACRON*
REG U.S. PAT OFF
with COTTON

LOOK FOR THIS GUIDE
TO EXTRA BENEFITS!
This and similar fiber-content tags featured on suits and slacks indicate that
the fabric contains sufficient "Dacron"
to provide the extra benefits that have
made "Dacron" a national favorite.

*"Dacron" is Du Pont's registered trademark for
its polyester fiber. Du Pont makes fibers, does not
make the fabric or suit shown here.

1958

*Dacron was introduced in 1951. Early promotion often featured models being
hosed down or thrown into lakes and happily dry in a matter of minutes.*

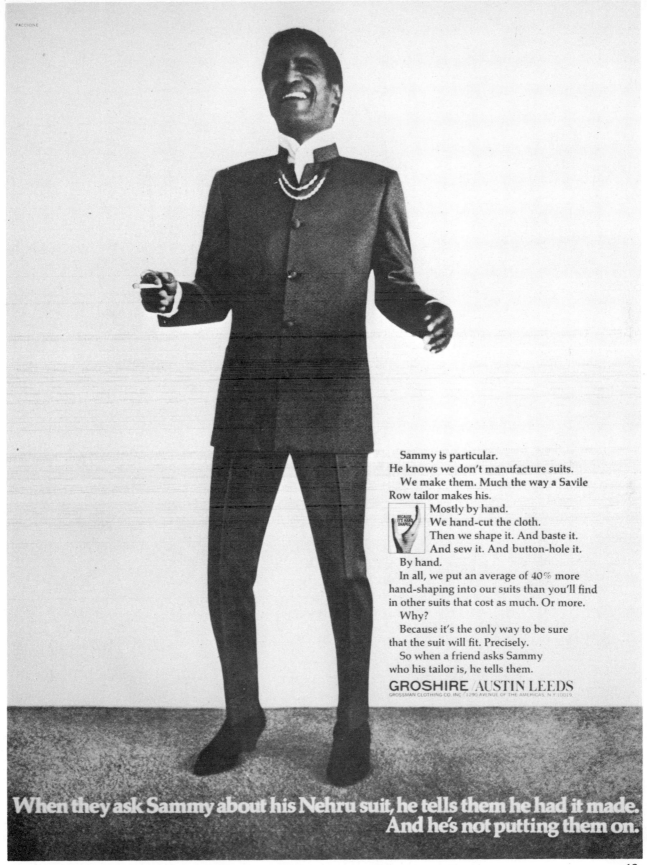

Sammy is particular.

He knows we don't manufacture suits.

We make them. Much the way a Savile Row tailor makes his.

Mostly by hand.

We hand-cut the cloth.

Then we shape it. And baste it.

And sew it. And button-hole it.

By hand.

In all, we put an average of 40% more hand-shaping into our suits than you'll find in other suits that cost as much. Or more. Why?

Because it's the only way to be sure that the suit will fit. Precisely.

So when a friend asks Sammy who his tailor is, he tells them.

GROSHIRE / AUSTIN LEEDS

GROSSMAN CLOTHING CO. INC / 1290 AVENUE OF THE AMERICAS, N.Y. 10019.

When they ask Sammy about his Nehru suit, he tells them he had it made. And he's not putting them on.

1968

Despite Sammy's endorsement, this is one male fashion that never caught on.

242

After Six would like to take a moment to humble the dinner jacket.

For years, the average man has revered the dinner jacket as the private property of the country club set. To be worn only at very posh affairs.

A dinner jacket is a lot more democratic than that. Actually, a dinner jacket should be thought of as a good suit. Like your dark blue one, only a touch more dressy.

A dinner jacket is for the guy who has an occasional big night out, and wants to make it as big as possible.

A dinner jacket can be worn any-where you'd wear your good suit. A good restaurant. A night club. A cocktail party. A play. A friend's wedding.

You know, maybe we should stop calling it a dinner jacket.

1970

When you have to wear clothes. h.i.s

Corduroy jocko jacket, $25; White swabby jacket, $20; Safari jeans, $10; Striped flares, $13; Sunset body shirt, $9. Higher in the west. Talon zipper. For retailers names, write h.i.s., 16E. 34 St., N.Y., N.Y. 10016. Available in Canada. Boys' sizes, too.

Swiss Precision—Lee presents the Swiss Knit Leesure Suit, so named because of its precise attention to detail. Note the neat rib and sleeve pockets on the jacket (about $30) and the fluid lines of the slacks (about $20). Both of 100% texturized Dacron® polyester with the classic Oxford cloth look and feel. Top them off with a Lee herringbone print knit shirt (about $16) and you've got another great Lee Leesure Suit going for you. The Lee Company, 640 Fifth Avenue, N.Y., N.Y. 10019. (212) 765-4215.

Lee A company of vf corporation

1975

"One interesting index of [the other-directed person's leisure behavior] is the decline of evening dress, especially among men, and conversely the invasion of the office by sports clothes. This looks like an offshoot of the cult of effortlessness, and of course men say 'it's too much trouble' in explaining why they don't change for dinner or the evening. But the explanation lies rather in the fact that most men today simply do not know how to change roles, let alone make the change by proper costuming. Another reason may be the fear of being thought high-hat; one can wear gaudy shirts but not stiff ones. Thus, the sport shirt and casual dress show that one is a good fellow not only on the golf course or on vacation but in the office and at dinner, too."

David Reisman, *The Lonely Crowd* (1950)

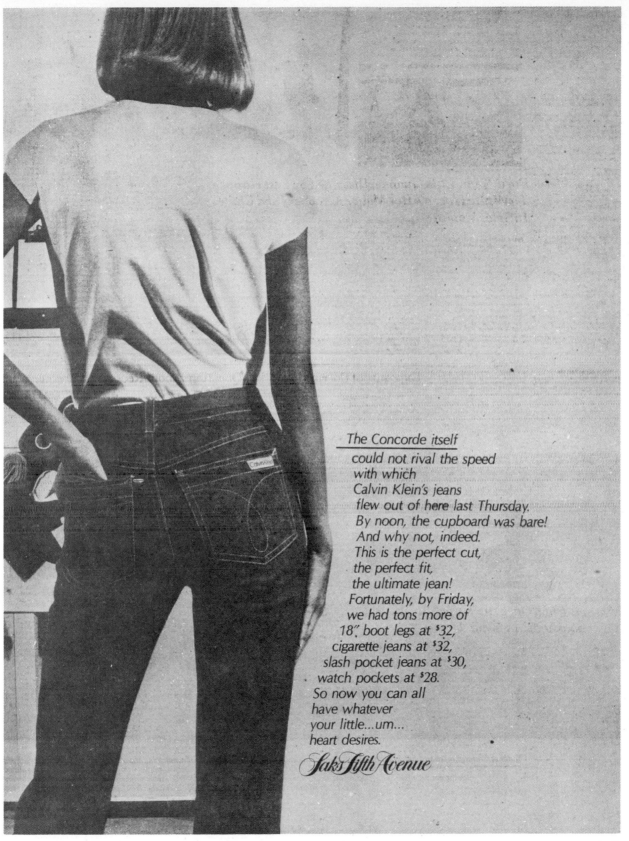

The Concorde itself
could not rival the speed
with which
Calvin Klein's jeans
flew out of here last Thursday.
By noon, the cupboard was bare!
And why not, indeed.
This is the perfect cut,
the perfect fit,
the ultimate jean!
Fortunately, by Friday,
we had tons more of
18" boot legs at $32,
cigarette jeans at $32,
slash pocket jeans at $30,
watch pockets at $28.
So now you can all
have whatever
your little...um...
heart desires.

Saks Fifth Avenue

1978

"When [Calvin Klein's] blue jeans appeared in the stores in February, 200,000 pairs were snapped up in a week."

Newsweek, May 8, 1978

246

adidas 3-stripe warm ups, made in the exciting new Keyrolan fabric. Outside, Keyrolan shines like tinsel. Inside, it's as soft as feathers, with an Arnel nap, and is extra light and comfortable.

Horizontal fabric stretch provides a perfect fit for any figure — male or female. Durable and very easy to look after, they are ideal gifts for this festive season — for jingling or jogging!

The all-sports people

KEYROLAN®

made for adidas by
BLUE RIDGE WINKLER
using ARNEL
TRIACETATE from CELANESE

adidas®

1978

Sportswear has been a staple of the American fashion industry ever since the bicycle fad of the 1890s dramatically altered women's apparel. For most European designers, sportswear is American fashion. "Sweat chic," by now a recognizable style of the 1970s, developed out of two socio-cultural phenomena: a predominately urban physical-fitness fad symbolized by a jogging mania, plus a 1950s nostalgia that finds sexiness in satin boxing shorts and quilted baseball jackets.

Part
THREE

Advertising and the Strategies of Persuasion

WOLCOTT'S INSTANT PAIN ANNIHILATOR.

Fig 1. Demon of Catarrh. Fig 2. Demon of Neuralgia. Fig 3. Demon of Headache. Fig 4. Demon of Weak Nerves. Fig 5.5 Demons of Toothache.

1863

AFFLICTIONS
AND ANXIETIES

Over-the-counter nostrums, mail-order remedies, and coupon cures have accounted for an enormous portion of the American health industry ever since an enterprising Boston coffeehouse proprietor began advertising a bottled treatment for that "woeful distemper, the Dry Belly-ache," in 1691. Throughout the eighteenth and nineteenth centuries foreign visitors were continually amazed to find no matter where they traveled such a vast assortment of advertised products promising to cure so many diseases and common discomforts. Columns crammed with announcements for the latest purgatives invaded otherwise respectable newspapers; walls, fences, cliffs —every available surface—praised the virtues of Hostetter's Bitters, Buchu, Ayer's Cherry Pectoral, and the mysterious St. X 1860. Acres of valuable mountain timber in Pennsylvania were leveled to treat railroad passengers to a four hundred foot proclamation of the medicinal powers of "Plantation Bitters."

In the beginning the stomach was the main target. Most common ills could be traced to its vacillations, its whimsies, its insolence. And each age had its favorite abdominal distress; advertising documents the destiny of the American stomach as it passed from the dry belly-ache of the Puritans, through the biliousness of the Founding Fathers, to the dyspepsia of the Gilded Age and the acid indigestion of today. To foreign observers, who thought most Americans looked unhealthy, the problematical condition of the national stomach came as no surprise. Hyperactive Americans did not know how to eat reasonably, but, as one visitor noted, would just "gobble, gulp, and go."

The foundations for a multimillion-dollar "upset stomach" industry were established early. But advertisers refused to settle for only the stomach. As the boundaries of disease seemed to expand, more and more virgin anatomical territory became open to speculation, claims, and counterclaims. By the 1880s and 1890s, anyone who could devise a dosage, patent a pill, or merely attach a new name to an old notion could become what Dr. Oliver Wendell Holmes called a "toadstool millionaire." Evangelists, peddlers, quacks and sober reformers, mountebanks and mad scientists, respected doctors and druggists, and many advertising agents themselves conducted a brisk trade in miracles. A Texas gardener, convinced that decay-causing, evil, invisible microbes were at the root of all disease, patented a pinkish substance which he advertised as a "Microbe Killer" that would cure everything from cankers to cancer. Within a few years he owned seventeen factories, ran a New York outlet, and lived regally in a Fifth Avenue mansion. On subsequent examination, the "Microbe Killer" proved to be 99.381 percent water. Americans were discovering that advertising *could* perform miracles.

Since the demand for such medicines was stimulated largely by self-diagnosis, their placebo effect depended heavily on the before-after mesmerism of advertising. For the inert drug to be in any way "effective," the advertisement had to operate entirely on the suggestibility of the patient. Even today it is estimated that 20 to 40 percent of prescription medicines are little more than placebos that patients (and, not infrequently, doctors) believe possess intrinsic pharmacological value. But not all nineteenth-century proprietary medicine manufacturers required their formulas to be mixed with a good dose of suggestibility before taking. Some of the most popular remedies were strong medicine by any criteria: Cocaine, opium, hashish, chloral, and alcohol worked wonders on nineteenth-century colds and headaches. A teaspoonful of Smith's Glyco-Heroin could instantly stop any cough. Mrs. Winslow's Soothing Syrup did its soothing of hypertension with huge amounts of morphia. Victorian women, who would have been socially ostracized for drinking a glass of beer, could get respectably stoned on medicines that contained up to 70 percent alcohol. The addictive nature of these products not only ensured consumer brand-loyalty but created marketing opportunities for a host of anti-addictive remedies. The Pure Food and Drug Act of 1906 was naturally more concerned with strong medicines than with harmless placebos, even though both kinds depended on fraudulent advertising. So temperance-oriented was the Pure Food and Drug movement that succeeded in destroying the most potent nineteenth-century remedies, that the crusade itself could be considered a dress-rehearsal for Prohibition.

The relation between advertising and consumer medicines has always been a symbiotic one. Early advertising cut its teeth on patent medicines: "The greatest advertising men of my day were schooled in the medicine field," Claude C. Hopkins noted in his memoirs. He went on to observe that since "medicines were worthless merchandise until a demand was created" proprietary copy amounted to the "supreme test" of a copywriter's talent. By the end of the nineteenth century, copywriters had become masters of hypochondriacal suggestion, turning ordinary physical discomforts or irregularities into alarming symptoms ("If you feel dull, drowsy, debilitated, have sallow color of skin . . ."). Those pimples on the forehead ("humiliating eruptions") were probably the sign of a terrible blood disease; that sluggish feeling undoubtedly meant a deranged liver. Constipation developed into a serious national preoccupation. No bodily process, however innocent, normal, or negligible, could be ignored. To the worried reader of advertisements, every sneeze signaled catarrh, every cough was a symptom of consumption.

An industrial society that demanded uniformity and standardization in everything from pickles and corsets to railroad tracks and civil service bureaucrats could not help but expect the human body to conform to machine principles. As statistical norms (pulse, temperature, height, weight, frequency of elimination) became increasingly used to establish national standards of well-being, public tolerance for physical and psychological deviation declined. Advertisers learned they could count on people thinking themselves either too fat or too skinny, too tall or too short, too pale or too dark, too restless or too lethargic, too constipated or too diarrhetic. Nobody, they guessed, felt quite right, especially members of the "weaker sex." For medicine manufacturers, anxiety over ill health was just as profitable as ill health—even more so, since genuine ill health took its toll of steady customers.

To stimulate such profitable anxieties, late-nineteenth-century advertisers invented two enormously influential versions of the human body: the machine and the model. The human "machine," with its familiar assortment of gears, pipes, tubes, and levers (nervous-system wires came with the twentieth century), offered the public a convenient image of internal efficiency and precision—"runs like a machine" became synonymous with good health. The photogenic model, on the other hand, with her flawless complexion, sparkling teeth, and shapely limbs, represented the external standards of human presentability—the eternal "after" of countless advertisements. As usual, copywriters had fabricated something far more potent and durable than had the manufacturers who commissioned them. Few nineteenth-century "proprietary articles" have survived. But the popular idealizations of efficiency and appearance—the machine and the model —developed into indispensable features of health-and-beauty-aid promotion as well as into permanent fixtures in the iconography of everyday life.

Efficiency and presentability: Practically all twentieth-century pharmaceutical-goods advertising hinges on these two unchallengeable standards of daily life. Headaches, indigestion, the "blahs," "simple nervous tension," Kafkaesque angst—the manic-depressive phases of ordinary living—interfere more than anything else with the ability to perform one's job, to "cope." On the external front, bad breath, oily hair, body odor, dandruff, enlarged pores, and pimples destroy the fragile structure of presentability (the total body "package"), thus ruining all chance of social or romantic acceptance. Keep fit and fit in, run like a machine and look like a model. That is the cumulative message of drug and toiletry advertising. And so persistently and successfully has the message been promoted that by now it amounts to a fundamental principle of human behavior. The emulative appeal of efficiency and presentability figures, of course, is one of the most significant cultural consequences of a well-groomed, toned-up corporate life style. Along with the middle-class nuclear family, the modern corporation has supplied advertising with its most vital and normative "psychographic" images. As contemporary sociologists have recognized, the family and corporation reward the same virtues and instill the same anxieties. As two of the most formidable institutions of our society, they continually reinforce and validate each other. By falling into disrepair, one not only risks personal disgrace but jeopardizes the smoothly run home or office.

Although the toughly fought Food and Drug reform movement of the early twentieth century squelched some of the most outrageous patent-medicine advertising, it did not by any means put an end to the public's willingness to swallow panaceas and placebos. If medicine manufacturers toned down their claims to satisfy new federal regulations, they also boned up on their science. Leaving serious health problems to what was by now a respected medical profession (to be called on for expert advice and testimonials), advertisers turned instead to the thousand little diseases and disorders of everyday life. In the 1890s a cough warned of imminent consumption; by 1920 it was merely a "social blunder." Pimples and bad breath, no longer symptoms of internal deterioration, represented physiological nuisances that stood in the way of a young woman's marriage or a young man's career. A good example of the changes in pharmaceutical advertising can be seen most dramatically in early Listerine advertisements. At first, Listerine was promoted as a "safe antiseptic" with countless hygienic uses: in other words, a slow-selling product in search of an anxiety. Then in 1921 the Lambert Company decided to use a clinical term for the ordinary unpleasantness known as bad breath—"halitosis." An anxiety was not only stimulated, it was labeled. Listerine sales climbed from 115,000 a year in 1921 to 4,000,000 a year in 1927.

Nor were "Microbe Killers" completely obsolete. Gone were the exaggerated claims, but not the dirty, evil germs. As the nation attempted to rid itself of an infiltrating Red Menace and other un-American impurities in the 1920s, a powerful new product went to work purifying the doorknobs, chair arms, and banisters of the American home: "You must have a trustworthy disinfectant to drive germs out of your home," ads for Lysol insisted. Besides having to confront the dangers of a germ-infested home environment, mothers were also warned of the "gray spectre" of disease that pursued children with untended cuts and scrapes. Women could also rely on trustworthy Lysol as a protection against offensive feminine odors and, in emergencies, as a potent contraceptive.

Americans remain as sensitive as ever to the social embarrassments of body odors, unwanted hair, and blackheads. Contemporary advertisements refer less euphemistically to such hygienic problems. Ads for vaginal sprays and "jock itch" powders reproach the public for some of its most intimate "infirmities." The common cold, nervous tension, backaches, and headaches are viewed as mysterious phenomena ("When headache strikes . . .") that turn grown men into helpless children ("Honey, I dot a told") and patient housewives into Florence Nightingales ("Try this, dear"). And assisting the imperious American stomach on its gastronomic escapades ("I can't believe I ate the whole thing . . .") remains the most lucrative business of all.

Throughout proprietary advertising one message gets hammered home in vintage Anacin fashion: Our frangible bodies are in constant need of repair, from head to toe, from *pityrosporum ovale* (dandruff) to *tinea trichophyton* (athlete's foot). Styles, emphases, medical terms, even the diseases change, but the real underlying anxieties, the free-floating hypochondria, the desperate need to be converted from "before" to "after," to find "instant relief," have troubled the American body and soul from St. X 1860 to Ex-Lax and Excedrin and through all the Brand Xs discredited along the way.

HELMBOLD'S
FLUID EXTRACT BUCHU.

[From Dispensatory of the United States.]

MEDICAL PROPERTIES AND USES.—Buchu is gently stimulating. It is given in Gravel, Chronic Catarrh of the Bladder, Morbid Irritation of the Bladder and Urethra, Disease of the Prostate Gland, and Retention or Incontinence of Urine, from a loss of tone in the parts concerned in its evacuation. The remedy has also been recommended in Dyspepsia, Chronic Rheumatism, Cutaneous Affections, and Dropsy.

HOTTENTOTS SEEN GATHERING BUCHU LEAVES
AT THE
CAPE OF GOOD HOPE,
FOR
H. T. HELMBOLD, Druggist,
594 BROADWAY, New York.

☞ *Beware of Counterfeits.*

1870

Dr. H. T. Helmbold's "Buchu" was the biggest-selling patent medicine of the Gilded Age. It was advertised with gusto, and Helmbold acquired a Shah's fortune from his opulent New York City "Temple of Pharmacy" (acclaimed the most "buchuful" site on Broadway), where he sold his famous nostrum as a cure for just about everything. The official Dispensatory of the United States listed the South African plant as a gentle stimulant "with a peculiar tendency to the urinary organs, producing diuresis."

Look Here, Friend.
Are you Sick?

Do you have pains about the chest and sides, and sometimes in the back? Do you feel dull and sleepy? Does your mouth have a bad taste, especially in the morning? Is there a sort of sticky slime collects about the teeth? Is your appetite poor? Is there a feeling like a heavy load on the stomach, sometimes a faint, all-gone sensation at the pit of the stomach, which food does not satisfy?

Are your eyes sunken? Do your hands and feet become cold and feel clammy? Have you a dry cough? Do you expectorate greenish colored matter? Are you hawking and spitting all or part of the time? Do you feel tired all the while? Are you nervous, irritable and gloomy? Do you have evil forebodings? Is there a giddiness, a sort of whirling sensation in the head when rising up suddenly? Do your bowels become costive? Is your skin dry and hot at times? Is your blood thick and stagnant? Are the whites of your eyes tinged with yellow? Is your urine scanty and high colored? Does it deposit a sediment after standing? Do you frequently spit up your food, sometimes with a sour taste and sometimes with a sweet? Is this frequently attended with palpitation of the heart? Has your vision become impaired? Are there spots before the eyes? Is there a feeling of great prostration and weakness? If you suffer from any of these symptoms, send me your name and I will send you, by mail,

One Bottle of Medicine FREE

Send your address on postal card to-day, as you may not see this notice again.
Address, naming this paper, Prof. HART. 212 E. 9th St., N. Y.

1888

Makes Women Beautiful.

Marvelous development accomplished by the new and wonderful "Vestro" method of enlarging the Female Bust. Flat-chested and unattractive women are quickly developed into commanding figures that excite wonderment and admiration.——A new and surprisingly effective home treatment has been discovered that enlarges the female bust at least **six** inches. Women who are not lacking in this respect will not be particularly interested, but to those who by some unfortunate circumstance of health or occupation are deficient in this development will be very much fascinated by the peculiar prominence achieved by the treatment. It is called "Vestro" and is controlled by the well known Aurum Medicine Co.

There is no doubt about the marvelous power of this new treatment to develope the bust to a gratifying extent. Any lady who wishes to know more about Vestro should send her name and address to the Aurum Medicine Co. They will send free, in plain sealed envelope by mail a new "beauty book" they have just prepared, also photographs from life showing the actual development induced and a great number of testimonials from physicians, chemists and prominent ladies all commending the wonderful and remarkable power of Vestro to enlarge the bust no matter how flat the chest may be. Do not fail to write at once. The beauty book and portraits will delight you. All you need do is to send name and address and a two-cent stamp to pay postage. All correspondence strictly confidential. Address **AURUM MEDICINE CO.**, Dept. KE, 55 State St., **Chicago.**

1900

Early bust developers refrained from mentioning breasts (see p. 281 for a modern version). Like most bust-enlargers, this one probably "worked" by building up pectoral muscles. In 1973 Psychology Today polled 62,000 readers on their "Body Image" and discovered that 26 percent of the women responding were "dissatisfied" with their breasts.

Just prior to this advertisement the government began supervising the extraction of cocaine from the coca leaf. Early Coke apparently contained a small dose of cocaine, which helped give the drink its patent-medicine "flavor."

DON'T BE FAT

My New Obesity Food Quickly Reduces Weight to Normal, Requires no Starvation Process on Your Part, and is Absolutely Safe.

Trial Package Sent Free to all who write, by Mail, Postpaid, in Plain Wrapper.   Write to-day.

The Above Illustration Shows the Remarkable Effects of This Wonderful Obesity Food—What It Has Done for Others It Will Do for You.

Excess fat is a disease. It is caused by imperfect assimilation of food. Nutriment which should go into muscle, sinew, bone, brain and nerve does not go there, but piles up in the form of superfluous fat, which clogs the human machinery and compresses the vital organs of the body and endangers health and life.

My new Obesity Food, taken at mealtime, compels perfect assimilation of the food and sends the food nutriment where it belongs. It requires no starvation process. You can eat all you want. It makes muscle, bone, sinew, nerve and brain tissue out of excess fat, and quickly reduces your weight to normal. It takes off the big stomach and relieves the compressed condition and enables the heart to act freely and the lungs to expand naturally and the kidneys and liver to perform their functions in a natural manner.

My natural, scientific Obesity Food does the work. You will feel better the first day you try this wonderful home food.

Mrs. Grace Reid Gates, 6668 Dearborn Street, Chicago, Ill., says: "My dear Mr. Kellogg, I have been taking your wonderful remedy lacking two days of a month, and I have never felt so well and hearty and comfortable in years. I weighed nearly 195 when I began your Obesity Food and Treatment, and now I have reduced my flesh more than 48 pounds.

"It really seems almost a miracle. I did not suppose it possible to lose so much flesh and not be hungry, but your food is wonderful.

"I eat all I want but my weight is steadily decreasing. I have consulted a doctor several times, and he says my heart is very much stronger than ever before, and my color is the picture of health.

"I had tried so many things to get rid of my fat, and none of them did it. I had no notion of trying again, until I got your letters, and now I am very glad I did.

"I have the time and will take pleasure in answering letters to those who write me."

Send your name and address—no money—to-day to F. J. Kellogg, 2105 Kellogg Building, Battle Creek, Mich., and receive the trial package in plain wrapper free by return mail.

Children frequently suffer from headaches. Headaches cause wakefulness.

Next time your youngster is afflicted with wakefulness, bathe his feet in hot water, using Ivory Soap.

By no possible chance will harm follow; and it is almost a certainty that good will.

But please remember one thing: It is the hot water that soothes the child's nerves. Ivory Soap makes the bath more efficacious. But Ivory Soap has no medicinal virtue. No soap has.

For bath, toilet and fine laundry purposes; for the nursery; for shampooing; for everything and anything that necessitates the use of a better-than-ordinary soap, Ivory Soap is unequalled.

Ivory Soap . . . . It Floats.

1910

The girl with the clear skin wins

Many an otherwise attractive girl is a social failure because of a poor complexion. If *your* skin is not fresh, smooth and healthy, or has suffered from an unwise use of cosmetics, see if the daily use of Resinol Soap will not greatly improve it.

Resinol Soap is not only unusually cleansing and softening, but its regular use helps *nature* give to the skin and hair that beauty of perfect health which it is impossible to imitate. Tendency to pimples is lessened, redness and roughness disappear, and in a very short time the complexion usually becomes clear, fresh and velvety.

The soothing, restoring influence that makes this possible is the *Resinol* which this soap contains and which physicians have prescribed for over twenty years, in Resinol Ointment, for skin and scalp troubles.

This same gentle medication, together with its freedom from harsh, irritating alkali, adapt Resinol Soap admirably to the care of the hair and of a baby's delicate skin. If the skin is in really bad condition through neglect or improper treatment Resinol Soap should at first be aided by a little Resinol Ointment.

Resinol Soap is sold by all druggists and dealers in toilet goods. In trial-size cake, write to Dept. 5-K, Resinol, Baltimore, Md.

Discriminating men like Resinol Shaving Stick because it soothes and refreshes the face, while supplying a rich, creamy, non-drying lather.

Resinol Soap

1916

You will find the proper treatment for oily skin and shiny nose in the booklet around every cake of Woodbury's Facial Soap

Conspicuous Nose Pores

How to reduce them

COMPLEXIONS otherwise flawless are often ruined by conspicuous nose pores. In such cases the small muscular fibres of the nose have become weakened and do not keep the pores closed as they should be. Instead, these pores collect dirt, clog up and become enlarged.

To reduce enlarged nose pores: wring a cloth from very hot water, lather it with Woodbury's Facial Soap, then hold it to your face. When heat has expanded the pores, rub in very gently a fresh lather of Woodbury's. Repeat this hot water and lather application several times, *stopping at once if your nose feels sensitive.* Then finish by rubbing the nose for thirty seconds with a lump of ice.

Do not expect to change in a week, however, a condition resulting from years of neglect. Use this treatment *persistently.* It will gradually reduce the enlarged pores until they are inconspicuous.

You will find a 25c cake of Woodbury's Facial Soap sufficient for a month or six weeks of this treatment, and for general use for this time. Get a cake today. For sale everywhere throughout the United States and Canada.

Send for sample cake of soap with booklet of famous treatments and samples of Woodbury's Facial Cream and Facial Powder

Send 5 cents for a trial size cake (enough for a week or ten days of any Woodbury's Facial Treatment) together with the booklet of treatments, "A Skin You Love to Touch." Or for 12 cents we will send you the treatment booklet and samples of Woodbury's Facial Soap, Facial Cream and Facial Powder. Address The Andrew Jergens Co., 8202 Spring Grove Avenue, Cincinnati, Ohio.

If you live in Canada, address The Andrew Jergens Co., Limited, 8202 Sherbrooke St., Perth, Ontario.

Woodbury's Facial Soap

Ellert Printing Company, Inc., New York.

Her One Deformity

An Utterly Unnecessary Corn

© B&B 1918

Why Will Dainty Women Keep Them?

Don't you find it hard to explain a corn, when millions never have them?

A corn means one of these things:

That you merely pare it or pad it, and never try to remove it. Or that you use some old-time treatment, harsh and inefficient.

Science has solved the corn problem by the method used in Blue-jay. Now every corn ache can be stopped in a jiffy. Any corn can be ended completely, and usually in 48 hours.

To do this, you simply apply a Blue-jay plaster. Then forget the corn. In 48 hours the average corn will go. And the toughest corn cannot resist a second application.

You can have no possible objection.

The application takes but a moment. The toe is then comfortable, the pain is entirely gone. There is no mussiness. Simply ignore the corn, go your way, and let the Blue-jay end it.

Blue-jay is a famous chemist's invention. It is prepared by a surgical-dressing house of world-wide reputation. Don't confuse it with the shams which people try and quit.

Blue-jay has millions of users. To them corns are but incidents, needing only a moment's care. Make one test, and you will join this army who never suffer corns.

Don't wait longer—make the test tonight.

How Blue-jay Acts

A is a thin, soft pad which stops the pain by relieving the pressure.
B is the B&B wax, which gently undermines the corn. Usually it takes only 48 hours to end the corn completely.

C is rubber adhesive which sticks without wetting. It wraps around the toe and makes the plaster snug and comfortable.
Blue-jay is applied in a jiffy. After that, one doesn't feel the corn. The action is gentle, and applied to the corn alone. So the corn disappears without soreness.

Blue=jay
Corn Plasters

Stop Pain Instantly—End Corns Completely

Large Package 25c at Druggists'
Small Package Discontinued

Also Blue-jay Bunion Plasters

BAUER & BLACK, *Makers of Surgical Dressings, etc.,* Chicago, New York, Toronto

(922)

1918

A Cough is a Social Blunder

People who know have no hesitation in avoiding the cougher. They know that he is a public menace. They know that his cough is a proof of his lack of consideration of others.

And they know that he knows it too, so they are not afraid of hurting his feelings.

For there is no excuse for coughing. It is just as unnecessary as any other bad habit. For it can be prevented or relieved by the simplest of precautions—the use of S. B. Cough Drops.

S. B. Cough Drops are not a cure for colds. They are a preventive of coughing. True, they often keep a cough from developing into a sore throat or cold. And they are a protection to the public because they keep people who already have influenza, colds and other throat troubles from spreading them through unnecessary coughing. Have a box with you always.

Pure. No Drugs. Just enough charcoal to sweeten the stomach.

One placed in the mouth at bedtime will keep the breathing passages clear.

Drop that Cough
SMITH BROTHERS of Poughkeepsie
FAMOUS SINCE 1847

The Disease Germ Is More Dangerous Than the Mad Dog

IF a snarling, foaming-mouthed, wild-eyed mad dog charged at a crowd of children—children strangers to you—you know what you would do.

Every ounce of chivalry in your being would be in the quick spring that would land you between the children and danger.

But how about the *unseen* menace—more threatening, more fatal, more cruel than a million mad dogs—a menace that threatens your family, your community and yourself all the time—the disease germ?

A region-wide epidemic can start in an unsanitary garbage-can. A cuspidor that is not kept sterile not only can, but will, spread tuberculosis, grippe, *influenza*, and other grave diseases.

Other danger-spots in the home—places where germs positively will breed, unless these places are regularly disinfected—are toilets; sinks; drains; dark, sunless corners; and wherever flies gather or breed.

You can make the danger-places in your home completely germ-proof by the regular use of Lysol Disinfectant; for no germ, no matter what its nature, can live in its presence.

Big hospitals rely upon it, physicians everywhere prescribe it, and boards of health urge its systematic use in the home.

Lysol Disinfectant is invaluable for personal hygiene.

Lysol Disinfectant is economical—a 50c bottle makes five gallons of powerful disinfectant; a 25c bottle makes two gallons. Use it regularly.

Remember, there is but one, true Lysol Disinfectant—the product made, bottled, signed and sealed by Lehn & Fink, Inc.

Lysol Toilet Soap
Contains a small quantity of Lysol Disinfectant, and therefore protects the skin from germ infection. It is refreshingly soothing and healing and healthful for improving the skin. Ask your dealer. If he hasn't it, ask him to order it for you.

Lysol Shaving Cream
Contains a small quantity of Lysol Disinfectant, and kills germs on razor and shaving brush (where germs abound), guards the tiny cuts from infection, and gives the antiseptic shave. If your dealer hasn't it, ask him to order a supply for you.

Samples Mailed Free. Send us your name and address, and we will gladly send you samples of Lysol Toilet Soap and also of Lysol Shaving Cream for the men of your family.

LEHN & FINK, Inc., *Manufacturing Chemists,* 120 William St., New York
Makers of Pebeco Tooth Paste

Lysol **Disinfectant**
Reg. U. S. Pat. Off.

1919

Lysol was used to kill more than germs: "In their monumental study 'The Control of Conception,' Dr. Robert L. Dickinson and Dr. Louise Stevens Bryant say flatly that Lysol should be banned as a contraceptive. Not that it isn't a good antiseptic. It is indeed a powerful antiseptic—too powerful to be used for contraceptive purposes except in weak solutions which the average woman can scarcely be trusted to make with accuracy and not reliable in any case."
James Rorty, *Our Master's Voice* (1934)

"How in the world did you ever let your teeth get in that condition?"

Dentists of today don't hesitate to express surprise when they find a patient with badly neglected teeth.

Surely enough has been said and printed and taught and advertised about the proper care of the teeth for almost every person to know something about the subject.

Users of Pebeco Tooth Paste know a little more, we think, than the average.

When a Pebeco user goes to the dentist, his teeth are not likely to be in a generally bad shape—unless the visit has been postponed too long.

Pebeco cleanses the teeth and tends to check decay by counteracting the condition known as "Acid-Mouth."

Its use induces a healthy alkaline flow of saliva that keeps the teeth and gums in a bright, firm condition.

Are your teeth protected against "Acid-Mouth"? A simple test will tell. Send for the test papers.

LEHN & FINK, Inc.

635 Greenwich Street, New York

Harold F. Ritchie & Co., Selling Agents for the United States and Canada
171 Madison Avenue, New York City   10 McCaul Street, Toronto

Also Makers of Lysol Disinfectant, Lysol Shaving Cream, and Lysol Toilet Soap

Have You "Acid-Mouth" ?

It Is Thought To Be the Chief Cause of Tooth Decay

These Test Papers Will Tell You—Sent Free With Ten-Day Trial Tube of Pebeco

There are probably many causes that contribute to decay of the teeth, but dental authorities seem to agree that in the vast majority of cases decay results from over-acidity of the mouth. You can easily tell if you have "Acid-Mouth," and also see how Pebeco tends to counteract this tooth-destroying condition, by the simple and interesting experiment with the test papers, which we will gladly send to you upon request.

Moisten a blue Litmus Test Paper on your tongue. If it turns pink, you have "Acid-Mouth." Brush your teeth with Pebeco and make another test. The paper will not change color, thus demonstrating how Pebeco helps to counteract "Acid-Mouth." Just send a post-card for Free Test Papers and 10-Day Trial Tube of Pebeco.

FLAPPERS they may be—
but they know the art of feminine appeal!

I talked to 200 of them and learned some interesting things—revealing facts which their critics might well ponder

By Ruth Miller

Flappers! We talk of them a great deal, but do we really know them? Who are they? What makes them flappers?

I wanted to find out some things about them so I went out, not long ago, and talked with 200 of them. —Society flappers, working flappers, home flappers—flappers! And this is what I found.

First of all, of course, they're young. And next, they're smart. They know their way around. Judged by older standards, perhaps they are a bit sophisticated for their years.

A spade, to the flapper, is a spade. She speaks of it as such. No silly mid-Victorian stuff for her! Unafraid, she looks the 20th century in the face.

Of course not all flappers have beauty. But practically all have something even more to be desired—a more personal appeal.

And their art of appeal is based not only on outer appearance—they make the most of every bit of femininity they have!

They well know, for instance, that personal daintiness is one of their strongest points of appeal. And they know the ever-threatening danger of one foe.

The great danger of underarm odor is that you may so easily offend *unconsciously.* The unusually active perspiration glands here; lack of evaporation—these things cause a condition that ordinary cleanliness cannot reach. The underarm must have regular care, just as the teeth and fingernails.

A perspiration corrective is necessary. 3,000,000 people now find their one best means of maintaining perfect personal daintiness through regular use of Odorono, the Underarm Toilette.

Odorono—equally effective for moisture and odor

Odorono was the first perspiration corrective to be perfected. Originally a physician's prescription, it is antiseptic in action and *perfectly harmless.* Physicians and nurses use it in hospitals as a thoroughly effective, scientific corrective.

A liquid, Odorono is as easy and delightful to use as a toilet water. And the joy of it is that one application gives at least three days' protection!

By correcting the cause of excessive underarm perspiration, Odorono saves the discomfort of soaked clothing, the expense of stained and ruined gowns. And you need bother with no other protection. With Odorono you may be absolutely sure that you never offend with the slightest taint of perspiration odor.

As one enthusiastic user writes: "I have used liquid Odorono for four years now and find that it keeps me free from *all* perspiration annoyance. I wish every woman might give it a trial for her own sake as well as for those about her." You, too, will find it indispensable when once you use it. At all toilet counters, 35c, 60c and $1 or by mail postpaid.

Of further interest

Men also find Odorono indispensable for toilet use. Send for special men's booklet, "Perfect Grooming Consists of More Than Cleanliness."

For hurting feet.—Odorono used twice a week will give tender, perspiring feet permanent relief. It keeps them comfortably dry and free from odor.

Personal service.—If you have a special problem relating to perspiration or know others who are bothered to an unusual degree, I will gladly advise you. Write and tell me about it.

Send for generous samples

I will send you generous samples of Odorono and Creme Odorono together with booklet of complete information. Or, sample of either one for 5c. The coupon below is for your convenience.

RUTH MILLER
The Odorono Company
708 Blair Avenue, Cincinnati, Ohio

Expressly for perspiration odor—Creme Odorono

You may not be annoyed by excessive perspiration moisture. In that case you will find Creme Odorono effective for just what you need—simply a deodorant. For of course the fact that you do not have troublesome moisture does not mean freedom from underarm odor.

Creme Odorono is a fragrant, nongreasy cream which vanishes at once on the skin. You can use it when dressing, for quick use, or for an entire day's protection and be assured of perfect daintiness. Large tube, 25c.

RUTH MILLER
708 Blair Avenue, Cincinnati, O.
Enclosed 10c. Send me, please, samples of Odorono and Creme Odorono. Also booklet.

Name _____

Address _____
(Note: For sample of either one of above enclose 5c and cross out one not wanted.)

Underarm deodorants were a lucrative by-product of Jazz Age fashions.

What is your baby worth?

Priceless! A great gift that can never be replaced! Innocent and defenseless. Its comfort and health, even life itself, depend on little duties that constitute vigilant care and loving thoughtfulness.

In the summertime no greater service can be rendered than to shield the child and its food from the perilous contact with flies and mosquitoes.

The fly is the filthiest insect known. Literally hundreds—some scientists say, thousands—of deadly bacteria swarm in the putrescent ooze of a fly's spongy foot. It contaminates everything it touches. Sows the germs of disease on the very delicacies a child likes to eat.

The mosquito is no less an assassin. Whole epidemics have been traced by its ravages. Penetrating a child's tender skin, the bite is bitterly painful. And with the germ of fever firing their blood, little bodies writhe in the burning torture of flaming torment. The end—sometimes is tragic.

Flies and mosquitoes transmit typhoid fever, dysentery, infantile paralysis. Safety is only possible when these insects are killed. That is why devoted parents in millions of homes use Fly-Tox. It destroys flies and mosquitoes. It safeguards the health and comfort of our most precious possession—little children.

Wherever there are flies, use Fly-Tox

In many finely appointed homes spraying every room with Fly-Tox is a daily summertime accomplishment. This is not just an exceptional refinement. Indeed, it is considered a requisite to good housekeeping.

Spraying the entire room with Fly-Tox reaches and kills offensive household insects even in their places of hiding. That insures unmolested summer comfort. Musty, fly-tainted odors are displaced by an atmosphere of cleanliness. The draperies are unsoiled, spotless, beautiful. The upholstery fresh and bright, radiant with cleanliness. In the absence of unclean household insects, every room in the house glows with a refreshing, cleanly charm—a charm in which every housewife enjoys a rightful pride.

The Modern Safeguard to Health and Comfort

Fly-Tox is an established, efficient household insecticide. It was developed at Mellon Institute of Industrial Research. Stainless. Harmless to humans. Yet when its cleanly fragrant spray touches them these insect enemies to man's health and comfort crumple up and die. Fly-Tox has brought to millions of homes a new summer comfort—a house without flies or mosquitoes.

Most people prefer the hand sprayer. It gives better satisfaction. However, a trial sprayer is given free with every small bottle.

HALF PINT · 50C   PINT · 75C   QUART · $1.25   GALLON · $4.00
Gallons in glass jugs are especially suitable for hotels, restaurants, summer camps, institutions

FLY-TOX
KILLS FLIES
MOSQUITOES
MOTHS, ROACHES, ANTS, FLEAS

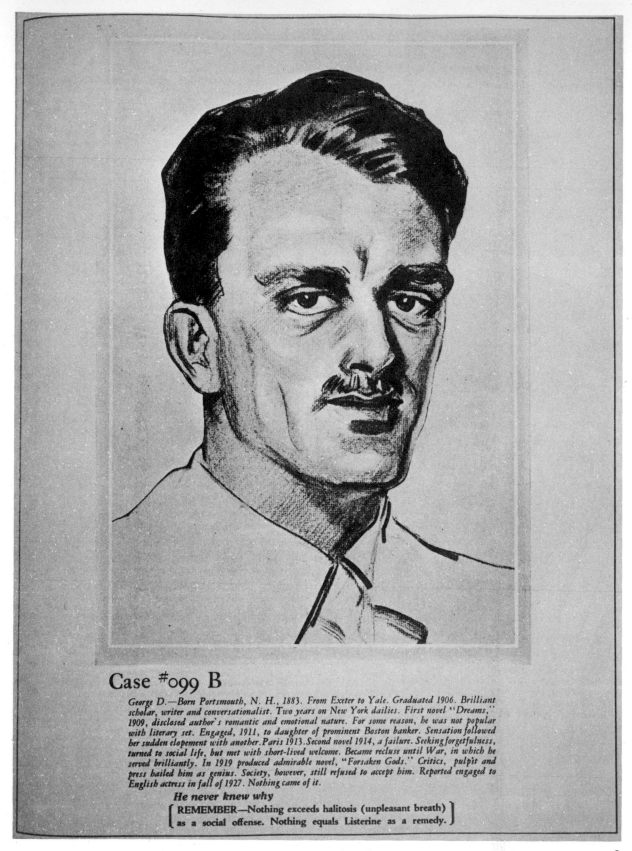

Case #099 B

George D.—Born Portsmouth, N. H., 1883. From Exeter to Yale. Graduated 1906. Brilliant scholar, writer and conversationalist. Two years on New York dailies. First novel "Dreams," 1909, disclosed author's romantic and emotional nature. For some reason, he was not popular with literary set. Engaged, 1911, to daughter of prominent Boston banker. Sensation followed her sudden elopement with another. Paris 1913. Second novel 1914, a failure. Seeking forgetfulness, turned to social life, but met with short-lived welcome. Became recluse until War, in which he served brilliantly. In 1919 produced admirable novel, "Forsaken Gods." Critics, pulpit and press hailed him as genius. Society, however, still refused to accept him. Reported engaged to English actress in fall of 1927. Nothing came of it.

He never knew why

[REMEMBER—Nothing exceeds halitosis (unpleasant breath) as a social offense. Nothing equals Listerine as a remedy.]

1928

Halitosis has long been an American obsession. In 1975 over 250 million dollars was spent in the United States on mouthwash—more than in the rest of the world combined.

Silent Purchase
A Modess Advantage

FOR the first time, a silent purchase plan for a sanitary napkin! And a napkin of wonderful improvements—soft, protective, absolutely disposable—Modess. Women are buying it, marveling at it, and buying again. But even with this new and ideal napkin the old embarrassment of purchasing was still a problem until Johnson & Johnson solved it so easily and ingeniously that you will wonder no one thought of it before.

In order that Modess may be obtained in a crowded store without embarrassment or discussion, Johnson & Johnson devised the Silent Purchase Coupon presented below. Simply cut it out and hand to the sales person. You will receive one box of Modess. Could anything be easier? Is there a woman anywhere who will not be grateful for this method of silent purchase?

Your first Modess will be a revelation of unhoped-for comfort. The great Johnson & Johnson laboratories worked four years to make the finest and most comfortable sanitary napkin ever offered to women. An entirely new substance, soft as the finest cotton, was invented for the disposable center. The gauze is specially softened and sides are gently rounded to prevent chafing. Modess has a moisture-resisting back. Once more the famous Red Cross trade-mark distinguishes a sanitary product of amazing superiority.

Fifty cents for a box of twelve.

Modess
so infinitely finer

SIX
SUPERIORITIES

1. Gauze specially softened with a film of down.

2. Pliant fluffy filler of amazing absorbency.

3. Rounded sides assuring comfort and no clumsiness.

4. A moisture-resisting back giving positive security.

5. Disposable—flushes away.

6. Silent purchase coupon.

© by J & J

SILENT PURCHASE COUPON

To Sales Person—
One box of Modess, *please*
The New sanitary napkin made by
Johnson & Johnson
NEW BRUNSWICK, N.J., U.S.A.

A serious business handicap
—these troubles that come from harsh toilet tissue

65% of all men and women over 40 are suffering from some form of rectal trouble, estimates a prominent specialist connected with one of New York's largest hospitals. "And one of the contributing causes," he states, "is inferior toilet tissue."

INTENSE SUFFERING usually accompanies most rectal ailments. Chronic pain that gradually wears down reserve energy . . . and handicaps a man in his daily work.

Specialists say that cases of this kind are astonishingly prevalent among all classes of people—men, women and children.

Often these troubles can be traced to the harsh-surfaced or chemically impure toilet tissues so frequently found in business or public toilets.

Why expose yourself to these dangers?

Speak to the superintendent at your place of work, or the man who does the purchasing. Ask him to install health-protecting Scott Tissues.

These famous toilet tissues are just as low-priced as the ordinary

"cheap" tissues, and they are absolutely safe from a health standpoint.

All three brands, ScotTissue, Sani-Tissue and Waldorf, are extremely soft—yet tough and strong in texture. Crumpled in the hand, they feel like old linen . . . suave and yielding.

They are unusually absorbent. Without this absorbent quality, thorough cleansing is impossible. This is why Scott Tissues are so much safer than ordinary toilet tissues.

Scott Tissues are chemically pure—neither acid nor alkaline in reaction. Made from the finest fresh materials. Each sheet is fully sterilized in manufacture.

Don't take chances with inferior tissue . . . at home or at the office. Be safe . . . always buy or use Scott Tissues. Scott Paper Company, Chester, Pa.

3 for 25¢

Sani-Tissue
A Scott Tissue

Soft as old Linen
Scott Tissue
The absorbent soft white Toilet paper
Scott Paper Company

2 for 25¢
Prices for U. S. only

© 1930, Scott Paper Company

The **Waldorf**
A Scott Tissue

3 for 20¢

Scott Tissues

They fit the built-in fixtures

NOTE: ScotTissue and Waldorf are the two largest selling brands in the world . . . Sani-Tissue is the new popular priced white toilet tissue embodying the famous *thirsty fibre* qualities.

1930

An example of how any product could find a new marketing identity during the Depression.

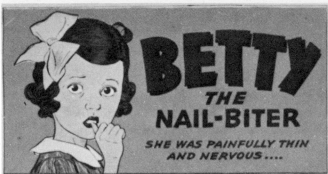

How Ovaltine Helps to Curb Child's Nervousness

Often Adding Weight at a Surprisingly Rapid Rate

OVALTINE is a pure food concentrate approved by more than 20,000 doctors. It is highly valued because of the very noticeable increases in both weight and nerve poise, which so frequently occur, when Ovaltine is added to the regular daily fare.

A series of scientific tests conducted with 48 school children in New York showed a decrease in nervousness, in some cases, of 25% in 2 weeks (as measured by the Olson-University of Minnesota checking system) when Ovaltine was added to the regular diet.

85% of all nervous under-par children treated in these New York tests responded almost at once. In one case, nervousness diminished as much as 18% in a single week.

While these results are of outstanding significance to mothers of nervous children, they are equally important to the mothers of underweight children, too. For child specialists have long observed that underweight and nervousness usually go hand in hand.

Thus, when a child is given Ovaltine, he frequently benefits 2 ways. For it acts to break up the "vicious circle" that nervousness and underweight always tend to create. And often, weight increases of a pound a week or more are reported when Ovaltine is added to the normal diet.

You simply mix Ovaltine with milk —either hot or cold—and children love it for its delicious taste. (Note the special offer of the genuine Little Orphan Annie Mug for serving hot Ovaltine.)

Special Offer FOR BOYS AND GIRLS!

MAIL FOR BRAND-NEW ORPHAN ANNIE MUG

Here's a chance to get the very latest Orphan Annie Mug with new and *different* colored pictures of Orphan Annie and Sandy. Made of genuine Beetleware. Our regular price 50c—now sent to Ovaltine users for *only* 10c.

To obtain—cut out and fill in the coupon below. Then get a can of Ovaltine at your drug or grocery store. Take out all of the thin aluminum seal you find under the lid of the can and mail it in to THE WANDER COMPANY, DEPT. H6-LHJ5, 180 NORTH MICHIGAN AVE., CHICAGO, together with 10c and the coupon below. In a few days the postman will bring you a brand-new Little Orphan Annie Mug as illustrated here.

(If you do not enclose aluminum seal from can of Ovaltine, send 50c, our regular price.) Mail coupon now.

OVALTINE

The Swiss Food-Drink—Now made in the U.S.A.

Don't neglect coated tongue! It usually indicates an unhealthy condition of your intestines. Correct this trouble with yeast.

"COATED TONGUE

—that's a symptom of self-poisoning!"

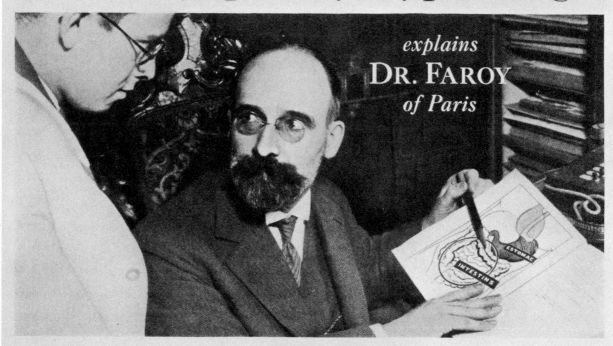

explains
DR. FAROY
of Paris

"—In such cases I advise fresh Yeast," declares this famous medical authority

That white, coated tongue of yours! It's a signal of bodily distress. *Heed it.*

That's the advice leading doctors—including world-famous medical authorities—are now giving.

For instance—here is the statement of Dr. Georges Faroy, author of the famous "Digestive Therapeutics." Dr. Faroy is head of the department for internal diseases in the great Hôpital Beaujon, Paris. *He says:—*

"Poisons that collect in the intestines undermine health . . . Headaches, coated tongue, indigestion and general loss of vitality are symptoms.

"I advise people suffering from these ailments to avoid cathartics and harsh laxatives. I know no safer means for permanently overcoming constipation than fresh yeast."

If you would "tone up" your system and keep it free of the poisons that lead to coated tongue, bad breath, bad skin, etc., try Fleischmann's Yeast!

Just eat it regularly, like any other food—3 cakes every day. Eat it before meals, or between meals and at bedtime—plain or dissolved in water (a third of a glass).

Won't you try it today?

DR. STRASSER, head of a well-known Austrian sanatorium, states: "Fresh yeast has a revitalizing effect on the intestines."

DR. WEICKSEL, of the University of Leipzig, Germany, states: "Fresh yeast increases secretion of gastric juices . . . purifies."

"My Experience Proves the Doctors are Right"

"Extra work, together with my studies, made a very full schedule," *writes* Miss Ethel A. Anderson, *of New York.*

"I felt very run-down . . . often had headaches. My system felt sluggish . . . I began eating three cakes of Fleischmann's Yeast every day . . . Now I don't believe I have ever felt better. I have no more headaches. My strength came back. Yeast cleared up my complexion beautifully!"

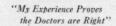

*Important Fleischmann's Yeast for Health is sold only in the foil-wrapped cake with the yellow label. It is yeast in its fresh, effective form, *the kind famous doctors recommend!* Every cake is rich in health-giving vitamins B and G and the "sunshine" vitamin D. At grocers, restaurants and soda fountains. Write for booklet. Dept. Y-CC-12. Standard Brands Incorporated, 691 Washington Street, New York City.
Copyright, 1932, Standard Brands Incorporated

1932

Inexpensive yeast was a miracle drug of the Depression. So heavily was it promoted during this campaign that the Journal of American Medicine *felt obliged to respond to the ads with a study disclaiming most of "Dr. Faroys'" evidence.*

Don't let Adolescent Pimples put a stop to YOUR good times

YOUNG PEOPLE are often plagued by unsightly pimples after the start of adolescence—from about 13 to 25, or longer.

Important glands develop at this time, and final growth takes place causing disturbances in the body. The skin gets oversensitive. Waste poisons in the blood irritate this sensitive skin—and pimples break out!

Fleischmann's fresh Yeast clears these skin irritants out of the blood. Then, the pimples go. Eat 3 cakes *daily*—one about ½ hour before meals—plain, or dissolved in a little water—until your skin clears. Start today!

Copyright, 1936, Standard Brands Incorporated

—clears the skin
by clearing skin irritants - out of the blood

Science now tells you what causes

NERVOUS B.O. (NERVOUS BODY ODOR)

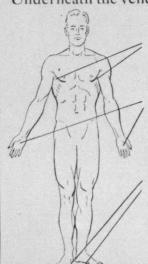

HOW TO WORRY ALL DAY—

I'll take a chance and wear these same underthings a second day—they _seem_ okay.

Oh dear, I wonder if it's possible for people to notice perspiration odor from these underthings so quickly.

The salesgirl gave me such a funny look. She actually seems to be avoiding me. _Am_ I offending?

Seems hot in here, and everybody's so unfriendly. Why _did_ I risk second-day underthings?

Jack's not at all like his usual self—seems so aloof. Is he noticing, too? It's the last time I'll ever take _that_ chance!

From now on, I'm Luxing my undies after every wearing. Then I'm _sure_ they're fresh!

It _NEVER_ pays to take a chance—

Two-day underthings never get by! We all perspire, especially in summer. Others soon notice the stale odor that clings to underthings. To protect daintiness, Lux underthings after _each_ wearing. Lux whisks away odor, yet saves colors. Avoid soaps with harmful alkali—cake-soap rubbing. Safe in water, safe in Lux!

Be sure of yourself in any situation . . . . Take NULLO Daily!

NEW PILL KILLS BODY ODORS AND BAD BREATH!

Absolutely Harmless! Take Nullo like a Vitamin!

FOR BODY ODORS: Take Nullo like a vitamin—1 or 2 tablets daily! Then never "back away" from close contact again! Nullo not only kills underarm perspiration odor—it controls all body odors, including odors of the feet and scalp. No amount of exercise, nervous excitement, or rushing can produce offensive body odor when you take Nullo regularly.

When used as directed women's special odor problems—during the "difficult" period, for instance—are solved once and for all! Even your socks, underwear, dresses, and sweaters will carry no odor. That's because you have no body odors when you take Nullo regularly.

FOR BAD BREATH: Chew Nullo for speedy breath cleansing. Be sure of your breath —even in contact as intimate as a kiss! Not even onions, alcohol or tobacco odors can last against Nullo. Try Nullo today. If not delighted your money back!

SAFE as a lettuce leaf. Nullo contains only an ingredient you eat every day in green vegetables—nature's chlorophyll, specially processed by Dr. F. Howard Westcott's formula. Nullo does not stop natural, healthy perspiration. Taken internally, it safely and effectively deodorizes.

The De Pree Company
Holland, Michigan

Established 1906—Manufacturers of Nurse Brand Drugs and Wheatamin Vitamins

30 day supply $1.25
Economical family size (100 tablets) $2.95

NEW POCKET SIZE 29¢

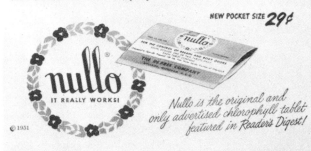

nullo ®
IT REALLY WORKS!

© 1951

Nullo is the original and only advertised chlorophyll tablet featured in Reader's Digest!

Get <u>fast</u> pain relief !

Bufferin
TRADE-MARK

Acts <u>twice as fast</u> as aspirin!
Doesn't upset the stomach!

Here's how Bufferin acts <u>twice as fast</u> as aspirin

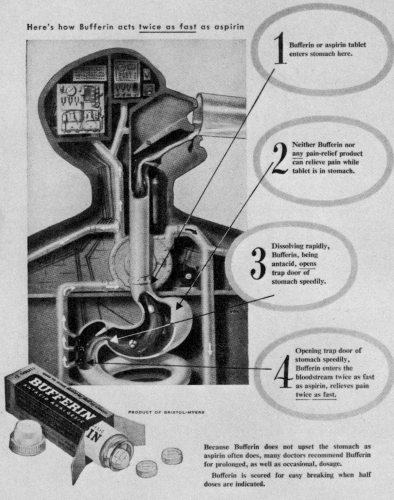

1 Bufferin or aspirin tablet enters stomach here.

2 Neither Bufferin nor any pain-relief product can relieve pain while tablet is in stomach.

3 Dissolving rapidly, Bufferin, being antacid, <u>opens</u> trap door of stomach speedily.

4 Opening trap door of stomach speedily, Bufferin enters the bloodstream twice as fast as aspirin, relieves pain <u>twice as fast.</u>

PRODUCT OF BRISTOL-MYERS

Because Bufferin does not upset the stomach as aspirin often does, many doctors recommend Bufferin for prolonged, as well as occasional, dosage.

Bufferin is scored for easy breaking when half doses are indicated.

No tablet or powder can give you relief from pain until the pain-relieving ingredient enters the bloodstream. Bufferin, being antacid, opens the stomach valve *speedily*, gets *into* the bloodstream *twice as fast* as aspirin! Therefore Bufferin acts *twice as fast* to relieve pain.

And Bufferin won't upset your stomach as aspirin often does, because Bufferin is antacid.

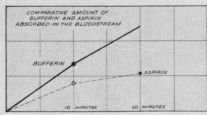

COMPARATIVE AMOUNT OF BUFFERIN AND ASPIRIN ABSORBED IN THE BLOODSTREAM

BUFFERIN

ASPIRIN

10 MINUTES   20 MINUTES

TIME OF ABSORPTION

Clinical studies prove that people who took Bufferin had more pain-relieving ingredient *actually in the bloodstream* in ten minutes than those people who took aspirin had in twenty minutes. That's why Bufferin acts *twice as fast* as aspirin to relieve pain.

For headaches, neuralgia, and ordinary muscular aches and pains, remember Bufferin for fast pain relief! Ask your physician or dentist about Bufferin. Get Bufferin from your druggist. Carry the 12-tablet, pocket-size package. Keep the economical 36- or 100-tablet package in your home medicine chest. Bufferin is also available in Canada.

IF YOU SUFFER FROM ARTHRITIS OR RHEUMATISM, ASK YOUR PHYSICIAN ABOUT BUFFERIN

1951

BAD BREATH
now made "Kissing Sweet" in seconds

Delicious New Chewing Gum, Contains Chlorophyll, That Magical Green Purifier. Banishes Bad Breath from:

ONIONS, GARLIC, SMOKING, ALCOHOL, AND MOST OTHER CAUSES

CLORETS is the delicious new chewing gum that contains Chlorophyll, the amazing green purifier found in growing plants. You simply chew CLORETS, and in seconds, your breath becomes "Kissing Sweet".

You'll find CLORETS the pleasantest way to enjoy the truly astounding benefits of Chlorophyll, Nature's own purifier.

AMAZINGLY EFFECTIVE...CLORETS rid your breath of unpleasant odors. They actually banish most odors that make your breath offensive.

CONVENIENT...Chew CLORETS just as you chew any gum. If you like gum, then you'll thoroughly enjoy delicious CLORETS. You'll want to adopt CLORETS as your regular chewing gum. They're *that* good! And how comforting to know that when you chew CLORETS, your breath will tell no tales.

LONG-LASTING PROTECTION...Keep CLORETS in pocket or purse. Chew one or two *after* you eat, drink or smoke and *before* every important date. CLORETS keep your breath "Kissing Sweet".

GARLIC LOVER: Enjoy garlic and other flavorful foods without broadcasting the smell. Simply chew CLORETS.

ALCOHOL: After drinking, chew 1 or 2 CLORETS. Your breath will tell no tales.

MORNING BREATH: Chew CLORETS. Your breath becomes "Kissing Sweet" almost instantly.

WE DARE YOU TO MAKE THIS "BREATH TEST"

Don't accept our word for what CLORETS will do. Make this convincing test yourself. Eat onions or garlic; smoke a cigar, take a drink. Then chew 1 or 2 CLORETS. Now ask your best friend to smell your breath. She's *sure* to tell you, "Your breath is Kissing Sweet."

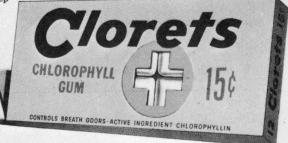

Clorets
CHLOROPHYLL GUM   15¢
CONTROLS BREATH ODORS · ACTIVE INGREDIENT CHLOROPHYLLIN

1951

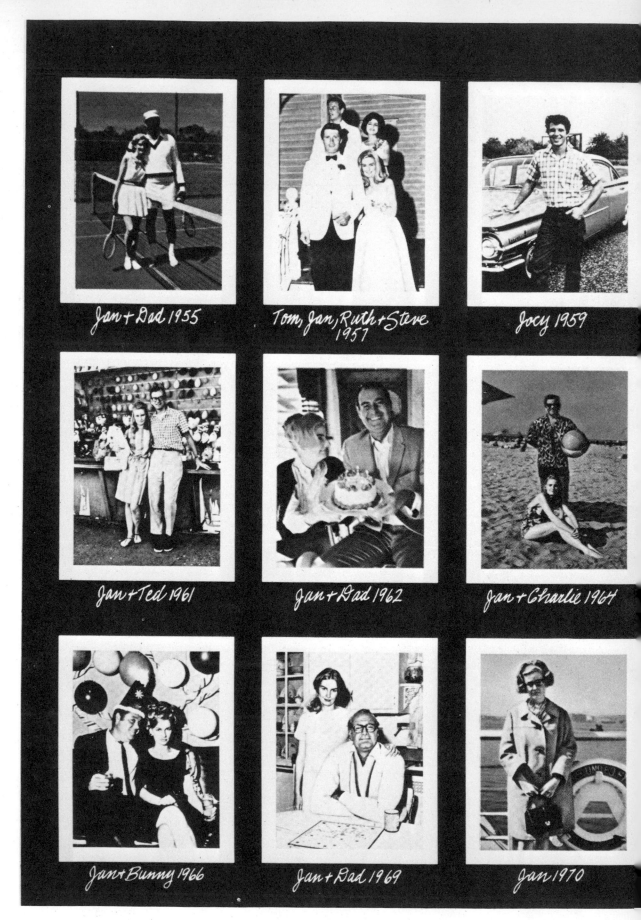

Jan + Dad 1955

Tom, Jan, Ruth + Steve 1957

Joey 1959

Jan + Ted 1961

Jan + Dad 1962

Jan + Charlie 1964

Jan + Bunny 1966

Jan + Dad 1969

Jan 1970

Valium is the most commonly prescribed tranquilizer. Recent studies show that 67 percent of the users of minor tranquilizers are women.

35, single and psychoneurotic

The purser on her cruise ship took the last snapshot of Jan. You probably see many such Jans in your practice. The unmarrieds with low self-esteem. Jan never found a man to measure up to her father. Now she realizes she's in a losing pattern—and that she may *never* marry.

Valium (diazepam) can be a useful adjunct in the therapy of the tense, over anxious patient who has a neurotic sense of failure, guilt or loss. Over the years, Valium has proven its value in the relief of psychoneurotic states—anxiety, apprehension, agitation, alone or with depressive symptoms.

Valium 10-mg tablets help relieve the emotional "storms" of psychoneurotic tension and the depressive symptoms that can go hand-in-hand with it. Valium 2-mg or 5-mg tablets, *t.i.d.* or *q.i.d.*, are usually sufficient for milder tension and anxiety states. An *h.s.* dose added to the *t.i.d.* dosage often facilitates a good night's rest.

Valium®(diazepam)
for psychoneurotic states manifested by psychic tension and depressive symptoms

Roche
LABORATORIES
Division of Hoffmann-La Roche Inc.
Nutley, New Jersey 07110

The most important minutes of your summer day

When hot weather makes you feel tense, irritable, headachy, two Bayer Aspirin and a short rest can help you feel better fast!

It happens to most of us on a hot, humid summer day, when the pressures of daily living mount up. By mid-afternoon we feel so headachy and edgy that we're in no mood to enjoy life or the company of others.

Here's how to turn that mood around: just take two Bayer Aspirin for your headache, sit down for a few minutes and relax. These few minutes can make a world of difference in the way you feel and act. You'll enjoy being with people, and they'll enjoy being with you.

When you get headachy and out of sorts on a hot afternoon, set aside a few minutes for Bayer Aspirin and a brief rest. These can be the most important minutes of your day.

Special Fortified Formula

TURNS OFF HEADACHE PAIN RELIEVES ITS NERVOUS TENSION AND DEPRESSION

What's best to take for tension headache pain? Why not take the pain relief compound doctors recommend most for headaches? You'll find it in Anacin* Tablets. And today's Anacin gives you *more* of it than any other leading headache tablet. In minutes Anacin breaks the grip of headache pain so relaxes its nervous tension and helps lift its depression. You can bounce back fast with Anacin. You see Anacin is a special fortified combination of ingredients and *only Anacin has this formula.* Next time a tension headache strikes, see if medically proven Anacin doesn't work better for you.

1964   1967

In the strident sixties, as prescription tranquilizers and new "over-the-counter" drugs such as Vanquish and Compoz helped sooth middle-class America's nerves, the standard headache remedy advertisers attempted to cash in on the Age of Anxiety by promoting their analgesics as mood changers and anti-depressants.

"Beauti-Breast boosted my ego almost as much as my bustline!"

"I shaped up my bustline— gaining 3 inches in just 14 days. I owe it all to Beauti-Breast of Paris!" says Sandy Dixon.

"This wonderful plan really worked—adding three firm, eye-catching inches to my bustline, and improving the appearance of my breasts, in just *two short weeks!*

"And there's no doubt about it! I was a volunteer, with 9 other women, on a medically conducted test to find out how much an average woman can improve her bustline within 14 days on the *Beauti-Breast* plan. At the start of the program, my bustline was measured by the doctor's head nurse in front of witnesses. Fourteen days later, the same nurse and witnesses measured it again. The tape measure proved my bustline went from 35 to 38 inches. A *full 3-inch gain!*

"But, of course, I already knew what to expect, because I had seen the delightful transformation taking place in my figure. And, to be perfectly frank, I noticed that *others* were beginning to notice, too!

"Beauti-Breast boosted my ego almost as much as my bustline. You can't imagine what an unbelievable experience it is to suddenly blossom out 'for real' after all those hopeless years of trying to look like what I wasn't.

"I'll never give it up! And I know that as long as I stick with the *Beauti-Breast Plan...* continue to use the hydro-breast-massager, the skin-softening cremes, and follow the exercise and diet suggestions in the 'Guide,' I'll never lose my firm, new look!

"One more thing—if you're like me, and have to diet from time to time to keep trim everywhere else, you've probably already discovered the same thing I learned. When you start shedding pounds, one of the first places you start losing is the *bustline!* Right?

"Well, thanks to *Beauti-Breast,* I've got that problem solved once and for all. Now, I can lose weight mainly *where it counts.* My bustline stays firm, shapely, and lovely.

"All I can say about the *Beauti-Breast of Paris* plan is...*I love it! I love it! I love it!"*

Sandy Dixon

"Dozens of tiny jets of pulsating water, swirling and dancing around my breasts, gently massaging them and part of my bustline, was a pleasure-filled and restful experience!"

I LOVE IT!

Our Clinically Tested BEAUTI-BREAST OF PARIS Kit Includes:
1. Bustline Developer Guide
2. Hydrotherapy Water-Massage Contour Cup
3. Beauti-Breast Cremes
SENT IN PLAIN WRAPPER

ALSO AVAILABLE AT BETTER BEAUTY SALONS

Patented. © Joe Weider 1975

WILL BEAUTI-BREAST PLAN REALLY WORK FOR ME AS WELL?

Yes, it will. And here's the proof. We asked 3 groups of women aged 19 to 58 to participate in 3 different 14-day tests conducted by eminent medical doctors and fitness experts. Results of these tests prove beyond a shadow of a doubt that our plan works ...and works fast! Gains reported from just one of these tests are reproduced below. Especially note the gains of Sandy Dixon, the fourth subject listed in this series of tests.

MEASUREMENTS

Subject	Initial	After First 15-Minute Treatment	After 14 15-Minute Treatments
K.S.	33½	34	34½
P.O.	35	36	38
M.B.	34½	—	36
S.D.	35	—	38
L.L.	35	35¼	36¼
D.R.	34	35	37
D.T.	32	32½	34
B.H.	32	32½	34½

Average bustline increase after 14 days: over 2 inches.

HOW CAN OUR BUSTLINE PLAN PRODUCE SUCH STARTLING RESULTS?

The prominent doctor who conducted this test explains it this way: "Breasts, having no muscles, are supported and totally dependent on your upper bustline musculature to give them a more pronounced appearance. These muscles can start deteriorating, even at the age of 19, which can result in a sagging, aged look. The Beauti-Breast Plan strengthens these muscles, adding the vital support that keeps the breasts lifted and the bustline higher, firmer, and better contoured. The posture muscles are also strengthened, lifting breasts that appear to be flattened against the rib cage. The Plan also affects the Cooper's ligaments that help support the breasts, moving them forward and upward, helping to further enhance breasts and bustline beauty."

The breasts are primarily made up of mammary glands and fatty deposits. It's the fatty deposits that control the size of the breasts. Since proper nutrition may affect fatty deposits, we have included a nutritional guide to help influence breast size growth if your breasts are small due to a lack of proper nutrition.

NOW...YOU CAN DEVELOP THE KIND OF BUSTLINE YOU ALWAYS WANTED! OUR GUARANTEE!

"Your very first use will give you an amazing temporary gain of ¼ to 1 inch. Continued use will result in a lasting increase of another 1 or 2 more inches, if you stay with the program. *We guarantee it...* or your $19.98 will be refunded immediately, no questions asked!" What can be fairer? What could be nicer to look forward to? DO IT NOW!

DON'T WAIT TO START MAKING GAINS. DO IT NOW!

Beauti-Breast of Paris DEPT. BY/LA
P.O. Box 8072, Van Nuys, Calif. 91409

I'LL TRY IT! What it did for Sandy and test subjects proves it will increase my bustline also. I am therefore enclosing $19.98 for the Complete Beauti-Breast Plan, including Hydrotherapy Contour Cup, Bustline Increaser Guide and Beauti-Breast cremes, to be sent in plain wrapper on your satisfaction or money back offer. Calif. res. add 6% sales tax. **Enclosed is** (Check one) ☐ **Check or ☐ Money Order.** (No C.O.D.'s Please) Complete plan mailed prepaid. Please allow 3 to 4 weeks for delivery.

Name _____ Age___ Bustline Measurement _____ (Optional)

Address _____

City _____ State _____ Zip _____

Master Charge ☐ Bank Americard ☐ Account # _____

Signature _____ Expiration date _____

Body Persuasion System, Inc., 21100 Erwin Street, Woodland Hills, CA 91364

IN CANADA: Beauti-Breast Plan, 2875 Bates Rd., Montreal, Que.

HEROES, HEROINES, AND CELEBRITIES

Most generalizations about America, or Americans, or the American Character, even those often-quoted ones made by such perceptive observers as Alexis de Tocqueville and James Bryce, usually end up only as good grist for the mills of future historians. But even with such a cautionary view at hand it still seems safe to say that Americans today are obsessed with the notion of fame. Who's famous? Who's *more* famous? Why are they famous? Do they deserve to be famous? These questions and a few variations seem to be a preoccupation of people in the intelligentsia and the working class alike, at least if one can believe the mass media. Entire magazines are now devoted to the fame game, while newspapers and television news programs have added special "people" sections that deal with the rich, the talented, and the merely well-known. Magazine circulations and Nielsen ratings can tumble or skyrocket on the basis of which personality agrees to appear on what cover and what talk show. In the advertising business—a traditional source of income and publicity for the famous—unprecedented sums of money are being spent to secure the endorsement of a whole range of celebrities, from superstars to has-beens. Today the choice of the right personality can literally mean the difference between profit and loss.

The nature of the endorsement technique and the reasons for its strong appeal to consumers and advertisers alike can best be understood by considering the over-all setting for most advertisements. Advertising usually exists within a context created by the media, so ads literally compete with the content of each medium for the attention of readers, listeners, and viewers. Because the American mass media devote only a small amount of time and space to news and information and are overwhelmingly committed to entertainment, the presence of a well-known personality in a sales talk gives the advertiser a chance of having his product's name and his message noted—and remembered. Furthermore, in today's heavily commercialized atmosphere, ads compete with each other whether or not they're for the same kind of product. Although all of this is now most obviously true on television, the history of celebrity endorsements dates back to the late nineteenth century.

In one sense the endorsement is as old as salesmanship itself. Patent-medicine showmen, drummers, and pitchmen often linked the names of the famous, the respected, or the legendary to whatever they were hawking; before the age of instant communications it was a moot point whether or not they were telling the truth. In the decades following the Civil War, as printed salesmanship evolved into modern advertising, pictures of the highly born, the powerful, and the celebrated became a permanent feature of America's system of selling. Occasionally a president or a ruling monarch, even the Pope, would be enlisted in support of some workaday product, usually without the famous person's consent. By the end of the century, however, such people in the public eye as President William McKinley and noted suffragette Elizabeth Cady Stanton willingly participated in the burgeoning new world of advertising. They turned out to be the first in a long line of newsworthy figures whose faces have appeared throughout the pages of advertising history. Politicians, politicians' wives, ex-politicians, politicians masquerading as movie stars, important writers, famous artists, daring adventurers, and renowned explorers have all lent their names and reputations to the promotion of America's never-ending cornucopia of goods and services.

But as everyone knows, the overwhelming number of celebrity endorsements has always been given by performers from the entertainment worlds of show business and big-league sports. This practice, too, dates back to the turn of the century, when the great stars of theater and opera—Sarah Bernhardt, Enrico Caruso, Lillian Russell, the idols of America's rapidly growing urban middle class—often offered an endorsement of some product. Some baseball players had attained a modicum of fame as early as the 1880s, and cards with their pictures were distributed by tobacco companies. However, only after 1910, as baseball became entrenched as the only true American game, did such popular players as Ty Cobb and Honus Wagner begin to appear in the print ads of the day. These early star performers proved to be the prototypes for a new breed of public personality whose presence in American life would be even more pervasive as new communications systems changed the very nature of fame and the meaning of celebrity.

During the 1920s film personalities began to make frequent appearances in advertising. Stars of the first rank—Mary Pickford, Douglas Fairbanks,

Charlie Chaplin—saw endorsements as an opportunity to promote themselves and their movies; "starlets" like the young Joan Crawford were eager to make some extra cash and to stay in the public eye in any way. Producers and directors, including D. W. Griffith, and later Walt Disney and Busby Berkeley, also relied on the publicity value of testimonials. This pattern of Hollywood's involvement in advertising was established very early and remained absolutely constant until about 1960. During that time almost every major star appeared in the print ads of the day: Gable, Bogey, and the Duke, archetypes of masculinity for a whole generation, together with Shirley Temple, Grable, Hayworth, and Monroe, the entire spectrum of American womanhood, all urged readers to buy a whole range of products (and to see their "latest picture"). More often than not, the men endorsed cigarettes or automotive products, the women beauty-care items or soft drinks.

In the 1930s radio rapidly emerged as the most popular of all the media. By the end of the decade almost 90 percent of all American homes had a receiving set and it was turned on more than four hours a day. Unlike film, radio was an advertising-supported medium, that is, the advertisers paid for the programs and the air time in order to attract potential customers for their goods and services. Not too much time passed before the advertisers required big-time radio stars to participate in the commercials, so in a real sense the endorsement technique was built directly into the broadcasting system. Fred Allen, Jack Benny, Major Bowes, Bing Crosby, Bob Hope, Kate Smith, Rudy Vallee, in fact just about every major radio personality, took part in at least one commercial during every weekly show. Most of them also appeared in print ads re-endorsing their sponsor's product and reminding readers of the day, time, and network for their programs.

Radio was the crucial instrument in the process that transformed famous sports figures into big-name celebrities. Ruth, Dempsey, Gehrig, Grange, and Louis would certainly have been legendary heroes of their game in any age, but radio enabled their exploits to be heard by millions of people. As their popularity increased, so too did their salaries and the number of advertisers who wished to have their products associated with the greats of their time. Radio had made them—like the singers, comedians, and actors—entertainers who performed in an advertising medium. During radio's heyday, other, lesser names in sport also became well-known to the listening audience and received financial benefits from advertisers. Interestingly enough, athletes did more endorsements for cigarettes than for any other product.

Television, as the child of commercial radio, was predestined to imitate the structure, styles, and habits of the earlier medium. By 1950 most of the popular radio talent had moved over to television, which in the early days was simply radio with pictures. Often these pictures contained the sponsor's name in enormous letters and, whenever possible, the star of the show holding the product. A few celebrities like Arthur Godfrey and Art Linkletter were especially adept at doing commercials and so were always able to find sponsors for their programs. Naturally, the tradition of popular broadcasting people appearing in print ads continued, and soon the magazines were filled with endorsements by Lucille Ball, Sid Caesar and Imogene Coca, Bert Parks, Hal March, Dinah Shore, Red Skelton, Hopalong Cassidy, and Howdy Doody. Baseball players, too, benefited from exposure on TV, and as set sales zoomed, endorsements piled up for the likes of DiMaggio, Williams, and Mantle. A few black players also began doing testimonials, because on television the greatness of Robinson, Mays, and Aaron could not be hidden behind a color line.

During the cultural upheavals of the 1960s, celebrity endorsements suffered a severe loss in prestige, especially among the young, whose heroes —the Beatles, Dylan, the Rolling Stones—openly mocked advertising and the whole business system. In addition, the Hollywood star factory died (helped to its grave by television), and film's most important actors now either shunned publicity or openly espoused radical political beliefs. Finally even the greediest of athletes found it difficult to endorse smoking in the face of vigorous government assertions that long-term use of tobacco poisoned the human body. In such a hostile atmosphere, many thought that the best endorsements were satires on the genre, such as Braniff's "When You've Got It, Flaunt It" campaign, which featured a hodgepodge roster of new celebrities like Sonny Liston, Andy Warhol, and Joe Namath.

By making it plain that he only did it for the money, Namath, more than anyone else, helped to make the endorsement respectable again. His continued success is indicative of the way advertising on television has developed. Because TV had the power to create a national mania for football, the game's most famous player could become the medium's most frequently visible salesman. Because TV could take us to the Olympics and teach us about all kinds of sports, endorsements from ice skaters, swimmers, skiers, and decathlon winners became highly desirable. Television also took us into space and finally to the moon, and many of the men who manned the ships became like other celebrities, visiting TV talk shows and, after leaving the service, doing testimonials.

Of course, television changed all the established rules about fame. When a person can be seen by twenty or thirty million viewers simultaneously, it doesn't much matter what he or she is doing or how talented: They are ipso facto well-known. Because advertising has always played a central role in television history, many commercial "stars" have benefited from the medium's ability to create instant celebrities. Even in the earlier days a few advertising spokesmen like Rex Marshall and "Speedy Alka-Seltzer" became as well-known as the entertainers; some, like Ed McMahon, became show-business personalities in their own right. These days the power of television advertising has, unfortunately, made Mr. Whipple, Madge the Manicurist, and Morris the Cat more familiar to the American people than the names and faces of most senators or cabinet members.

Today the distinction between entertainer and salesperson is increasingly blurred, because the same performers play the same roles on the programs that they do in the commercials. Nancy Walker, for example, has been familiar to television watchers as the smart-aleck maid on *McMillan and Wife*, the smart-aleck mother on *Rhoda*, the smart-aleck agent on *Blansky's Beauties*, and the smart-aleck waitress in the Bounty paper-towel ads. Another example is Farrah Fawcett-Majors, who as Noxzema's first "Great Balls o' Comfort" girl displayed all of the assets essential to being cast as one of *Charlie's Angels*; from there she went on to make commercials for companies, not as a nameless pretty face but as a famous, sexy television performer. Some role-switching can have more serious implications, as when Robert Young, known to tens of millions as Dr. Welby, was employed to sell a health-care product. Vigorous complaints by the Federal Trade Commission, consumer groups, as well as the competition, attest to the fact that most of us know the power the tube can exercise over our perception of the world—and of the characters in it.

According to *Advertising Age*, about 20 percent of today's most effective television commercials use celebrities to attract the attention of the enormous viewing audience. An increasing number of these are the already familiar faces from television's most successful programs: Karl Malden, Telly Savalas, and Bobby "Baretta" Blake. However, as the air waves become cluttered with strident program announcements and with more commercials of shorter duration, advertisers are spending outlandish amounts of money to get the biggest stars and most important names. John Wayne and Sophia Loren have recently been paid over $300,000 each, while Elizabeth Taylor, Barbra Streisand, and Carol Burnett have each reportedly turned down $1 million to do one testimonial. The ability of entertainers to refuse this kind of money may tell us something about the nature of celebrity life in America, but offering a seven-figure inducement clearly reveals just how deeply embedded the tradition of endorsements has become, and how important they are to advertiser and consumer alike.

In the pages that follow we have provided a very short history of the advertising business's devotion to the cause of fame. Our criteria for inclusion have been personal and therefore, strictly speaking, arbitrary. We did strive to show a broad range of personalities, but we confess a partiality for the endorsers who came from outside the realms of sports and entertainment. We decided that the slight distortion was worth it since the nontraditional endorsements give a sharper sense of how the advertising business employs contemporary people and events to sell products. On the other hand, most of the athletes and entertainers included were extraordinarily famous, even legendary, and many, such as Jackie Robinson and Ronald Reagan, have had importance outside the celebrity world.

McKinley and Waterman

FOR PRESIDENT.   **FOR PENS.**

IT IS THE ONE FOUNTAIN PEN ENTIRELY SATISFACTORY.
A TRIAL PERMITTED; EXCHANGES ARE INVITED.

I have been using one of your fountain pens for several months, and take pleasure in saying that I find it an invaluable pocket companion.

Very truly yours,

W. McKinley

Inquire at your local dealer's, or write for booklet.

EXHIBITED AT THE INTERNATIONAL EXPOSITION UNIVERSELLE, ESPLANADE DES INVALIDES.

L. E. Waterman Co.,

157 Broadway, New York, N. Y.   12 Golden Lane, London, E. C.

1900

Although it seems outlandish to us to see an incumbent President appearing in an advertisement, McKinley was up for reelection when he appeared in the above ad, so his desire for any kind of public attention is at least understandable. But Stanton's motives, like those of other notables who appeared in ads at this time, remain a matter of conjecture. Was it merely a desire for fame? Or money? (How much, if anything, she received is not known.) Was she seeking to publicize the women's movement or simply a forum to express her views on the "perfumed woman"?

290

His Majesty King Edward VII

Chooses an

ANGELUS
PLAYER-PIANO

In December, a few days too late to publish a suitable announcement for an earlier issue of this magazine, we received the following cablegram from our European representatives:

" Sir Herbert Marshall Sons & Rose have had the distinguished honor of supplying one of their own make of pianos fitted with the ANGELUS player, to His Majesty, King Edward VII."

Although this is by no means the first time a King, or member of royalty, has purchased an ANGELUS, nevertheless this most recent royal tribute is doubly impressive and particularly significant, in view of the fact that all the leading piano-players, both American and foreign are sold in London.

Therefore, in selecting the ANGELUS, King Edward made his choice from all of the piano-players of the world which could make any claim whatsoever for consideration.

Can any intending purchaser of a piano-player or player-piano afford to overlook this most remarkable indorsement and convincing testimonial to the superior merits of the ANGELUS?

Only the ANGELUS instruments are equipped with the Melodant, the Phrasing Lever, and the Artistyle Music Rolls.

THE WILCOX & WHITE CO., Meriden, Conn.
The Pioneers in the Manufacture of Piano-playing Devices

Regent House   Regent Street   London

PREMIER

1910

292

1910

TY COBB Famous Ball Player, says:

"Tuxedo is a good, pure, mild tobacco and makes a wonderfully pleasant pipe-smoke."

Ty Cobb

The World's Greatest Ball Player Smokes the World's Best Tobacco

There isn't a cross-roads village in the entire country that doesn't know and respect the name of Ty Cobb. This man has aroused the admiration of an entire sport-loving nation by his wonderful mental and physical alertness in the cleverest outdoor game man has yet devised. Ty Cobb has the two qualities most highly prized by Americans—Brains and Speed. He leads his league in batting; he is the champion base-runner; and all the time his wits and muscles work in perfect co-ordination.

Tuxedo
The Perfect Tobacco for Pipe and Cigarette

Ty Cobb's approval of Tuxedo is added to that of thousands of other prominent Americans who testify that here is a wholesome, beneficial, pleasing tobacco.

SAMPLE TUXEDO FREE— Send us 2c in stamps for postage and we'll mail you prepaid a souvenir tin of TUXEDO tobacco to any point in U.S.A. Address

Tuxedo Department
Room 1187
111 Fifth Ave.
New York

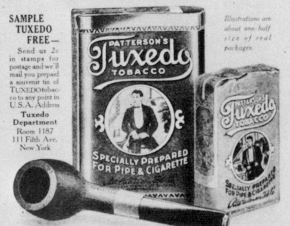

Illustrations are about one-half size of real packages.

Tuxedo has made thousands of men happy, temperate and comfortable converts to the pipe, because it has made pipe-smoking not only possible but pleasant to them.

There isn't a speck of irritation, scorch, sting or bite in a pound of Tuxedo. All that is removed by the famous original "Tuxedo Process"—a process that has had imitations galore—but the original "Tuxedo Process" is still the best.

YOU CAN BUY TUXEDO EVERYWHERE

Convenient, glassine-wrapped, moisture-proof pouch . . . **5c**   Famous green tin, with gold lettering, curved to fit pocket **10c**

In Tin Humidors, 40c and 80c   *In Glass Humidors, 50c and 90c*

THE AMERICAN TOBACCO COMPANY

The true portrait of Caruso's art

When you hear a Victor Record of Caruso's voice *played on the Victrola*, you hear the great tenor exactly as he wishes you to hear him. Only the Victor process of reproduction can bring out *all* the wonderful beauty of tone which the Victor process of recording put into the record.

After their records have passed the critical judgment of the officials of the Victor Recording Laboratory, the great artists who make Victor Records pass judgment upon themselves as they are heard on the Victrola and they must give the final approval before any of their records are released to the public.

Victrolas $25 to $1500. Victor dealers everywhere.

"HIS MASTER'S VOICE"
This trademark and the trademarked word "Victrola" identify all our products. Look under the lid! Look on the label! VICTOR TALKING MACHINE CO. Camden, N. J.

Victor Talking Machine Co., Camden, N. J.

How Famous Movie Stars Keep Their Hair Beautiful

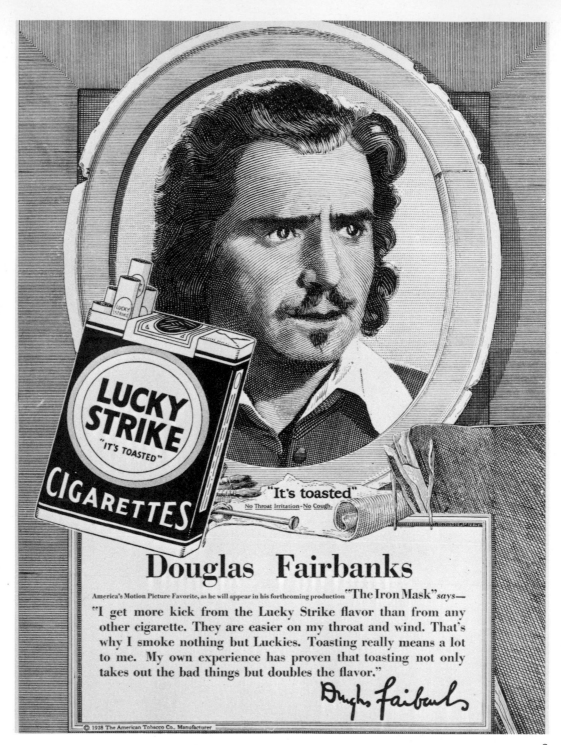

1928

"No one has quite recaptured the freshness, the sense of perpetually innocent, perpetually adolescent narcissism that Douglas Fairbanks brought to the screen. There was, of course, an element of the show-off in what he did, but it was (and still remains) deliciously palatable because he managed to communicate a feeling that he was as amazed and delighted as his audience by what that marvelous machine, his body, could accomplish when he launched into the trajectory necessary to rescue the maiden fair, humiliate the villain or escape the blundering soldiery that fruitlessly pursued him. . . .

MARY PICKFORD *and the costume*
that could not be duplicated

TINY, clinging hands—oh! so dirty—soiled the soft, silken folds of "Our Mary's" gorgeous gown. It could not be replaced . . . the scenes must all be retaken at a cost of thousands of dollars. Consternation reigned. Then someone . . . but read Miss Pickford's own story of how this seemingly tragic situation turned out to be only an amusing incident!

"BEFORE making 'Little Annie Rooney,' my latest picture, I did two costume plays, and the silks and satins I wore were a continuous source of care.

"However, I knew from experience with my own gowns, that there is a remedy when accidents happen—that Lux dissolved in hot water will restore dainty fabrics to their original state of spotlessness.

"When a costume is made of the only piece of silk of its kind in Los Angeles and a dozen scenes have been made showing that costume, an accident to it brings a difficult and often costly situation. Such an occasion came to my attention recently.

"A costume had been used in a very expensive picture, when a child rubbed a dirty little hand on my dress. Consternation reigned. The director saw visions of retakes costing thousands of dollars if the costume could not be duplicated.

"A lady who was standing nearby approached and said: 'I'm so very, very sorry! Let me take the dress and see what can be done about it.' She took the gown and in the course of time returned it as good as new.

"She explained that Lux had accomplished the result. 'But why were you so sorry?' she was asked. 'Why, you see it was my little girl that soiled it,' she explained."

Mary Pickford

From a photograph by Strauss-Peyton Studios, Kansas City

MISS PICKFORD as "Little Annie Rooney"

In her newest picture "Little Annie Rooney," which has just been released, Miss Pickford achieves one of the finest screen characterizations of her career.

All of Monday's Laundry treated like fine fabrics now

Your hands, too, deserve the utmost kindness

ONE day "Why not Lux for the hardest job of all—Monday's laundry?" you said. "All my things are so nice and cost so much nowadays—they simply cannot stand the wear and tear of strong soap." Joyfully you call on Lux to work its wonders. And it does!

Your becoming little housedresses, the children's cheery ginghams, your nice house linens —all come out of its cleansing suds fresher looking than ever before, colors unfaded, whites snowy clean. Everything lasts longer, too.

There's nothing in Lux to injure the delicate fibres—just the same bubbling suds you've always trusted your fine things to—gentle, magically cleansing. And Lux is such a relief to your hands after harsh laundry soap! Really, they don't mind Monday any more. Such a little Lux does the whole laundry, too.

Gone! those in-the-dishpan HANDS

Now dishwashing has lost its old terrors. Three times a day you plunge your hands into the dishwater and Lux leaves them soft and white. No tell-tale in-the-dishpan look. Just one teaspoonful of Lux is enough! Lever Bros. Co., Cambridge, Mass.

Now the Big New Package, too

LUX

A little Lux goes so far it's an economy to use it

"*Mary Pickford, with whom he was to contract Hollywood's first royal marriage, had created, of course, the classic American girl—spunky, virginal, with a beauty bathed in golden sunlight—but she was, in fact, a tough, shrewd woman.*"
Richard Schickel, *His Picture in the Papers: A Speculation on Celebrity in America, Based on the Life of Douglas Fairbanks, Sr.* (1973)

> "When the movies came, the entire pattern of American life went on the screen as a nonstop ad. Whatever any actor or actress wore or used or ate was such an ad as had never been dreamed of."
>
> Marshall McLuhan, *Understanding Media*

Presenting...
CHARLIE CHAPLIN
in the blindfold cigarette test

Famous star selects
OLD GOLD

"One cigarette of the four I smoked in the blindfold test was like shooting a scene successfully after a whole series of failures. It just 'clicked' and I named it as my choice. It was OLD GOLD. Which clears up a mystery, for the supply of OLD GOLDS in my Beverly Hills home is constantly being depleted. It seems that Strongheart and Rin-tin-tin are the only motion picture actor stars who don't smoke them."

Charlie Chaplin

MR. CHAPLIN was asked to smoke each of the four leading brands, clearing his taste with coffee between smokes. Only one question was asked: "Which one do you like best?"

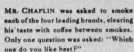

© P. Lorillard Co., Est. 1760

Made from the *heart-leaves* of the *tobacco plant*

CHARLIE CHAPLIN... movie favorite the world over, in one of his best-loved pictures ... "The Circus."

How does OLD GOLD do it?

WHAT'S the secret of OLD GOLD's winning charm? The answer is very simple. Three types of leaves grow on the tobacco plant ... coarse, heavy *top-leaves*, irritating to the throat ... withered *ground-leaves*, without taste or aroma...and the *heart-leaves*, rich in cool and fragrant smoking qualities. These golden-ripe *heart-leaves* give Old Golds their *honey-like smoothness*. That's why so many famous people choose them. And that's why you too can pick them ... even in the dark.

SMOOTHER AND *BETTER*—"NOT A COUGH IN A CARLOAD"

"Lucky Strikes were the cigarettes carried on the 'Friendship' when she crossed the Atlantic."

Amelia M. Earhart

Amelia M. Earhart,
first woman to fly the Atlantic by aeroplane

For a slender figure—
Reach for a Lucky instead of a sweet

"It's toasted" No Throat Irritation-No Cough.

© 1928, The American Tobacco Co., Manufacturers

LONE EAGLE: 15 jewel; radium dial; handsomely engraved; flexible link band . . . $37⁵⁰

"My Bulova keeps accurate time and is a beauty"
COLONEL CHARLES A. LINDBERGH 1927

Many advertisements in 1927 used Lindbergh's name and the name of his plane, "The Spirit of St. Louis," but Bulova was the first to use his picture and to commemorate the flight with a product named after the pilot. Five thousand "Lone Eagle" watches were sold in the first three days after Lindy's flight, and fifty thousand over the next few years.

Courtesy Bulova Watch Co.

1932

"The Girl or the Car" *A Mobiloil Movie with*

CLARK GABLE & UNA MERKEL

Clark Gable now co-starring with Jean Harlow in M.G.M.'s "Hold Your Man"

Una Merkel now featured in Metro-Goldwyn-Mayer's "Lady of the Night"

1 HE: "Five bucks for that lunch! What an expensive luxury you are!"

2 SHE: "And now let's get that lovely wrist watch I told you about."

3 SHE: "Look, isn't it beautiful! We've just time to make the matinee!"

4 HE: "Supper at the Ritz! Impossible! I've just enough money left to get gas and Mobiloil."

5 SHE: "Oh, look across the street! You could buy some of that cheap oil. Then you'd at least be able to get me a soda!"

6 HE: "Listen, little girl. This car's got to keep rolling for a couple of years more. You don't catch me using anything but Mobiloil."

Today's speeds give oil double the beating it took 3 years ago. That's why you need Mobiloil. Ordinary oils break down. If you are using ordinary oil the chances are 10 to 1 you are paying more for oil per year than you would with Mobiloil at 30¢ a quart. In addition you risk expensive repairs and shortened car life.

Mobiloil SOCONY-VACUUM CORPORATION

MERGER OF STANDARD OIL COMPANY OF NEW YORK AND VACUUM OIL COMPANY

The public excitement over the birth of the Dionne quintuplets in May, 1934, lasted for about six or seven years. In that time they made several movies, appeared in dozens of newsreels, and endorsed products for anyone who had the right fee: Lysol, Colgate Dental Cream, Quaker Oats, Carnation milk, Palmolive Soap, Pure-Test Cod-Liver Oil, Musterole, Remington Rand typewriters, Karo syrup, and General Motors.

The quintuplets' doctor, Allan Roy Dafoe, also endorsed many products in addition to having a syndicated newspaper column and his own radio show as a result of his participation at the birth.

First Lady of the Land, First Lady of the Air, who has enjoyed the refreshing ease and comfort, the time- and money-saving economy of almost 100,000 miles of air travel in the past four years. Mrs. Roosevelt says: "I never cease to marvel at the airplane."

1939

In addition to this institutional ad for the fledgling air-travel business, Mrs. Roosevelt also lent her support and prestige to the Zenith hearing aid; for a short while in the 1930s she conducted radio shows sponsored by Pond's Cold Cream, and in the early 1950s she appeared in a television commercial for Parkay margarine in exchange for air time to promote a charitable cause.

1944

FRIDAY NIGHT WHEN "THE HOUR" IS OVER, KATE SMITH THRILLS A SMALL ADMIRER WITH AN INVITATION TO JOIN HER IN HER DRESSING ROOM FOR SUPPER.

THE MOST HEARTFELT COMMERCIALS ON THE AIR

Kate Smith really loves the products she talks about

ONE OF the liveliest and most popular of network shows is "The Kate Smith Hour," now in its seventh year. Its music, drama, comedy, novelties, and guest stars are a regular Friday night diet for millions of Americans.

And millions of Americans have discovered that the fervor and sincerity of Kate's personality extend right into her selling. When she gives forth with her rhapsodic commercials describing the glories of Jell-O, Jell-O Puddings, and Sanka Coffee, she's telling you how a good cook and a practicing housekeeper really feels about them.

Graciously giving autographs and receiving congratulatory messages, Kate winds up a busy day. She is perfectly willing to talk about her success in selling over the air. "I guess it's just that I enjoy good things to eat myself. So naturally I like to talk about 'em to other folks. I know they're always keen for new food ideas—especially the kind that save time and trouble."

"Here comes my supper tray. M-m—Sanka Coffee. And Jell-O Chocolate Pudding! Now you take this pudding, for example. It's the most delicious you ever ate. It has an old-fashioned, homemade taste that's perfect. And *anyone* . . . even this little girl here . . . can make this pudding in only 8 minutes. Do you know it would take a half hour or more the old, fussy way?"

"And another thing, now that rations and shortages have made meals so slim, women are always looking for a satisfying, nourishing dessert. These Jell-O Puddings made with milk fill the bill perfectly! There are three marvelous flavors, chocolate, vanilla, and butterscotch—and, there are so many different ways to fix 'em up and serve 'em! Oh, yes, I have lots to talk about."

"So is it any wonder I enjoy my commercials? And I'm extra proud to be sponsoring Jell-O Puddings right now," Kate says, "because their deliciousness hasn't been affected one bit by wartime conditions! They taste just as luscious as ever—and that's something to shout about nowadays!"

JELL-O PUDDINGS
THREE MARVELOUS FLAVORS

1944

1947

"Champion of the world. A Black boy. Some Black mother's son. He was the strongest man in the world. [After one of his victories] People drank Coca-Colas like ambrosia and ate candy bars like Christmas. Some of the men went behind the Store and poured white lightning in their soft-drink bottles. . . .

"It would take an hour or more before the people would leave the Store and head for home. Those who lived too far had made arrangements to stay in town. It wouldn't do for a Black man and his family to be caught on a lonely country road on a night when Joe Louis had proved that we were the strongest people in the world."

Maya Angelou, *I Know Why the Caged Bird Sings* (1970)

Champion of the Year

JACKIE ROBINSON! One of the most talked about . . . one of the most applauded . . . one of the greatest names in baseball. Many honors have been bestowed upon him, but perhaps the most significant of all, is this:

The nationwide audience of "Jack Armstrong—All-American" recently voted Jackie Robinson BASEBALL CHAMPION OF THE YEAR!

Jackie Robinson is the first person upon whom such an honor has been bestowed by the boys and girls of America.

And—this famous Dodger star is a *Wheaties* man! "A lot of us ball players go for milk, fruit and Wheaties," says Jackie. "Nourishing and swell eating the year around."

Famous for nourishment, these 100% whole wheat flakes provide three B vitamins, also minerals, food energy, protein. Plus second-helping flavor! Had *your* Wheaties today?

General Mills

Listen to "Jack Armstrong—All-American". Sponsored by Wheaties and heard over the ABC Network—Coast to Coast—5:30 P.M. weekdays.

"Breakfast of Champions"

310

VACATION for GARY COOPER . . . and You!

WHETHER you slip away to Sun Valley for a Holiday-on-Skis —like Mr. and Mrs. Gary Cooper— or enjoy winter sports at home— you'll find Pabst Blue Ribbon is always a pleasant, friendly companion.

That ever-faithful, *real beer flavor* you enjoy in Pabst Blue Ribbon

was achieved by 104 years of pioneering in the *Art of Brewing*... and the *Science of Blending*.

By tasting, by comparing, you will understand why millions the world over have settled down to the real beer enjoyment that comes only with blended, splendid Pabst Blue Ribbon.

33 FINE BREWS BLENDED INTO ONE GREAT BEER

Pabst
Blue Ribbon

1948

"Here's how I Remember! Why don't YOU?"

John Wayne

JOHN WAYNE
in a scene from
"HONDO"
*A Wayne-Fellows Production
Distributed by Warner Bros.
in WarnerColor*

"It Says What You Want to Say—in a Way Folks Like!"

"Twenty-five years in pictures is a long time—by anybody's watch. And in these many years I've had many a helping hand. For don't let 'em kid you—nobody gets to be a star all alone. It takes a tip here, a suggestion there, a pat on the back and a kick in the shins, too—*both* when they're deserved.

"Anyway, I like to remember the folks who remember me, and a Sampler's a grand way to do it. I find a Whitman's Sampler says just what I want to say in a way folks understand and appreciate."

Started in 1842

CHOCOLATES
delicious, nutritious and energy-giving
FOOD

Here, in a scene between "takes", the big 6-foot-4 star John Wayne offers refreshment in the form of a Whitman's Sampler to a fellow worker. Just the kind of hospitality a girl can enjoy, yes?

COPR. 1954, STEPHEN F. WHITMAN & SON, INC., PHILA.

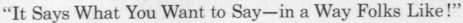

A WOMAN NEVER FORGETS THE MAN WHO REMEMBERS

1954

"Duke" Wayne has been doing testimonials for three decades. Recently he reportedly received $400,000 for his support of Datril 500.

Thrilling Beauty News *for users of* <u>Liquid</u> Shampoos!

LUSTRE-CREME is the favorite beauty shampoo of 4 out of 5 top Hollywood stars... and you'll love it in its new Lotion Form, too!

Marilyn Monroe
starring in
"GENTLEMEN PREFER BLONDES"
A 20th Century-Fox Production
Color by Technicolor

MARILYN MONROE says, "Yes, I use Lustre-Creme Shampoo." When America's most glamorous women use Lustre-Creme Shampoo, shouldn't it be *your* choice above all others, too?

<u>Now!</u> Lustre-Creme Shampoo *also* in New Lotion Form!

NEVER BEFORE—a liquid shampoo like this! Lustre-Creme Shampoo in new Lotion Form is much more than just another shampoo that pours. It's a *new* creamy lotion, a fragrant, satiny, easier-to-use lotion, that brings *Lustre-Creme glamour* to your hair with every heavenly shampoo!

VOTED "BEST" IN DRAMATIC USE-TESTS!
Lustre-Creme Shampoo in new Lotion Form was tested against 4 leading liquid and lotion shampoos ... all unlabeled. And *3 out of every 5 women preferred Lustre-Creme* in new Lotion Form over each competing shampoo tested—for these important reasons:

✶ Lather foams more quickly!
✶ Easier to rinse away!
✶ Cleans hair and scalp better!
✶ Leaves hair more shining!
✶ Does not dry or dull the hair!
✶ Leaves hair easier to manage!
✶ Hair has better fragrance!
✶ More economical to use!

Prove it to Yourself...
Lustre-Creme in new Lotion Form is the best <u>liquid</u> shampoo yet!

Yes! Now take your <u>choice</u>:
Famous <u>Cream</u> Form...or new <u>Lotion</u> Form

Famous Cream Form in jars or tubes, 27¢ to $1. (*Big economy size, $2.*)

New Lotion Form in handy bottles, 30¢ to $1.

POUR IT ON—OR CREAM IT ON! In famous Cream Form, Lustre-Creme is America's favorite cream shampoo. And all its beauty-bringing qualities are in the new Lotion Form. Whichever form *you* prefer, lanolin-blessed Lustre-Creme will leave your hair shining clean, eager to wave, never dull or dry.

1953

It's a Great Year for Wedding Pictures

Photographed in Monaco on Anscochrome, April 1956, by Howell Conant

The happy day springs to radiant life, all the gayety and movement just as it was, all the color completely, charmingly true-to-life. 3-times-faster Anscochrome, the amazing new color film, makes all the difference . . . in all of your color pictures. Ansco, A Division of General Aniline & Film Corp., Binghamton, N. Y.

Slides to view and project...   Prints to cherish and share...

Super-speed successor to traditional color films.

get <u>more</u> than you bargained for—

GIVE YOUR EYE TEETH to be sitting pretty? There's an easier way—painless, too. Sit down in Hanes Fig Leaf briefs. Double-panel seat. Knit from soft, lustrous cotton. Live elastic in waistband and leg openings. 89c*. Boys' 65c.*

ANY WAY YOU LOOK at it, you can bank on a Hanes athletic shirt for real comfort. And still save money! Full-combed cotton yarns. Highly absorbent. Trim-fitting Swiss rib. Only 75c. Boys' 59c.

SEE FOR YOURSELF! Hanes broadcloth shorts s-t-r-e-t-c-h your dollar—but good. Full-cut and Sanforized. Three comfortable styles in solid colors, whites or stripes. 85c to $1.

*Slightly higher in the Far West

get  **HANES** UNDERWEAR

And get more than you bargained for—on television! See Sid Caesar and Imogene Coca on NBC-TV every Saturday night.

P. H. Hanes Knitting Company, Winston-Salem 1, N. C.

1952

Ricky Jr.

Lucille Ball and Desi Arnaz with the Ricky Jr. Baby Doll

the baby all America loves... Ricky Jr. is wonderful! Ricky Jr. is famous! Ricky Jr. is the baby that stars on the "I LOVE LUCY" television show. Now your little girl can have Ricky Jr. for her very own. She can do all the wonderful things with Ricky Jr. that Lucy does. Ricky Jr. is LIFESIZE, 21 inches tall and drinks, wets, sleeps, cries, bathes, blows bubbles. Ricky Jr. is made of unbreakable vinyl plastic that feels as soft, silky, tender as his adorable namesake. **14.98**

An American Character LIFESIZE doll

THE RICKY JR. DOLL FOR ENDLESS HOURS OF PLAY. The Ricky Jr. doll—makes a wonderful playmate for your little girl. Ricky Jr. is wonderful fun on the "I LOVE LUCY" television show and will be just as much fun in your home. **14.98**

RICKY JR'S. PLAYTIME PRODUCTS DOLL CARRIAGE. No prouder little girl ever walked Main Street than your little girl, when she takes Ricky Jr. for an airing in his own Ricky Jr. carriage. **12.98**

RICKY JR'S. TRIMBLE DOLL BATH. There's a world of fun in keeping Ricky Jr. clean and bathing him just like Lucy does. It is a replica of Ricky Jr's. own bath on the "I LOVE LUCY" show. **11.98**

EXTRA CLOTHES FOR RICKY JR. She'll love to dress up Ricky Jr. in his Sunday suit and play with the many accessories that go with it—booties, bubble pipe, wash cloth, soap, extra bottle. **3.98**

WRITE FOR 32 PAGE, DOLL CATALOG. Fun and information galore. Send 10c in stamps or coin to cover postage and handling to **AMERICAN CHARACTER DOLL CO., LI, 200 FIFTH AVE. NEW YORK 10**

1953

ERNEST HEMINGWAY, who has been called the greatest living American writer, is also internationally famous as a deep-sea fisherman. Since publication of *The Sun Also Rises* in 1926, his novels and short stories have enriched the literature of the English language consistently, year after year. His latest best seller is *Across the River and Into the Trees*.

In every refreshing glass... Purity, Body and Flavor

Hemingway also did testimonials for Pan Am and for Sheaffer Pens, but he was not the only famous writer to lend his name to the pages of advertising. Recently Lillian Hellman appeared in a fur-coat ad that extolled her as a "legend." F. Scott Fitzgerald was featured in early Book-of-the-Month ads as a famous writer and in the 1930s was a judge in a beauty contest sponsored by a facial cream.

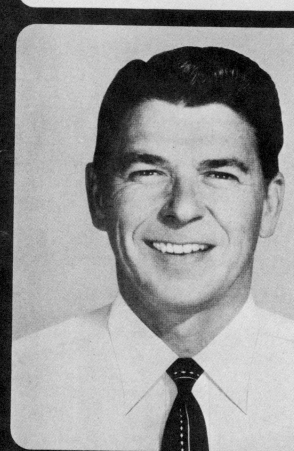

"The neatest Christmas gift of all!," says Ronald Reagan

You can twist it... You can twirl it... You can bend it... You can curl it...

The new revolutionary collar on **Van Heusen Century shirts**

won't wrinkle... ever!

RONALD REAGAN starring in Universal International's "LAW AND ORDER," Color by Technicolor

THE Van Heusen Century is the *only shirt in the world* with a soft collar that *won't wrinkle . . . ever!* It fits smoothly always, without starch or stays.

Soft as a fine handkerchief, and as easy to launder—because the fold-line is *woven in*. Just iron the collar flat, flip it, and it folds perfectly every time.

Also, it gives you up to *twice the wear* of ordinary shirts. Whites, **$3.95.** Superfine Whites and colors, **$4.95.** Tie shown: Van Heusen Shirt-Mate, **$1.50.**

Van Heusen Century shirts

Phillips-Jones Corp.; New York 16, N. Y., Makers of Van Heusen Shirts • Sport Shirts • Ties • Pajamas • Handkerchiefs • Underwear • Swimwear . . . and the famous Van Heusen Century Shirt with the soft collar that won't wrinkle ever.

1954

Ronald Reagan became governor of California in 1966. In the late 1940s and early 1950s he had been a well-known B-movie star who, like so many others, often did endorsements. In 1955 he became the host of the very popular General Electric Theater, a function that gave him enormous national exposure. On the show he introduced both the plays and the commercials, and every program ended with his uttering the famous line, "At General Electric progress is our most important product."

"How to achieve conviction and a point of view in troubled times"

Adlai E. Stevenson

Adlai E. Stevenson, United States Representative to the United Nations
Member, Board of Directors, Encyclopaedia Britannica

"When I visited Dr. Albert Schweitzer in his primitive jungle hospital in French Equatorial Africa, he told me he considered this the most dangerous period in history—not just modern history, but all human history. Why? Because, he said, heretofore nature has controlled man, but now man has learned to control elemental forces—before he has learned to control himself.

"Striving to understand how our mastery of elemental forces can be made to serve humanity in these troubled times, we instinctively turn to the sources of Western thought, to the searchings of great and immortal minds on the origins of government, the tenets of philosophy, and the nature of man. For man can control himself only if he understands both himself and the civilization he has created out of his longing for justice and peace.

"Here, in the GREAT BOOKS OF THE WESTERN WORLD, is the mainspring of our civilization—the collective conscience which makes it run. In the pages of these beautiful volumes truth stands out—ready to guide anyone concerned with where our world is going."

Published by the Encyclopaedia Britannica in collaboration with the University of Chicago

GREAT BOOKS

Now available direct from the publisher with great new
SYNTOPICON

A mind is filled and enriched by a new concept only if the concept is fully understood. And only a disciplined scholar can ordinarily stick to the task of absorbing great abstract ideas without an instructor. Guidance, interpretation and discussion are usually necessary to give these great ideas meaning and application to one's life. That is why this Private Library Edition of the GREAT BOOKS was published.

THE SYNTOPICON

The key to its enormous value is the "teacher" it provides—the amazing SYNTOPICON—a new concept in self-education. Created by 100 scholars over a period of eight years, it is like a "teacher" living in your home . . . always ready to interpret to you the great ideas contained in the GREAT BOOKS.

As you begin to absorb and understand these great ideas, you will begin to reflect their greatness in your own ability to think, speak, and act with new and impressive weight. You will have sounder judgment on political and economic issues as the great minds make the whole great idea of government clear to you. You will develop a sounder philosophy of life as *your* mind is illuminated by the great minds of the ages.

You will not be limited in business progress by your own narrow specialty, but will be prepared to handle the daily problems of top level management which call for broad general thinking rather than limited technical knowledge. Even in your personal life, the great ideas can guide you to greater success and contentment.

Don't miss this opportunity to learn the details of the Private Library Edition of the GREAT BOOKS. Mail the attached card for a free descriptive booklet showing how you can find new understanding of yourself and the world through the great ideas which have engrossed men since the written record of man began. It is in this way that one stretches both mind and soul.

Mail the attached card now for FREE BOOKLET

Simply tear out the attached card along perforated line, fill in and mail for your free, colorfully illustrated booklet describing the GREAT BOOKS and the SYNTOPICON. Or write to GREAT BOOKS OF THE WESTERN WORLD, Department 35-F, 425 N. Michigan, Chicago 11, Illinois.

Andy Warhol and Sonny Liston always fly on Braniff. (When you got it– flaunt it.)

We see them a lot, and they always enjoy themselves.
They like our vigor, and they like our verve.
Good. That's why we paint our planes different colors
and make the interiors so plush.
That's why we pick the sharpest girls we can find
and dress them in Pucci's.
And that's why the whole airline harps
on service, service, service.

Make every drink ice cold.
Serve every meal piping hot.
Bring them a magazine. Fling them a pillow.
Get them there on-time. And guess what.
It works. They keep coming back.
They keep asking their Travel Agent:
"Does Braniff fly there too?
Put me on it."

A quality company of Ling-Temco-Vought, Inc
LTV

1969

The Dingo Man. He's no ordinary Joe.

Boots are his thing.
They're part of his image.
He knows just how to wear boots. With style.
He knows when to wear them too.
Whenever he feels like it. But don't try to con
The Dingo Man into a boot made
by a shoemaker. His boots are real.
The label inside all of them reads "Dingo."
If you don't believe us, ask any girl
Joe Namath knows.
For store near you, write:
Acme Boot Co., Inc., Dept. PL 91,
Clarksville, Tenn. 37040.
A subsidiary of Northwest
Industries, Inc.

dingo®

From Acme.® Ⓐ The World's Largest Bootmaker.

"After our first Moon landing, I resolved I would never publicly endorse any product or service unless I sincerely believed in it."

Apollo 11 Astronaut, Buzz Aldrin, discusses the Computerized Self-Analysis system in every 1972 Volkswagen.

**"Everything after a Moonwalk is a letdown.
You can't top it.
So instead, you adjust.
You adjust to a world that's a far cry from perfection."**
Or at least the kind of perfection that took Buzz Aldrin to the Moon and then brought him back within a quarter mile of an aircraft carrier carrying the President of the United States.

Then it's over and there he is. With a Doctor of Science degree from MIT and a walk on the Moon under his belt, in a world, that at times, seems absolutely chaotic.

Then, something comes along that makes a great deal of sense to him.

And he becomes enthused:

"In analogy with the manned space flight programs, past, present and future—of Mercury, Gemini, Apollo, Sky Lab and Space Shuttle—which pioneered computer check-out systems, the present VW system compares with the early Mercury flight of Shepard, Grissom and Glenn."
Volkswagen's new Computerized Self-Analysis system.

To Buzz Aldrin, it's a **"great step forward in the area of troubleshooting of automobiles."** To you, if you own a 1972 Volkswagen, it means getting the most advanced automotive check-up there is.

"The car, truly, is wired along the same principle of a space craft."
(Nothing like asking the man who manned one.)

How the system will work at VW Dealerships:
In its simplest terms, it's a network of check points and sensors throughout the car; each sensor reporting the condition of various key points in the car to one central socket in the back of the car.

The socket, when plugged into a computer, which will be at Volkswagen dealers starting later this year, will actually report the condition of your car directly to you.

Things like your electrical system, cylinder compression and front wheel alignment will all be checked without human error.

Altogether, 60 vital service points will be checked. The results will then be printed out on a sheet of paper, in plain English, for you to read.

"Keeping that print-out sheet after each check-up is like checking-in with Mission Control when you're 200,000 miles out in space. It gives you a nice, secure feeling." It also gets you home quicker.

"The technical advances of the system amaze me, of course, but the speed of operation amazes me even more." To check cylinder compression the conventional way today, a mechanic has got to do the following: remove each spark plug, insert a gauge, crank the engine, take a reading, make a decision and then put each spark plug back.

At top speed, the procedure takes 10 minutes and 40 seconds for four cylinders.

With the new VW system, it takes 60 seconds.

To check out your electrical system, you need a great deal of knowledge, equipment, and 9 minutes and 40 seconds.

With the new VW system, your electrical system is checked out in less than 2 minutes.

At top speed, it takes the best mechanic using the best equipment 4 minutes to check out your front wheel alignment.

With the new VW system, elapsed time is 60 seconds flat.

So there you have it.

Instead of a mechanic telling you what's wrong with your car, now your car and your dealer's computer can tell you.

It took Volkswagen 7 years and enough money to develop and market an entirely new automobile to come out with the Computerized Self-Analysis system.

Why such a concentrated effort on service instead of, let's say, a new, longer, lower, wider Beetle?

Basically for the same reason Colonel Buzz Aldrin decided to publicly support it.

The reason is known as progress.

———————————

Postscript: Earlier this year, Volkswagen felt it had something advanced enough to show, not only to a man who walked on the Moon, but also a man who was intimately familiar with the subject of computerized check-out and testing.

After a series of meetings and after seeing the system in operation and after learning of the plans to bring in the computers starting later this year, Colonel Aldrin's response, very simply, was: **"I'm impressed."**

© VOLKSWAGEN OF AMERICA, INC.

PHOENIX SILK HOSE

Every desirable feature of merit with the unusual advantage of durability.

Women's 75¢ to $2 pair
Men's 50¢ to $1.50 pair
Misses' 75¢ pair
Infants' 25¢ & 50¢ pair

AT THE BEST SHOPS
"MADE IN THE U.S.A."
BY THE
PHOENIX KNITTING WORKS
246 BROADWAY, MILWAUKEE

© 1915 P. K. W. MILWAUKEE

A "HOLD-UP" ON THE AVENUE

SEX

America has become a sex-conscious society. Evidence surfaces everywhere: in the erotic lyrics and rhythms of popular tunes; suggestive bantering in television situation comedies; nude figures flashing across stage and screen; explicit magazine covers competing for rack space and the public eye; adult bookstores, peep-shows, massage parlors, and sex supermarkets catering to any fantasy or fetish; motels and hotels renting rooms by the hour. It seems as though nearly everyone has gotten in on the act. Americans are undoubtedly spending more time and money on sex than ever before. What started as a revolt against Victorian propriety in the early decades of the twentieth century has gradually turned into what Henry Miller, that long-time champion of sexual liberation, has dispiritedly called "a tyranny of the flesh."

Advertising has played a decisive role in both intensifying and extending America's attentiveness to sexuality in the twentieth century. Sex in advertising has had a far greater impact on American life than its use as an unexcelled attention-getting device would at first suggest. Rather than simply reflecting American sexual attitudes and standards of behavior, advertising has, in the interests of corporate enterprise, aggressively helped establish them. Over the years, advertisements have exerted considerable influence on this nation's changing tastes in sexual matters and have largely determined what is sexually appealing. In addition to its traditional fixation on parts of the female anatomy, advertising now frequently highlights the alluring features of the male torso. Sex in advertising has also moved from indirect association to overt identification with consumer products. A good number of recent advertisers have gone so far as to establish sexual lives for their products. Sex, if it was used in ads at all, was once discreet and anatomical; it is now more often explicit and situational. What began as an effective strategy of persuasion has evolved, as the current advertisements for sexual paraphernalia and self-help books suggest, into a commodity in itself.

Before its evolution into a commodity, sexual suggestion was used to stimulate sales, launch new products, reinvigorate sagging campaigns, and generally establish a competitive edge for different brands of increasingly standardized products. But in addition to these conventional functions, sex has served as an important stratagem when advertisers set out to create attractive identities for otherwise undistinguished products. Sex has also been a prominent feature of advertisements aimed at expanding markets for such products as cigars, cigarettes, perfumes, and hair sprays by redirecting the product's appeal from exclusively one sex to both, without threatening either's respective identity. But whatever its use, sex in advertising remains embedded in corporate realities and contrivances rather than in some vaguely masculine or feminine sense of what seems "naturally" alluring. Sex as a selling tool lies at the core of America's economy of abundance, and advertising has been instrumental in putting it there.

Sex has moved merchandise for years. From the silk-stocking advertisements in the early decades of this century to the recent seductive urgings of the Noxzema girl to "take it off, take it all off," advertisers have consistently traded on sex appeal. A late 1960s research study showed that 30 percent of all advertisements capitalized on some form of "sexiness," be it an appreciable degree of nudity, suggestive copy, alluring symbols, or erotic situations. In one sense there is nothing new in these findings. It's not that there is so much more sex in ads now than in the past; it's simply that the sexual content is now more explicitly defined. A 1915 ad for Evinrude outboard motors shows a young bather expressing her brand-loyalty by writing love letters in the sand. A recent Fabergé ad for "Bedtime Perfume" guarantees to "keep you looking your loveliest no matter *when*." A 1921 ad for Holeproof Hosiery coyly speaks of "demurely alluring" ankles that will "fascinate" and "captivate." Contemporary ads for Centaur perfume reassure men that the scent "transmits its virile message only in moments of close and intimate contact." The playful ambiguities of Clairol's "Does she . . . or doesn't she?" have yielded to such direct fare as the more recent "Fly me" advertisement for National Airlines. When Mamie Van Doren beckoned, "Gentlemen, come a little closer . . . I've got something nice for you," many may well have been disheartened to discover that she was actually peddling samples of Aqua Velva shaving cream. The message is now more unequivocal. Mail-order houses routinely fill men's magazines with such advertisements as "How to Have THE SEXUAL DRIVE YOU ALWAYS DREAMED

OF," with the assurance of a money-back guarantee for those willing to admit yet another sexual failure.

The current preoccupation with sex is not the result of continuous movement toward greater and greater explicitness. Sex, like fashions, moves in cycles. The tailored look of the 1950s, for example, was far less "sexy" than the flapper style of the 1920s. In fact, the oscillations of sexuality in advertising are seen most reliably in fashions, and more particularly in the length of women's clothes. Contrast Victorian bloomers and bustles to the silk and satin chemises of the 1920s and 1930s; the sack and sheath of the 1950s to the mini and micro of the 1960s and to the ill-fated maxi and hot pants of the 1970s. With every rise in the hemline, more products surfaced to tend to each newly exposed area of skin.

Sex in advertising began with women's ankles and slowly worked its way up. As late as the 1890s decorum had still confined women to tailored shirtwaists with leg-o'-mutton sleeves and amply cut, floor-length skirts that regularly swept the streets. But by the 1920s, the Gibson girl had become a flapper: A woman who could vote, work, drink, smoke, and, as reform groups began to attack the "double standard," could also think more about her own pleasure. Manufacturers and advertisers responded to the practicalities of working lives and the freedom and quickening tempo of leisure-time activities with striking ads for lighter, shorter clothes. But each inch of a shortened skirt represented miles of moral change. Glaring at newly trimmed knee-length skirts, much of the conservative, male-dominated press expressed outrage at women wearing what seemed like a minimum of clothes and a maximum of cosmetics, head-decorations, and jewelry. Permanent waves, they groaned, had made the beauty parlor the newest shop in town as well as one of the busiest and costliest. Ads for silk and rayon underwear helped put the petticoat out of business. But perhaps the most durable change, at least in terms of its impact on sex in advertising, came when dark cotton stockings were exchanged for silk hosiery. Stunning graphics in widely circulated advertisements helped make legs the focal point of the new, sexy pencil-thin look.

The commercial facts of life dominate sex in advertising. The democratization of silk was largely responsible for the "invention" of legs as a sexual appendage in the years immediately preceding World War I. As a 1915 advertisement for Phoenix Hose makes clear, silk stockings had traditionally been regarded as a luxury item, available principally to upper-class women, few of whom felt any great compulsion to display their social status in such terms. But since silk stockings carried class status, once they were made available to middle- and lower-class women, display became almost a necessity—in accordance with Veblen's theory of conspicuous consumption. Initially women didn't buy silk stockings to show off their legs but displayed their legs because they could buy silk stockings. In this preference for silk, "class" was initially a more important factor than sex appeal. But these distinctions gradually faded. Women would become increasingly self-conscious about their legs. And with the sexualization of legs came a significant decline in the buttocks and hips as focal points for sex appeal. From that point on, advertisers variously shifted female sex appeal from the legs to the bosom to the nape of the neck to the mouth to the navel to the underarm and back to whatever area best suited their commercial interests. But it was the sight of a well-turned ankle that first excited advertisers. The exquisitely illustrated advertisements for silk stockings soon made a name for such artists as Coles Phillips, earned huge profits for the industry, started America on its way to "cheesecake," established the basic tactics for most subsequent uses of sex in advertising, and showed how readily corporate enterprise could manage prevailing tastes in sexuality.

Advertising in the Jazz Age irrevocably tied sex to consumption. In contrast to women in earlier ads who had been shown assuming more directly productive roles in the economy, the vast majority of twentieth-century women were relegated in advertisements to their "proper place" in the American home. Despite the fact that more women were working than ever before, advertisers most frequently cast them as wageless managers of consumer purchases and regarded them as prime targets for their sales pitches. Accordingly, advertisements urged women to define their success as homemakers by the number of mass-produced items they could accumulate. Yet advertising also encouraged this same mythic figure—described by Thomas Edison as "the woman of the future" soon to be "liberated" by his inventions—to rely increasingly on the sexual images provided in ads for more gratifying self-identities. Trading on developments in psychology, and more particularly on those of Freud, advertisers conditioned women to look to the trappings of sex for self-definition. Advertisers seemed as eager as Freud to penetrate the unconscious—but for decidedly different reasons. Sold on what Freud had uncovered, advertisers have consistently profited from commercial applications of his theories of sexual repression. And most have remained devout disciples to this day.

By Victorian standards, women were not supposed to be interested in the sexual aspects of their own lives. Yet the more women wrapped themselves up in what one social commentator described as "veritable straitjackets of tweed, flannel and boned corsetry," the more bulges and curves surfaced in the material objects around them. Furniture, for example, took on the outlines of female figures. Table and chair legs appeared so similar to "thighs and calves that squeamish housewives made the resemblance all the stronger by fitting them with skirts." Freud located in such evidence reserves of repressed sexuality. Given this theoretical support, advertisers went to work on making women more self-conscious consumers.

Advertisers in the 1920s used sex not to extol either the special qualities of womanhood or the particular features of a product but rather to create an overriding sense of insecurity in women about their sexual attractiveness. This notion is perhaps most readily seen in the well-known contemporary Certs ad: "If he kissed you once, / Will he kiss you again? / Be Certain. Use Certs." But the precedent had been set decades before in such ads as the ones for Mary Garden perfume (1919) and Woodbury soap (1922), in which what were then daring poses and suggestive promises were offered as ways for women to build enough confidence in their sexual identities to face the social world and to make the grade with an "enduring love." Such ads implicitly suggest that women ought to spend as much time tending to their appearance as practicing their skills as homemakers. Women were captivatingly depicted in front of mirrors or in bathtubs dreamily cultivating their sex appeal. Advertising eventually led women to the belief that their most important task each day was the creation of an alluring self-image. As the advertisements for Chesterfield (1926), Lucky Strike (1932), and Old Gold (1935) cigarettes make apparent, women were shown in seductive positions to remind others that smoking was an equally acceptable sign of femininity. But these ads also implicitly served notice that femininity would be judged in just such provocative terms. Significant increases in the sales of cosmetics, jewelry, and the other finely appointed accouterments of sexuality were upshots of the sexual competitiveness promoted among women by advertisers in the 1920s. "Charm," "beauty," and "loveliness" were linked with purchasable goods. Advertisers soon could measure sex appeal in the cash value of the commodities it spawned.

Advertisements made it quite clear that the primary responsibility of women was to be sexually attractive. In *Voices of Civilisation* (1943), Denys Thompson quotes one advertisement's definition of sex appeal:

> *Woman's deep-seated instinct urging her to the use of perfumes is a manifestation of a fundamental law of biology. The first duty of a woman is to attract. . . . It does not matter how clever or independent you may be, if you fail to influence the men you meet, consciously or unconsciously, you are not fulfilling your fundamental duty as a woman.*

Consumption quickly became an accustomed compensation for those unable to satisfy the conditions of such "duty." Characteristically, advertising would have it both ways: Products became a means both to express and to sublimate sexual desire and frustration.

Advertisements constituted the major source of popular sexuality well into the 1940s, when pinups and the movie industry's sexual interludes provided stiff competition. But advertising continued as the "sexiest" thing in print. Ads easily outpaced the editorial matter in magazines—at least until the late 1960s, when high-gloss "girlie" magazines upped the ante in the sexual explicitness of articles and photo features. Through the years, enticing illustrations have been the leading attention-getting device used in advertising. The work of such distinguished commercial artists and photographers as George Petty, Hayden Hayden, Earl Moran, Coles Phillips, and Edward Steichen undoubtedly helped win public approval for the feminine ideals established in ads. In particular, Steichen's captivating photographs (see the 1936 ad for Woodbury's facial soap) prepared the public for the time when nudity no longer would be regarded as shockingly offensive.

Nudity in advertising has most often been used to promote women's products. (Until recently, advertisers have made little effort to trade on male nudity—what Helen Gurley Brown, editor of *Cosmopolitan*, affectionately calls "beefcake.") And yet, while nudity has become a proven means to gain the consumer's eye, its effectiveness as a strategy of persuasion remains questionable. By the late 1960s, when the shock of public nudity had worn off, one advertising executive could matter-of-factly state that something more was needed: "A nude is not news. . . . Either you're going to have to go into much more specific expressions of the sexual relationship to get attention, or fit it in where it is pertinent to the product." Recent research studies confirm this judgment: Nudity in advertising negatively affects brand recall.

Once nudes had made more than cameo appearances, advertisers could hardly resist having phallic symbols pop up in their work. For example, they frequently depicted women holding everything from cigars, long-necked bottles, and guns to keys, knives, and assorted fruits and vegetables —all in the service of selling goods and the sexuality attached to them. And what advertisers have not been able to show, they talked about.

The language of twentieth-century advertising has buried in it sexual allusions, puns, innuendo, double entendres, and what advertisers call "near words" (for example, Smirnoff's ad: "What's a Horseshot?"). When in the late 1930s men repeated the slogan "Please Give Me Something to Remember You By," there was no doubt about what they had in mind. Such earlier slogans as "See That Hump," "He won't be happy till he gets it," "Eventually—Why Not Now?" "You Press the Button, We Do the Rest," and "Blow Some My Way," whether intended by advertisers to be risqué or not, got picked up by the public and turned into suggestive catchphrases. They often found their way into early vaudeville routines, burlesque acts, and musical comedies. Such expressions have remained prominent features of advertising strategy ever since.

Sex in advertising consistently creates a verbal world in which language pays rich dividends—sexual messages which invite the reader's vicarious imaginative participation: "When should a blonde give in?" (Clairol); "Be careful how you use it!" (Hai Karate); "Flick Your Bic." Recently advertising copy has become even more explicit. A current ad for Speidel watches shows an aspiring bridegroom rushing in to announce proudly to his fiancée, "Honey, this is the day. Today, I'm going all the way." But once the watch is displayed, the theme shifts to "Speidel goes all the way." Gillette ads urge us to "Shower with a Friend," and the woman in the English Leather ads boasts, "My men wear English Leather or they wear nothing at all." Advertisers design such hyperbole to be humorous. But often such ads make the product seem irrelevant.

The impetus for much of the verbal fireworks in advertising comes from the psychological advice firms have acquired over the years. Such prominent psychologists as Daniel Starch and Walter Dill Scott had long associations with advertising. But it was not until Alfred Kinsey and his colleagues published their work on human sexuality in 1948 that advertisers were provided with another important clinical basis for appealing to consumers' instinctual drives. Before the 1950s were over, advertisers came to rely more frequently on the research of such figures as Ernest Dichter, Louis Cheskin, Pierre Martineau, and James Vicary. Each developed effective techniques to plumb the recesses of consumer consciousness for their "real reactions" to products and for indications of the latent sexual symbolism they attached to certain products. Dichter declared that the prosperous ad agency "manipulates human motivations and desires and develops a need for goods with which the public has at one time been unfamiliar—perhaps even undesirous of purchasing." In one celebrated campaign, Chrysler used Dichter's findings to project an image of their convertibles as "mistresses" and their sedans as "wives." In another instance, Dichter urged that Ivory not advertise soap but rather the pleasures associated with taking baths.

James Vicary developed an even more subtle form of manipulation during the same period. "Subliminal seduction," as its most ardent critics call it, formulates consumers' needs, often without their knowledge. It embeds commercial or sexual messages in such a way that they are either displayed so rapidly or printed so lightly that they are not readily visible to the conscious eye. But the unconscious eye does notice and "read" them. The most persistent critic of subliminal advertising claims that agencies routinely retouch the photographs in their ads to plant nude figures, genitalia, and a host of obscenities in the props and bodies surrounding their products. By the end of the 1950s, sex had permeated nearly every creative phase of advertising: copy, graphics, and even product design.

While researchers studied the sex lives of Americans, advertising increasingly associated products with sexuality. Advertisers focused on what science-fiction writer Arthur C. Clarke called "the sexiness of things." The sexualization of a product can perhaps be most readily seen in the Old Gold ad (1950) featuring a dancing pack of cigarettes. And, as the ad for Wolfschmidt's vodka (1962) shows, the human body gradually was displaced in many ads. In such instances advertisers ventured so far as to create sex lives for their products. A mid-1960s ad for Sprite promoted a drink called the "Tom Jones: wherein gin and Sprite have a merrie tumble on the rocks." Even product technology was considered for the sexual impact it could create. For example, hard, shiny plastic surfaces soon dominated the assembly lines. Writing at the end of the 1950s, Norman Mailer observed that "the phallus has come to the supermarket and the drugstore in a thousand hand-sized plastic cylinders which give a spray or a shoot of insecticide, meringue, shaving cream, 'or roll on out of a deodorant with a ball-shaped tip." The sexual identification would eventually be so complete that, as the Dodge ad (1968) makes clear, the distinctions between the object and the person connected to it disappeared. Although he is writing about the late 1950s, Mailer's explanation seems appropriate: "A car is sold not because it will help one to get a girl, but because it is already a girl. The leather of its seats is worked to a near-skin, the color is lipstick-pink, or a blonde's pale green, the taillights are cloacal, the rear is split like the cheeks of a drum majorette."

The sexual energy associated with products has been repeatedly advertised as one way for the solitary housewife to get through daily routines. The midday visits of Mr. Clean, the Man from Glad, FTD's golden Mercury, and Ajax's White Knight brighten the life of what market researchers fondly describe as "Mrs. Middle Majority." One Ajax executive offered the following explanation for the appeal of his product and its slogan ("stronger than dirt"): "Every housewife has been waiting for a white knight since she was a little girl. . . . Actually we are saying to her 'stronger than your husband.'" In such instances, the association of products with sexuality is designed to provide consumers with a welcome relief from a highly impersonal, technological society.

By the late 1960s, co-ed dorms, women's liberation, men's magazines, singles bars, four-letter words, topless waitresses, go-go dancers, and the pill—among other factors—were responsible for dramatic changes in what *Time* called "spectator sex—what may be seen and heard." With Frank Sinatra crooning "All the Way" and Planned Parenthood ads touting oral contraception as the way to "Take the Worry Out of Being Close," advertising was hard-pressed to keep pace with the fast-changing cultural scene and sexual attitudes. After forty years of assault, the Victorian code of sexual behavior was in disarray, reduced to Hemingway's notion that

"What is moral is what you feel good after." As the ads for Tiparillo (1968) and Relax-A-Cizor (1969) suggest, sex in advertising fluctuated between desire and fatigue. But the one for Champion Slacks (1969) made it clear that advertising had also entered a new frontier of "meaningful relationships." As one Congregationalist minister put it, the 1960s were an "orgy of open-mindedness."

Sex clinics have done a brisk business in the 1970s. Saturated with the erotica of films, magazines, theater, and sex manuals, Americans seemed to be "having" sex more but enjoying it less. In a recent interview, one prominent sex counselor remarked that "a lack of desire" now accounts for nearly half the problems therapists treat. But one consolation, according to William Masters, who with his wife Virginia Johnson directs the noted Reproduction Biology Research Foundation, is that more people now seem willing to acknowledge their problems and seek help. For many of them, sex has apparently taken on the identity of a commodity and is becoming as dehumanized as the corporate production line. Sex in advertising has followed suit. Most of the following ads dated in the 1970s show how sexist sexuality has continued to be. Perhaps the pendulum is now swinging back. Legalized abortion has been challenged in several states; dresses are longer again; the pill is out; the condom is back in.

Attacks on sex in advertising date back at least as far as the mid-eighteenth century, when one newspaper editor, reacting to the spate of ads for "Prolifik Elixir," a herbal aphrodisiac, noted, "I cannot excuse my fellow laborers for admitting into their papers several uncleanly advertisements not at all proper to appear in the works of polite writers." Since that time, the charges against sex in advertising have remained fairly consistent: It will corrupt public morals, weaken the family, and threaten the social fabric. A 1978 agency survey, "Sex on the Airwaves," ranks sex right behind violence as the most serious viewer dissatisfaction with television. A 1969 study conducted for *Mediascope*, a communications trade journal, revealed that "half of America notices a lot of sex in advertising. . . . Women notice it more than men, the old more than the young, and the South more than any other quarter of the country. The rich are less easily offended than the poor." Significantly, the poll found that fewer than half the respondents were offended by sex in advertising. Such demographics indicate that sex in advertising is embedded in everyday life in America. And despite the fact that few of our lives can hardly measure up to the sexual images promoted in scores of alluring advertisements and commercials, sex will undoubtedly continue to occupy center-stage in the theatrics of advertising.

Cozy
and
Happy

CHASE
Plush
Motor Car
Robes

Made by Sanford Mills

BEAUTIFUL : COMFORTABLE : DURABLE : SANITARY

Beauty—Robes of wonderful colorings and designs with rich plush surfaces.

Comfort—Shields you like the coat of fur given Arctic animals by Mother Nature.

Durability—A Chase Plush Robe will outwear three or four other woven fabric robes.

Sanitary—Nothing adheres to the bright, smooth facings —a simple shaking removes dust.

The best stores now featuring a complete stock.

·L·C·CHASE & CO·

Ask your dealer about Chase Robes.

NEW YORK   BOSTON   CHICAGO
Leaders in Manufacturing Since 1847

1917

"The first social revelation [of the Jazz Age] created a sensation out of all proportion to its novelty. As far back as 1915 the unchaperoned young people of the smaller cities had discovered the mobile privacy of that automobile given to young Bill at sixteen to make him 'self-reliant.' At first petting was a desperate adventure even under such favorable conditions, but presently confidences were exchanged and the old commandment broke down. . . . Only in 1920 did the veil finally fall—the Jazz Age was in flower."

F. Scott Fitzgerald, "Echoes of the Jazz Age" (1931)

336

NOW that discretion is the better part of buying, men and women should learn the difference between this pure-dyed silk hosiery and "loaded" silk hose.

The soft effulgence and the grace of Luxite Hosiery commend it to all who have an eye to beauty. And its unrivaled serviceability prompts them to recommend it to their friends.

So Luxite has become the great American hosiery success—and is today an international favorite.

Ask your dealer to supply you. If he cannot do so, write for price list and descriptive booklet today.

Men's Silk Faced 50c, and Pure Thread Silk 75c and $1.00. Other styles at 35c up.
Women's Pure Thread Silk, $1.00 to $2.50. Other styles, 40c up. Children's, 35c up.

LUXITE TEXTILES, Inc., 652 Fowler Street, Milwaukee, Wisconsin

NEW YORK   CHICAGO   *Makers of High Grade Hosiery Since 1875*   SAN FRANCISCO   LIVERPOOL
Luxite Textiles of Canada, Limited, London, Ont.

Carl Naether's Advertising to Women (1928) offered this analysis of the famous Woodbury campaign: "It is a lure to make women believe that, by using the soap in question, she will be able to cultivate a skin sufficiently beautiful to constitute an infallible safeguard against the waning of male affection. . . . Because of the overwhelming pictorial appeal to woman's strongest emotion, the illustration may succeed in laming the reader's reasoning faculties . . . to make woman believe the unreasonable assertion that she will be able to keep warm and active her man's feelings toward her by bringing the advertised soap in contact with her skin at stated intervals!"

338

BLUE MOON
Silk Stockings

1926

"*Nature in the Raw is seldom MILD*"

THE PILLAGE OF PARIS

"*Nature in the Raw*"—*after the great French artist Luminais . . . inspired by the savage fierceness of untamed Norsemen in the ruthless capture of Paris—845 A. D.*

—and raw tobaccos have no place in cigarettes

They are *not* present in Luckies . . . the *mildest* cigarette you ever smoked

WE buy the finest, the very finest tobaccos in all the world— but that does not explain why folks everywhere regard Lucky Strike as the mildest cigarette. The fact is, we never overlook the truth that "Nature in the Raw is Seldom Mild"—so these fine tobaccos, after proper aging and mellowing, are then given the benefit of that Lucky Strike purifying process, described by the words—"It's toasted". That's why folks in every city, town and hamlet say that Luckies are such mild cigarettes.

"It's toasted"
That package of mild Luckies

LUCKY STRIKE
"IT'S TOASTED"
CIGARETTES

Copr., 1932, The American Tobacco Co.

"*If a man write a better book, preach a better sermon, or make a better mouse-trap than his neighbor, tho he build his house in the woods, the world will make a beaten path to his door.*"—RALPH WALDO EMERSON. Does not this explain the world-wide acceptance and approval of Lucky Strike?

Science enriches Woodbury Formula
with Benefits of "**Filtered Sunshine**"

Nature's source of beauty for the skin!

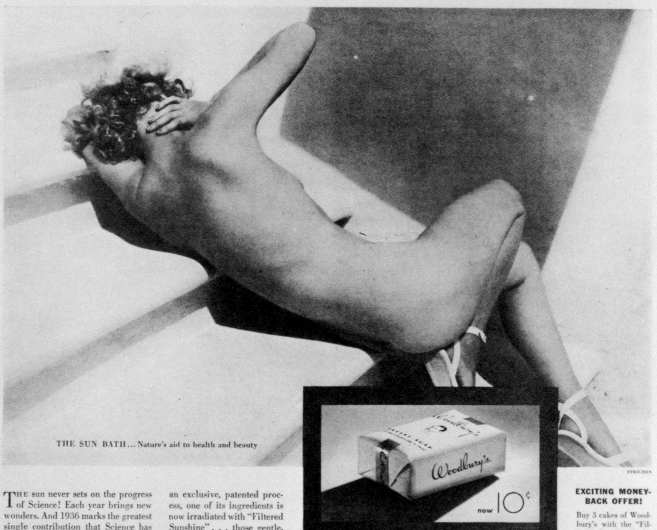

THE SUN BATH...Nature's aid to health and beauty

Woodbury's Facial Soap

now 10¢

STEICHEN

THE sun never sets on the progress of Science! Each year brings new wonders. And 1936 marks the greatest single contribution that Science has ever made to the charm and loveliness of American women.

Today, a soap you have long known and loved...Woodbury's Facial Soap ...gives your complexion, all your skin, the marvelous, beauty-enhancing benefits of "Filtered Sunshine."

Now Endowed with Benefits of "Filtered Sunshine"

For more than 50 years Woodbury's creamy lather has coaxed finer texture and clear radiance to faulty complexions, improved every normal skin.

Now the original Woodbury formula brings you a new refinement. By an exclusive, patented process, one of its ingredients is now irradiated with "Filtered Sunshine"... those gentle, kindly rays that are Nature's aid to skin loveliness.

This "Filtered Sunshine" element is released from Woodbury's lather as you wash and bathe. The skin readily absorbs it, as extensive tests by a leading university have proved.

A Luxurious Economy

Try this amazing new scientific soap! You *can* at very little cost and on Woodbury's promise to refund your money, if you're not delighted! The new Woodbury's is only 10c for the same big, long-lasting cake for which, in years past, you paid twenty-five cents.

Your complexion will soon become "A Skin You Love to Touch"...your skin all over will be softer, smoother. And don't be selfish! Let your whole family use the new "Filtered Sunshine" Woodbury's for face, hands and bath. It's splendid for the baby's bath, too, leading authorities agree. At all drug, department and ten-cent stores, and at your grocer's! Get 3 cakes today!

EXCITING MONEY-BACK OFFER!

Buy 3 cakes of Woodbury's with the "Filtered Sunshine" element in it. Use 2 cakes. If your skin is not smoother, finer, noticeably lovelier, then do this: Mail to us before August 31, 1936, the unused cake in wrapper (seals unbroken) and the wrappers from the two used cakes. Tell why Woodbury's did not suit you, also amount paid for 3 cakes. We will then refund to you the full purchase price, plus postage. Address, John H. Woodbury, Inc., 167 Alfred St., Cincinnati, Ohio. In Canada, John H. Woodbury, Ltd., Perth, Ontario.

TUNE IN on PAUL WHITEMAN, NBC Network—every Sunday evening, 9:45 E. D. T.

Look for the head and signature, *John H. Woodbury, Inc.* on all Woodbury products. © 1936, John H. Woodbury, Inc.

1936

This photograph, taken by Edward Steichen, is most probably one of the first photographs of a nude woman used in advertising.

Stop, Look and Kiss 'em

LOOK OUT FOR THE JARS and jolts in inferior Technical Merchandise. The Keuffel and Esser line of Drafting Materials and Engineering Instruments is always dependable—and we are their exclusive selling agents.

H. H. SULLIVAN INC.

TECHNICAL MERCHANDISE

QUALITY BLUE PRINTS AND PHOTO COPIES

"EVERYTHING FOR THE DRAFTING ROOM"

HARDWARE - ARTISTS SUPPLIES - HOUSE PAINT

65-71 SOUTH AVE. - ROCHESTER, N. Y. - STONE 550

1936

Commercial artists, such as Earl Moran, George Petty, Hayden Hayden, and Coles Phillips, helped turn "cheesecake" into a feminine ideal for generations of American men. Their alluring advertisements decorated the walls of locker rooms, dormitories, prison cells, and military barracks.

ARTCRAFT

Stockings of Elegance

For personal-sized fit . . . Demi for the small.   Debutante for the medium.   Damsel for the tall.

1950

"To the mind of the modern girl, legs, like busts, are power points which she has been taught to tailor, but as parts of the success kit rather than erotically or sensuously. She swings her legs from the hip with masculine drive and confidence. She knows that 'a long-legged gal can go places.' As such, her legs are not intimately associated with her taste or with her unique self but are merely display objects like the grill work on a car. They are date-baited power levers for the management of the male audience."

Marshall McLuhan, *The Mechanical Bride* (1951)

NO SEAMS TO WORRY ABOUT!

I'VE FALLEN FOR SEAMLESS STOCKINGS BY *Hanes*

HANES HOSIERY INC. · 350 FIFTH AVE., NEW YORK · $1.35 TO $1.95 AT LEADING STORES

BOTTLE OF THE SEXES

Here is the "his" and "her" scotch. Ambassador Deluxe, *uniquely*, has her lightness without compromising his flavor — a brilliant new achievement of Scotch distilling skill.

Get together with Ambassador tonight...see how diplomatic the world's lightest scotch can be.

1962

"You sweet doll, I appreciate you. I've got taste. I'll bring out the real orange in you. I'll make you famous. Kiss me."

"Who was that tomato I saw you with last week?"

Wolfschmidt Vodka has the touch of taste that marks genuine old world vodka. Wolfschmidt in a Screwdriver is an orange at its best. Wolfschmidt brings out the best in every drink. GENERAL WINE AND SPIRITS CO., NEW YORK 22. MADE FROM GRAIN, 80 OR 100 PROOF. PRODUCT OF U.S.A.

1962

Should a gentleman offer a Tiparillo to a dental hygienist?

"The doctor is a little late, sir. Will you have a seat?"

She's the best thing to hit dentistry since novocaine. "Hey Dummy," your mind says to you, "why didn't you have this toothache sooner?"

Maybe if...well, you could offer her a Tiparillo.® Or a Tiparillo M with menthol. An elegant, tipped cigar. Slim. And your offer would be cleverly psychological. (If she's a bit of a kook, she'll take it. If not, she'll be flattered that you *thought* she was a bit of a kook.) And who knows? Your next visit might be a house call.

Mother warned me...

that there would be men like you driving cars like that. Do you really think you can get to me with that long, low, tough machine you just rolled up in? Ha! If you think a girl with real values is impressed by your air conditioning and stereo . . . a 440 Magnum, whatever that is . . . well—it takes more than cushy bucket seats to make me flip. Charger R/T SE. Sounds like alphabet soup. Frankly, I'm attracted to you because you have a very intelligent face. My name's Julia.

Join the fun . . . catch

DODGE *fever*

1968

348

"Why don't you take the 8:45 instead?"

It's a great day in the morning when you use Kings Men After Shave Lotion. Its subtle, manly fragrance underscores the vigorous way you feel after soothing and cooling your just-shaved face. What's more, Kings Men is the first 24-hour skin tonic, and no other After Shave Lotion gives you a lift that lasts so long. You'll feel great when you start your day with Kings Men After Shave Lotion. $1 plus tax.

It's so nice to have a King's Man around the house

KINGS MEN®
for good grooming

After Shave Lotion • Pre-Electric Shave Lotion • Cologne • Aerosol Luxury Shave
Hairdressing • Deodorants

1961

**Bill Page
won't be president of the company
until 1987.**

**But with "Young Exec Slacks"
(and the boss' wife in his corner)
who knows?**

Bill Page is pretty smart. He knows what it takes to get ahead. That's why he wears Young Exec slacks by Champion. They make him look important. Like he belongs on top. The smart styling and tapered fit of Young Exec slacks earmark him for success. All-worsted fabrics in reverse twists, club checks and muted plaids give him the look he wants. He knows who to impress and how. He's not one to footsie around. The Young Exec will make it big...even if the boss' wife invites someone else to dinner next week. Champion Young Exec slacks, from 17.95 at all smart stores.

CHAMPION SLACKS
49 West 23rd Street, New York, N.Y. Another fine product of K R Kayser-Roth.

1969

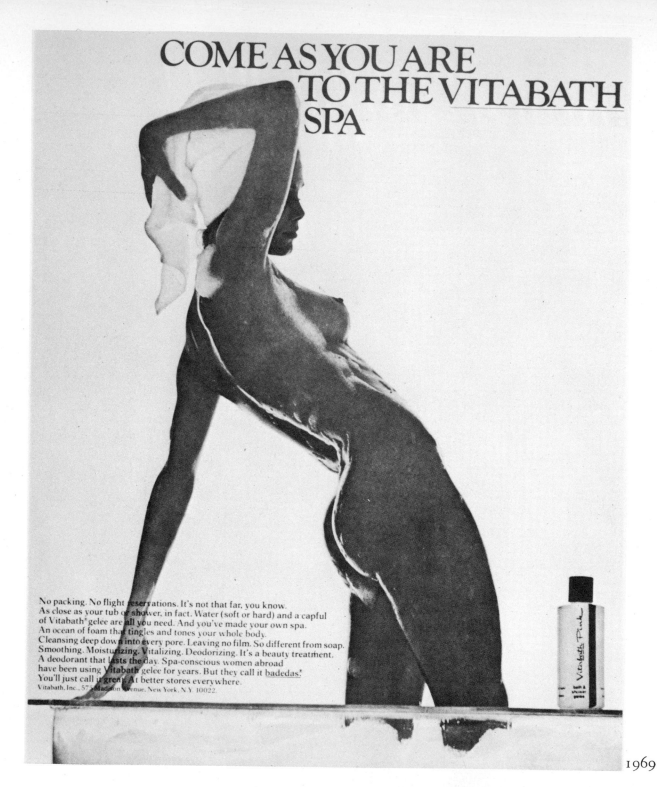

COME AS YOU ARE
TO THE VITABATH
SPA

No packing. No flight reservations. It's not that far, you know.
As close as your tub or shower, in fact. Water (soft or hard) and a capful
of Vitabath® gelee are all you need. And you've made your own spa.
An ocean of foam that tingles and tones your whole body.
Cleansing deep down into every pore. Leaving no film. So different from soap.
Smoothing. Moisturizing. Vitalizing. Deodorizing. It's a beauty treatment.
A deodorant that lasts the day. Spa-conscious women abroad
have been using Vitabath gelee for years. But they call it <u>badedas</u>.
You'll just call it great. At better stores everywhere.
Vitabath, Inc., 575 Madison Avenue, New York, N.Y. 10022.

1969

Nude women in advertising are most often used to promote women's products. In the midst of the sexual revolution in the late 1960s, Helen Gurley Brown, editor of Cosmopolitan, offered the following explanation: "Women don't get to see nearly as many naked women as they would like to. You never have a chance to look at another naked woman. I don't think 80 percent of the women in this country have any idea what other women's bosoms look like. They have this idealized idea of how other people's bosoms are, but we are now beginning to see that there are hundreds of thousands of different shapes, colors, and structures. You know, nipples are all different. Well, that knowledge is just now being disseminated. My God, isn't it ridiculous to be an emancipated woman and not really know what a woman's body looks like except your own?"

Now Relax-A-cizor invents...
sexy exercise
for the man.

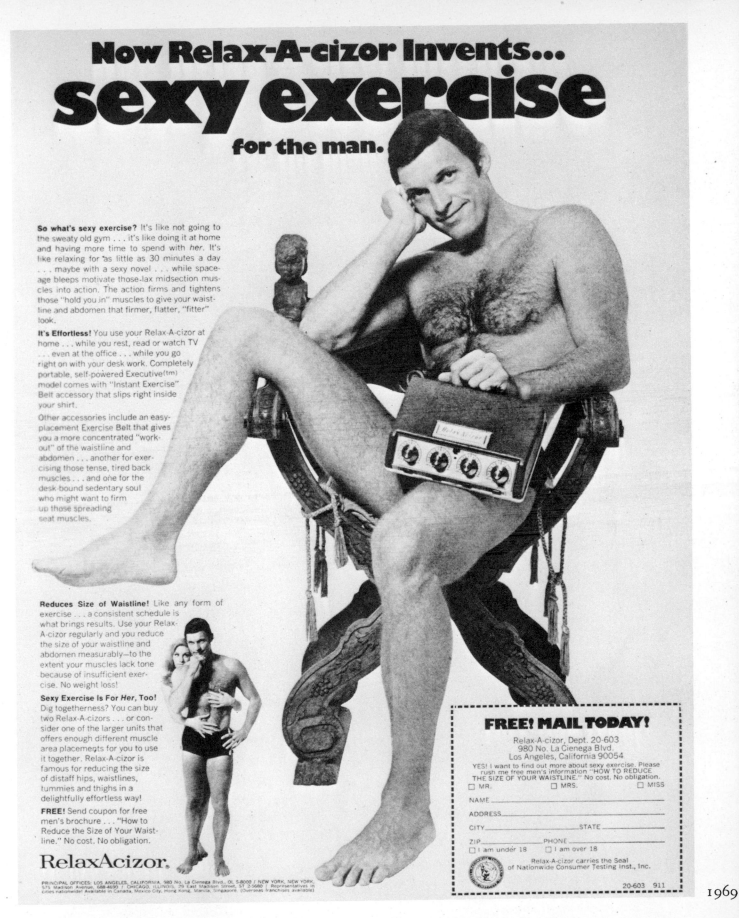

So what's sexy exercise? It's like not going to the sweaty old gym . . . it's like doing it at home and having more time to spend with *her*. It's like relaxing for 'as little as 30 minutes a day . . . maybe with a sexy novel . . . while space-age bleeps motivate those lax midsection muscles into action. The action firms and tightens those "hold you in" muscles to give your waistline and abdomen that firmer, flatter, "fitter" look.

It's Effortless! You use your Relax-A-cizor at home . . . while you rest, read or watch TV . . . even at the office . . . while you go right on with your desk work. Completely portable, self-powered Executive(tm) model comes with "Instant Exercise" Belt accessory that slips right inside your shirt.

Other accessories include an easy-placement Exercise Belt that gives you a more concentrated "work-out" of the waistline and abdomen . . . another for exercising those tense, tired back muscles . . . and one for the desk-bound sedentary soul who might want to firm up those spreading seat muscles.

Reduces Size of Waistline! Like any form of exercise . . . a consistent schedule is what brings results. Use your Relax-A-cizor regularly and you reduce the size of your waistline and abdomen measurably—to the extent your muscles lack tone because of insufficient exercise. No weight loss!

Sexy Exercise Is For *Her*, Too! Dig togetherness? You can buy two Relax-A-cizors . . . or consider one of the larger units that offers enough different muscle area placements for you to use it together. Relax-A-cizor is famous for reducing the size of distaff hips, waistlines, tummies and thighs in a delightfully effortless way!

FREE! Send coupon for free men's brochure . . . "How to Reduce the Size of Your Waist-line." No cost. No obligation.

RelaxAcizor.

PRINCIPAL OFFICES: LOS ANGELES, CALIFORNIA, 980 No. La Cienega Blvd., OL 5-8000 / NEW YORK, NEW YORK, 575 Madison Avenue, 688-4690 / CHICAGO, ILLINOIS, 29 East Madison Street, ST 2-5680 / Representatives in cities nationwide! Available in Canada, Mexico City, Hong Kong, Manila, Singapore. (Overseas franchises available)

FREE! MAIL TODAY!

Relax-A-cizor, Dept. 20-603
980 No. La Cienega Blvd.
Los Angeles, California 90054

YES! I want to find out more about sexy exercise. Please rush me free men's information "HOW TO REDUCE THE SIZE OF YOUR WAISTLINE." No cost. No obligation.

☐ MR.   ☐ MRS.   ☐ MISS

NAME _____

ADDRESS _____

CITY _____ STATE _____

ZIP _____ PHONE _____
☐ I am under 18   ☐ I am over 18

Relax-A-cizor carries the Seal of Nationwide Consumer Testing Inst., Inc.

20-603   911

1969

"A woman is a woman until the day she dies, but a man's a man only as long as he can."

Moms Mabley

This little cigar brings out the Tall N' Slim in you.

TALL N' SLIM CIGARS

TALL N' SLIM Menthol CIGARS

Tall and slim in today's modern style, our little cigar gives you 100mms of rich, mild tobacco you don't have to inhale to enjoy. Treat yourself soon to America's first 100mm little cigar with a charcoal filter. United States Tobacco Co., Greenwich, Conn. 06830.

I'm Margie.

I'm Margie.

Fly me.

I'm a girl. I'm an airplane.

I'm an airline.

I'm a fresh new way of getting you where you want to go (New York, Miami, New Orleans, Los Angeles, San Francisco—even London).

My name is Margie. Chances are you'll meet and fly Carol, Sally, Michelle and Gayle, too. Chances are you won't meet Leroy, Don, Peter or Lee, because they're working for you behind the scenes. But you'll be flying them all the same.

And soon you'll be able to fly Barbara, the first of our new fleet of DC-10's. She's this year's airplane. This winter she's joining her sister ships, National's 747's, with the only DC-10 service between New York and Florida and between Florida and California.

The idea is to make your next flight a nice personal experience, person-to-person.

So next time you're going someplace, give us a call. And call us by our first name: National.

Fly Margie. ✸ Fly National.

National honors American Express, BankAmericard, Carte Blanche, Diners Club, Master Charge/Interbank, UATP, our own card and cash.

1971

Women's groups attacked as sexist National's "Fly Me" slogan, its sequels "We were born to fly" and "I'm going to fly you like you've never been flown before," as well as Continental's "We really move our tail for you." Stewardess organizations protested that such ads conditioned men to ignore safety instructions from those they regarded as "objects of their sexual fantasies" and that women would view flight attendants as a corps of "man-stealers." As the controversy roared, sales took off.

354

Ask me about archery

America's second most challenging sport.
It's fun! It's exciting!

I'd like to learn more about the challenge of the bow and arrow.   Age_____ Do you own a bow now?_____Yes_____No

Name_____Street Address_____City_____State_____Zip_____

Mail to: Bear Archery, Department PB-5, Rural Route One, Grayling, Michigan 49738.

1974

PUT YOUR GUN
INTO SOMETHING SOFT.

Like a beautiful Bull Llama grain holster.
It's soft, with a full suede lining yet completely waterproof, unscratchable and indestructable. It's designed for strength and durability and has enough finished quality for wear with your finest business suit. Unlike other holsters on the market, ours will not cause damage to the finish of your handgun, and it's interchangeable from shoulder harness to belt to ankle.

Whether you choose luxurious brown or black, choose an interchangeable Universal holster.

Send $1.00 for 1977 catalogue.

UNIVERSAL LEATHERGOODS, INC

Drawer 35747
Tulsa, Okla. 74135
(918) 492-7870

1977

"I feel that where advertising is concerned, sex is something like garlic. You can't argue that it doesn't add flavor, but you can certainly argue about how much to use and when. The combination of ever-increasing competition from new products, and the traditional worry that consumers are being inundated by too many advertising claims, have many admen today convinced that the flavor is a must."

Donald Keenan of Beecham Products, makers of Macleans toothpaste and Brylcreem

1977

"One of the main jobs of the advertiser in [the] conflict between pleasure and guilt is not so much to sell the product as to give moral permission to have fun without guilt."

Ernest Dichter, president, Institute for Motivational Research

ELECT THE NEW MISS MURIEL

One of these girls can fulfill your wildest dreams if you help fulfill hers.

Jan Daley   Susan Anton   Margaret Davies

Vote for one of these girls to be the new Miss Muriel and you could win some pretty incredible prizes. Like a new Corvette plus a trip to Europe.

For the past few months you've seen them dancing and singing on Muriel television commercials. Now you can choose your favorite.

To vote, just follow the instructions on the coupon. Or pick up a ballot wherever you buy Muriel® cigars.

If the girl you vote for wins, you'll become eligible to be a winner in the big Miss Muriel Election Sweepstakes.

FIRST PRIZE is a new Corvette plus a week in Europe. There are also five second prizes — brand new Camaros. And ten third prizes — one week sports vacations for two, to any resort in the Continental U.S.A.

So choose your favorite and vote today. You could end up being the big winner in the new Miss Muriel Election Sweepstakes.

MURIEL CORONELLA

FIVE CIGARS

To pick the girl you'd like to become Miss Muriel send this coupon, or a facsimile, along with either one Muriel cigar band or a plain 3x5-inch piece of paper containing the words "Muriel Election Sweepstakes" to the Post Office Box listed under your candidate's name below. If your choice wins, you become eligible for all the valuable prizes.

Jan Daley   Susan Anton   Margaret Davies
P.O. Box 148   P.O. Box 202   P.O. Box 363
New York, N.Y. 10046   New York, N.Y. 10046   New York, N.Y. 10046

Name_____
Address_____
City_____ State_____ Zip_____

Vote for Miss Muriel. You may win a new Corvette and a trip to Europe.

"Muriel" Election Sweepstakes. Official Rules. No purchase required. 1. You've seen them on television. Now pick the girl you'd like to be Miss Muriel. Complete the ballot entry form (or facsimile) and mail it together with either one Muriel cigar band or 3x5 plain piece of paper containing the words "MURIEL ELECTION SWEEPSTAKES" to the Miss Muriel of your choice at her address listed below. If your choice wins, you become eligible for all the valuable prizes. "MURIEL ELECTION SWEEPSTAKES" — Jan Daley — P.O. Box 148, N.Y., N.Y. 10046 or Susan Anton — P.O. Box 202, N.Y., N.Y. 10046 or Margaret Davies — P.O. Box 363, N.Y., N.Y. 10046. 2. Sweepstakes winners will be selected from among all ballot-entry forms and facsimiles received for the winning girl in the "Muriel" election. Random drawings to determine the winners will be held by an independent judging organization whose decisions are final. All prizes will be awarded. Winners will be notified by mail. Limit one prize per family. 3. Enter as often as you wish but each entry must be mailed separately. All entries must be postmarked by October 1, 1976 and received by October 8, 1976. 4. This sweepstakes is open to residents of the U.S.A. except employees of Consolidated Cigar Corporation, its affiliated companies, its advertising, sweepstakes agencies and their families. This offer is subject to all Federal, State and local laws and is VOID in the States of Missouri, Ohio, Wisconsin, Maryland and wherever prohibited and/or restricted by law. No substitution of prizes permitted. Taxes are the responsibility of the prize winner. 5. For a list of winners, send a separate stamped, self-addressed envelope to: Muriel Winners List, P.O. Box 411, New York, N.Y. 10046. (Note: Do not send request with your ballot-entry form.)

1977

In 1973, when singer Edie Adams whispered her last sultry "Why don't you pick one up and smoke it sometime," Muriel cigar profits dropped appreciably. Its agency responded by developing a more youth-oriented advertising campaign based on consumer sweepstakes to elect a new Miss Muriel. Now Susan Anton, who dreamed of teaching nursery school, can be seen slinking through locker rooms inviting men in a smoldering voice to "Let Muriel turn you on/That is my desire." But when CBS refused to run the commercial, its creators offered no apologies: "We set out to fulfill a guy's sexual fantasies." The publicity generated by the election pushed sales up and turned an ad campaign into a news event.

HOW TO HAVE
The Sexual Drive You Always Dreamed Of

Dear Friend,

If you have sex problems, potency problems, or even prostate problems, I'd like to send you something that comes in a plain brown wrapper.

No, it is not dirty pictures or anything like that. It is the last thing in the world that I am interested in, because I have something much better—the real thing.

But it is something that you won't want your friends, or especially your wife to know about.

Not for a while anyway. Here's why.

I'm going to send you a single evening's worth of reading material that shows you how I became much stronger sexually at 68 than I was at 40. And how I believe that you can do the same. And do it so fast that your wife may think you've been taking hormone shots from a world-famous doctor.

But I want you to make me one promise first—that you give my method of attaining new sexual strength and health a fair try, before you tell anyone—especially your wife—what you're doing.

That's because if you tell anyone about my secret method, before you give it a fair try, they might just be able to talk you out of it. They'll try to tell you that there just is no "at-home, do-it-yourself" way to overcome sexual and prostate problems, and get back the sexual powers of a 35-year-old, the way I did. And keep that sexual drive undiminished all the way up to 68, which is the age I am today.

But there is. And I have proved it in my own life. And my second wife—30 years my junior—will give testimony that I have.

And I'm sure that if you try it privately for even a few weeks—that no one in the world will ever be able to talk you out of it again.

But, Before I Go On, Let Me Tell You That I Am Not A Doctor, Or A Sex Therapist, Or Anything Like That.

I'm a businessman. An adult male, just like you.

An adult male whose day of "sexual reckoning" seemed to occur when I was in my early forties.

Until that time, I prided myself on being one of those rare men who was "always ready". However, suddenly, in my forties, I began to be plagued by most of the "classic" sexual problems. More and more, I found myself unable to achieve an erection, or maintain sexual intercourse long enough to satisfy my wife. I acquired a prostate problem that began to make sex, as well as urination, a painful process. And worst of all, my sexual desire itself was diminishing. Sex was becoming a thing of the past.

I still shudder when I think back on those days. But no more.

What I did first was consult a physician about my difficulties. He recommended hormone shots and tablets for my sexual inadequacies, but said that the only means of solving my prostate problem would be an operation.

I had seen friends of mine who had been operated on before. So I decided against the operation till I could get more facts. But I did take the hormones for a while.

They were certainly not the answer. I believed the reason for this was because they were artificial stimulants, given to my body from the outside. So I had to find another means of solving my problem. A natural means.

Thank God I Have Always Had An Inquisitive Mind. So I Studied The Problem Day And Night. And Slowly I Began To Get A Clear Picture.

After months and even years of work, I learned thrilling facts. Some came from the medical field. Others came from such great natural healers as Adele Davis, J. I. Rodale, George Watson, Irwin Stone, Linus Pauling and Lelord Kordel.

Some even came from the greatest healing manual of them all—the Bible.

But I had never seen anyone put them all together in one common-sense plan before.

For example, I learned that, given certain special foods, the male body can produce its own sex hormones. That it does not have to go outside itself for these vital hormones.

I learned that I had been unknowingly pouring into my body a crippling collection of chemical "sex killers." The same type of chemical, for example, that is fed to prisoners to destroy their sex drive. Or another chemical that causes the genital organs to shrink away, sometimes to the point where they no longer function at all.

Or another chemical that overtaxes the kidneys and thus painfully irritates the prostate.

I read with joy medical studies that showed that a man's virility should not normally decline until after the age of 75. That there is no such thing as the "male menopause." That a healthy man (and I memorized the step-by-step instructions these studies contained) can expect to have full sexual potency right through his sixties!

And then I went on, to discover the common vitamin that reduced prostate swelling. And it worked wonders for me. Along with the other vitamins I discovered, it was absolutely fantastic in the way it reduced the swelling, and pain, of my prostate. And in my case, once the swelling of the prostate was gone, the entire problem was gone. From that moment on, for example, neither sex nor urinating was any longer a problem.

When I Think That Over 25 Years Ago, I Almost "Gave Up" On Sex—And Today I Can Easily Satisfy My Second Wife, Who Is 30 Years My Junior...

Then all I can say is this:

It's wonderful.

And I want you to try it too.

Of course, when I first put together this complete plan, it all seemed too simple and too inexpensive to really work. But I was in such desperate condition then that I had no choice but to try it. And try it I did. Just as I ask you to do now.

It was astonishing. After just a few months on this amazingly simple plan, I was no longer plagued by a single one of those problems which had sent me rushing to my doctor. I suddenly gained—and continued to maintain—strong sexual desire. I can easily achieve and hold an erection. My second wife, Ellen, who is twelve years younger than my own daughter, reveres me in bed as though I were a young man.

My prostate problem continues to be completely under control, through the use of vitamins and minerals alone, without having undergone surgery.

And I received marvelous side benefits, which are almost equally valuable to me as the sexual ones.

For example, my blood pressure, pulse and blood count compare to that of average men almost 30 years younger.

I have a better appetite, a keen interest in life, and the energy I need to do whatever I desire to do. In fact, I literally "go" all day—whether I am working around the house, in the yard, or travelling for business, or even trout fishing.

I stand straighter than I did at 40. I am far thinner. I am still considered attractive by my wife's friends, who are her own age. And there is a definite improvement in the male quality of my voice.

But the most important point is this—Failures—sexual failures—are now a thing of the past. I am like a 35-year-old again. And I'd like to pass on the research and experience that did this for me to you, for your personal benefit.

Again, I Know This Sounds Incredible... But This Complete Plan Is So Simple That You Can Learn It In A Single Evening.

It's so simple, in fact, that I haven't yet figured out why no one ever put it all together before. Perhaps because the research itself was just too much work for someone who wasn't as desperate as I was, some 28 years ago.

But, since I discovered it, I've continued to read every new book I could find—even doctors' reports—and I've still never seen this complete secret printed anywhere at all.

Also, of course, it didn't take long for my friends to notice that a dramatic change had taken place in my sex life. They saw the results in my first wife, and then they saw even greater results in my second. They were eager to know "what kind of meat I was eating."

I told them simply that all I had really done was just "strengthen" my sexual input (through the secrets I mentioned above, and a few others), and therefore was able, in turn, to "strengthen" my sexual output.

Then I finally told them the complete details of what I had found—the step-by-step method—and let them prove it themselves.

At first they were downright skeptical that anything so simple could be so effective. But then they found it to be very helpful. In fact, it wasn't long before they were coming back and telling me that someone very important had been smothering them with compliments for "a job well done".

For them too, failures were now a thing of the past.

But Why Should I Restrict This Proven Plan To Only Myself And My Friends?

In fact, one of my friends said to me, "You know, Marvin, I would have paid you a thousand dollars for what your secret did for me."

Well, I don't want anything like a thousand dollars for it, but I do want men who need it to get it, and prove it themselves, at no risk of their money whatsoever. So what I've done is this—

I've completely re-written every detail of the complete plan. Everything that helped myself and my friends. For want of a better name, I've called it "How to Have the Sexual Drive You've Always Dreamed Of."

I feel certain that it makes no difference whether you are now younger or older than I am—or how long your problems have been crippling you—or how painful and embarrassing they may be today. This method must work for you, or it won't cost you a single penny.

By the way, because of its personal nature, there is only one way for you to see if I'm right—to get your guaranteed copy of "How to Have the Sexual Drive You've Always Dreamed Of"—and that's to order it now, by mail. It is not available in any book store or health food shop in the world, at any price. And when I send it to you, no one except yourself will know what the package that brings it to you really contains.

Also, you might be interested to know that this Plan has already been registered and copyrighted with the U.S. Government, so its secret cannot be copied or stolen.

Why put up with embarrassment, failure and pain one moment longer? Send for your guaranteed copy as soon as you can—TODAY if possible.

Sincerely,

Marvin Freeman

Marvin Freeman, INSTANT LEARNING, Inc., 380 Madison Ave., New York, N.Y. 10017

THIS LADY IS NOT MY DAUGHTER, BUT MY WIFE.

For the thrilling true story of the 68-year-old man who "regained the sexual powers of a 35-year-old," read this page.

MAIL 100% NO-RISK DOUBLE GUARANTEE COUPON TODAY! NYN-109

Marvin Freeman, INSTANT LEARNING, Inc., 27 Milburn St., Bronxville, N.Y. 10708

Alright, Marv—please rush me in a plain wrapper a copy of your Confidential Report "HOW TO HAVE THE SEXUAL DRIVE YOU ALWAYS DREAMED OF!" I enclose $9.98 in full payment. In addition, I understand that I may examine this Confidential Report for as long as I wish, since I'm fully protected by your 100% No-Risk Double guarantee shown below.

You are fully protected by this 100% no-risk Double Guarantee:
1. If you don't like my SEXUAL DRIVE report when it arrives, return it for a full refund - no questions asked.
2. Or, keep and use it for a full year. You are still protected. You MUST get all I've promised—or send it back NEXT YEAR. You still get every penny back.
☐ If you wish your order sent C.O.D., CHECK HERE! Enclose $1 good-will deposit now. Pay postman balance, plus postage and handling charges. Same money back guarantee, of course!

NAME _____

ADDRESS _____

CITY _____ STATE _____ ZIP _____

N.Y. res. please add appropriate sales tax.

1977

"I have read, literally, hundreds of volumes upon it [sex], and uncountable numbers of pamphlets, handbills and inflammatory wall-cards, and yet it leaves the primary problem unsolved, which is to say, the problem as to what is to be done about the conflict between the celibacy enforced upon millions by civilization and the appetites implanted in all by God. In the main, it counsels yielding to celibacy, which is exactly as sensible as advising a dog to forget its fleas."

H. L. Mencken, *In Defense of Women* (1918)

Sears has gone wild!

The Adventuress set: Go lean. Go lacy. Go live with color. Go wild! With Sears Adventuress Set.

The bra: lace cups on a stretch frame, stretch straps, scoop back. Natural cup with Cordtex® lift. Or contour cup with Wonder-Fil. Both styles under $6. (D cup higher)

The girdle: a new kind of power net that stretches to your measure for proportioned fit, all-over comfort. Spot controlling panels front, side and back. Under $12.

Choose the Adventuress Set (and matching lingerie!) in Adventuress Pink, Bravado Blue, or Desert Beige, all with Beige Lace or Snow Leopard White with White Lace. Charge

it on Sears Revolving Charge at any of over 2,500 Sears, Roebuck and Co. locations.

Go wild! At Sears.

COME WITH ME.

Introducing The Rough Rider Condom. Studded for more pleasure.

Come with me. And let me take you on the most sensuous ride of your life. A ride like you've never before experienced. Because there's never before been anything like ROUGH RIDER... the first condom with 468 exotic, orgasmic studs that cover every inch of you. And send sensual signals that make me tingle with ecstasy from the tips of my toes to the top of my head.

With ROUGH RIDER, it's easy to unleash the sexual animal inside me. And, because ROUGH RIDER is made of latex so thin it clings to you as closely as I do, you'll feel the throbbing excitement deep within me from the moment we begin to make love. Finally, ROUGH RIDER has a silky smooth lubricant called SK-70 that actually works with our own body secretions. So loving always comes naturally and effortlessly.

Come with me and join the ROUGH RIDERS. And together we'll experience the most adventurous, sexual ride of our love lives. With ROUGH RIDER, the first condom studded from head to shaft for more pleasure than you've ever dreamed of.

Also advertised in PENTHOUSE, *oui*, *Playgirl* and many others...

1978

Fears about health risks associated with oral contraception and intra-uterine devices led to a 15 percent increase in condom sales in 1977—to $160,000,000. While recent court decisions have made male contraceptives available in supermarkets, gas stations, and vending machines, a ban on radio and television advertising remains in effect.

SELECTED BIBLIOGRAPHY

Advertising:

Stephen Baker, *Visual Persuasion*, 1961.   J. A. C. Brown, *Techniques of Persuasion*, 1963.   Yale Brozen, ed., *Advertising and Society*, 1974.   E. E. Calkins, *The Business of Advertising*, 1915; *Louder Please! The Autobiography of a Deaf Man*, 1924. Jerry Della Femina, *From Those Wonderful Folks Who Gave You Pearl Harbor*, 1970. Ernest Dichter, *Psychology of Everyday Living*, 1947; *Strategy of Desire*, 1960.   Doyle Dane Bernbach, Inc., *Sex on the Airwaves*, 1978.   Stuart Ewen, *Captains of Consciousness: Advertising and the Social Roots of the Consumer Culture*, 1976.   William Freeman, *The Big Name*, 1957.   D. P. Gibson, *The $30 Billion Negro*, 1969.   John Gunther, *Taken at the Flood: The Story of Albert D. Lasker*, 1960.   Claude C. Hopkins, *Scientific Advertising*, 1921; *My Life in Advertising*, 1927.   Ralph M. Hower, *The History of an Advertising Agency*, 1939; 1949.   Fred Inglis, *The Imagery of Power: A Critique of Advertising*, 1972.   Wilson Bryan Key, *Subliminal Seduction*, 1973; *Media Sexploitation*, 1976.   Albert D. Lasker, *The Lasker Story*, 1953.   Geoffrey Leech, *English in Advertising: A Linguistic Study of Advertising in Great Britain*, 1966.   Varda Langholz Levmore, *Hidden Myth: Structure and Symbolism in Advertising*, 1975.   Marshall McLuhan, *The Mechanical Bride*, 1951.   Pierre Martineau *Motivation in Advertising*, 1957.   Martin Mayer, *Madison Avenue, U.S.A.*, 1958. Carl Naether, *Advertising to Women*, 1928.   David Ogilvy, *Confessions of an Advertising Man*, 1963.   Vance Packard, *The Hidden Persuaders*, 1957.   Otis Pease, *The Responsibilities of American Advertising*, 1958.   Shirley Polykoff, *Does She . . . Or Doesn't She?*, 1976.   Frank S. Presbrey, *The History and Development of Advertising*, 1929.   *Printer's Ink, Advertising: Today/Yesterday/Tomorrow*, 1963.   Rosser Reeves, *Reality in Advertising*, 1961.   James Rorty, *Our Master's Voice*, 1934. George P. Rowell, *Forty Years an Advertising Agent: 1865–1905*, 1906.   Denys Thompson, *Voice of Civilisation: An Enquiry into Advertising*, 1947.   Thomas Whiteside, *The Relaxed Sell*, 1954.   Janet Wolff, *What Makes Women Buy*, 1958.   James P. Wood, *The Story of Advertising*, 1958.

General:

Frederick Lewis Allen, *The Big Change*, 1952.   American Tobacco Company, *Sold American!*, 1954.   Roland Barthes, *Mythologies*, 1957; 1972.   Daniel Bell, *The Coming of Post-Industrial Society*, 1973.   Daniel Boorstin, *The Image: A Guide to Pseudo-Events in America*, 1962; *The Americans: The National Experience*, 1965; *The Americans: The Democratic Experience*, 1973.   Mvra Brenton, *The American Male*, 1966.   W. Elliott Brownlee, *Dynamics of Ascent: A History of the American Economy*, 1974.   Roger Burlingame, *March of the Iron Men: A Social History of the Union Through Invention*, 1938.   William H. Chafe, *The American Woman*, 1972.   John Chamberlain, *The Enterprising Americans: A Business History of the United States*, 1963.   Stuart Chase, *Prosperity: Fact or Myth*, 1929.   Thomas C. Cochran, *Social Change in America*, 1972.   James H. Collins, *The Story of Canned Foods*, 1924.   Reuel Denney, *The Astonished Muse*, 1957.   Alexis de Tocqueville, *Democracy in America*, 1862; 1976.   Charles Dickens, *American Notes*, 1842.   Ann Douglas, *The Feminization of American Culture*, 1977.   W. E. B. DuBois, *The Souls of Black Folk*, 1903.   Warren Farrell, *The Liberated Man*, 1975.   Marc Fasteau, *The Male Machine*, 1974.   Marshall Fishwick, *The Hero, American Style*, 1969.   Stuart B. Flexner, *I Hear America Talking*, 1976.   John Hope Franklin, *From Slavery to Freedom*, Fourth Ed., 1974.   John K. Galbraith, *The Affluent Society*, 1958; *The New Industrial State*, 1967; 1971; *Economics and Public Purpose*, 1973.   Betty Friedan, *The Feminine Mystique*, 1963.   Siegfried Giedion, *Mechanization Takes Command*, 1948.   Charlotte Perkins Gilman, *Women and Economics*, 1898.   John S. and Robin M. Haller, *The Physician and Sexuality in Victorian America*, 1977.   Edward C. Hampe and Merle Wittenberg, *The Lifeline of America: The Development of the Food Industry*, 1964.   Robert K. Heimann, *Tobacco and Americans*, 1960.   Shere Hite, *The Hite Report*, 1976.   Godfrey Hodgson, *America in Our Time*, 1976.   Rosabeth M. Kanter, *Men and Women of the Corporation*, 1977.   Elaine Kendall, *The Upper Hand*, 1965.   Kenneth Kenniston, *All Our Children*, 1977.   Alfred C. Kinsey, *Sexual Behavior in the Human Male*, 1948; *Sexual Behavior in the Human Female*, 1953.   Conan Kornetsky, *Pharmacology: Drugs Affecting Behavior*, 1976.   Leonard Kriegel, *The Myth of American Manhood*, 1978.   Henri Lefebvre, *Everyday Life in the Modern World*, 1968.   Robert S. and Helen M. Lynd, *Middletown: A Study in Contemporary Culture*, 1929; *Middletown in Transition*, 1937.   Marshall McLuhan, *Understanding Media*, 1964.   Norman Mailer, *Advertisements for Myself*, 1959.   Margaret Mead, *Male and Female*, 1949.   H. L. Mencken, *In Defense of Women*, 1926.   James Monaco, *How to Read a Film: The Art, Technology, Language, History, and Theory of Film and Media*, 1977; *Celebrity*, 1978.   Frank L. Mott, *A History of American Magazines*, 5 vols., 1957–68.   Gunnar Myrdal, *An American Dilemma*, 1944.   Robert Nisbet, *Community and Power*, 1953; 1962.   Paul H. Nystrom, *Economics of Fashion*, 1928.   Carl J. Palmer, *A History of the Soda Fountain Industry*, 1947.   Theodore Peterson, *Magazines in the Twentieth Century*, 1964.   David M. Potter, *People of Plenty*, 1954; *History and American Society*, 1973.   John B. Rae, *The American Automobile: A Brief History*, 1965.   David Riesman, *The Lonely Crowd*, 1950.   William Robbins, *The American Food Scandal*, 1974.   Joseph C. Robert, *The Story of Tobacco in America*, 1949.   Ishbel Ross, *Taste in America: An Illustrated History*, 1967.   Richard Schickel, *His Picture in the Papers: A Speculation on Celebrity in America Based on the Life of Douglas Fairbanks, Sr.*, 1973.   Jacob Schmookler, *Invention and Economic Growth*, 1966.   Tibor Scitovsky, *The Joyless Economy*, 1976.   Robert Sklar, *Movie-Made America*, 1977.   Alfred P. Sloan, *My Years at General Motors*, 1963.   Robert Sobel, *The Manipulators: America in the Media Age*, 1976.   Maurice Stein, *The Eclipse of Community*, 1960.   Keith Sward, *The Legend of Henry Ford*, 1948.   Frederick W. Taylor, *Principles of*

Scientific Management, 1911.   Frances Trollope, *Domestic Manners of the Americans,* 1832.   Thorstein Veblen, *Theory of the Leisure Class*, 1899; *The Theory of Business Enterprise*, 1904.   William H. Whyte, *The Organization Man*, 1956.   Susan Wagner, *Cigarette Country*, 1971.   Kathryn Weibel, *Mirror, Mirror: Images of Women Reflected in Popular Culture*, 1977.   Alfred North Whitehead, *Science and the Modern World*, 1925.   Raymond Williams, *The Long Revolution*, 1961; *Culture and Society 1780–1950*, 1958.   James Harvey Young, *The Toadstool Millionaires: A Social History of Patent Medicines in America Before Regulation*, 1961.

ABOUT
THE AUTHORS

ROBERT ATWAN is co-editor of *Popular Writing in America* with Donald McQuade and *American Mass Media* with Barry Orton and William Vesterman. A former teacher of English at Rutgers University, Mr. Atwan is now a professional writer in New York City.

DONALD MCQUADE is Director of American Studies at Queens College. He has published numerous articles on American culture in *Cross Currents* and *English Journal*, among other magazines, and is co-editor of *Popular Writing in America*. Mr. McQuade resides in New York City.

JOHN W. WRIGHT is an editor with a major New York publishing house. He has written a number of articles on the advertising business and its history, and is currently working on a book about the advertising industry. Mr. Wright lives on Long Island.